Islamic Resurgence

Sayyid Abul Ḥasan ʻAli Nadwī
and his Contemporaries

Islamic Heritage in Cross-Cultural Perspectives

1. Gandhi's Responses to Islam; by Sheila McDonough (ISBN 978-81-246-0035-1)
2. Fawā'id al-Fu'ād — Spiritual and Literary Discourses of Shaikh Niẕāmuddīn Awliyā; Originally Compiled by Amīr Ḥasan 'Alā' Sijzī Dehlawī; English Translation with Introduction and Historical Annotation by Ziya-ul-Hasan-Faruqi (ISBN 978-81-246-0042-9)
3. Change and Continuity in Indian Sūfism — A Naqshbandi-Mujaddidī Branch in the Hindu Environment; Thomas Dahnhardt (ISBN 978-81-246-0170-9)
4. Islamic Thought and Movement in the Subcontinent — A Study of Sayyid Abu A'lā Mawdudi and Sayyid Abul Hasan Ali Nadwi; Sheikh Jameil Ali (ISBN 978-81-246-0491-5)
5. Ṣūfī Thought of Shaikh Sayyid 'Abdu'l Qādir Jīlānī and Its Impact on the Indian Subcontinent; Manzoor Ahmad Bhat (ISBN 978-81-246-0545-5)

Islamic Heritage in Cross-Cultural Perspectives, no. 6

Islamic Resurgence

Sayyid Abul Ḥasan ʿAli Nadwī and his Contemporaries

Abdul Kader Choughley

D.K. Printworld (P) Ltd.
Publishers of Indian Traditions

Cataloging in Publication Data — DK
[Courtesy: D.K. Agencies (P) Ltd. <docinfo@dkagencies.com>]

Choughley, Abdul Kader.
Islamic resurgence : Sayyid Abul Ḥasan 'Ali Nadwī and his contemporaries / Abdul Kader Choughley.
p. cm. (Islamic heritage in cross-cultural perspectives ; no. 6.)
Includes bibliographical references (p.).
ISBN 13: 9788124605738
ISBN 10: 8124605734

1. Islam – 20th century. 2. Nadvī, Abulḥasan 'Alī, 1913- – Contemporaries. I. Title. II. Series. Islamic heritage in cross-cultural perspectives ; no. 6.

DDC 297.09 22

First published in India, 2011
ISBN 13: 978-81-246-0573-8 (HB) ISBN 10: 81-246-0573-4

Published and printed by:
D.K. Printworld (P) Ltd.
Regd. office : *Srikunj*, F-52, Bali Nagar
Ramesh Nagar Metro Station
New Delhi – 110 015
Phones : (011) 2545 3975; 2546 6019; *Fax* : (011) 2546 5926
E-mail: indology@dkprintworld.com
Web: www.dkprintworld.com

Acknowledgement

ALTHOUGH the idea of this research emerged from my reading of Sayyid Abul Ḥasan 'Ali's prolific writings, the nerve to carry it through was produced in the course of a detailed conversation with a colleague, Mufti Ayub Moola. His moral support and mentorship has guided me in many ways to complete this work.

I owe a special debt of gratitude to Maulānā Sayyid Muhammad Rabey, Rector of Nadwat-ul-'ulamā for his moral support during my stay at this prestigious institution. The Academy of Islamic Research and Publications, Nadwah, was kind enough to supply me with the books required for this research. I am equally under a sense of obligation to the personnel of Shibli Library who made copies of rare manuscripts and documents available at short notice.

My greatest source of support has been my family. I am grateful to my wife, Muniera, who was responsible for the typing of the manuscript and for her editorial assistance. To my daughters, Zainab, Safeera and Zaheera, there are no words to express my appreciation for their unwavering support during the years of my research. Without the encouragement of my family, the research would have taken much longer.

I would like to thank Susheel Mittal of D.K. Printworld (New Delhi) for facilitating the publication of this work.

Springs, 2010 **Abdul Kader Choughley**

Contents

Transliteration Table

Consonants, Arabic

initial: unexpressed medial and final:

ء '	د d	ض ḍ	ك k
ب b	ذ dh	ط ṭ	ل l
ت t	ر r	ظ ẓ	م m
ث th	ز z	ع '	ن n
ج j	س s	غ gh	هـ h
ح ḥ	ش sh	ف f	و w
خ kh	ص ṣ	ق q	ي y

Vowels, diphthongs, etc.

Short:	ـَ a	ـِ i	ـُ u
long:	ـَا ā	ـُو ū	ـِي ī
diphthongs:		ـَوْ aw	

A Note
From the Author

- ARABIC terms that deal with key concepts in the study have been italicised, e.g. *tajdīd.*
- Other Arabic and Islamic terms and words which are commonly used in Islamic Studies have been transliterated, e.g. Qur'ān.
- Anglicised words such as caliph have been treated as English words.
- For Urdu words the appropriate spelling has been used, e.g. Barelwi.
- Inconsistency may appear with author's names and titles of works which have been variously translated in international bibliographies — for example Abul A'lā Maulānā Maudūdī/Abul A'la Maududi. In such cases, correct Arabic transliteration has been invariably employed throughout the text, although in the endnotes and bibliography I have reverted to the spelling as published. The discrepancies in transliteration and spelling have become unavoidable due to inconsistencies in the original and translated sources consulted in the study.

Introduction

Islamic Resurgence: An Overview

THE phenomenon of Islamic resurgence during the nineteenth and twentieth centuries spawned multiple levels of Islamic discourse in response to the entrenched influence of Western civilisation and culture. The political hegemony of the West in the form of colonialism was a precursor to intellectual challenges it posed in the Muslim world. Thus contemporary Islamic thought added new dimensions to Islamic resurgence in context of the *iṣlāḥ* (reform) and *tajdīd* (revival) paradigm. The diverse backgrounds of Islamic scholars and movements contributing to Islamic resurgence provided a nexus for a traditionalist and Islamist understanding of these two concepts.

In view of the geo-political developments over the last century in the Muslim world, the rise of the Islamist group advocating a return to an Islam expressed by the *ṣalf-al-ṣāliḥ* (earliest representatives of Islam) has assumed significance in understanding the nature and scope of Islamic resurgence. Across this spectrum have been the contributions of the *'ulamā* in their articulation of *tajdīd*. The varied and often diverse interpretation of *tajdīd* by *'ulamā* and Islamists are manifestations of their pioneering roles in shaping the discourse of the Islamic resurgence.

The study seeks to examine the contributions of Maulānā Sayyid Abul Ḥasan 'Ali Nadwī (1913-99) to Islamic resurgence and his conception of an Islamic order. Maulānā Nadwī stands out as an outstanding *'ālim* combining traditional scholarship with established intellectual credentials. The focus on Maulānā Nadwī rests largely on his distinguished career of almost 70 years which encapsulates the dramatic geo-political changes sweeping across the Muslim world. Two emergent scenes are relevant to our study: the ascendancy of Islamic resurgent movements and efforts to establish an Islamic order. As a traditional *'ālim,* Maulānā Nadwī occupies an important position in relation to contemporary Islamic resurgence. Two important scholars, contemporaries of Maulānā Nadwī, Sayyid Abul A'lā Maudūdī (d. 1979) of Pakistan and Sayyid Quṭb (d. 1966) of Egypt have contributed significantly to influence the trends of Islamic resurgence. In a particular sense these scholars have made their respective contributions to the theme of the study and therefore allow a researcher to conduct a comparative analysis drawn largely from their important writings.

Biographical Profile of Maulānā Nadwī

Before we attempt to examine the concept of Islamic resurgence, it would be worthwhile to provide a brief biographical account of Maulānā Nadwī to understand his contribution to the *iṣlāḥī* (reform) and *tajdīdī* (revival) traditions. Chapter 3 contains biographical details of Maulānā Maudūdī and Sayyid Quṭb and their specific contributions to *tajdīd.*

Family Influences

Sayyid Abul Ḥasan 'Ali Nadwī was born in 1913 in Rai Bareilly, a town in northern India, in a prominent Sayyid family. Maulānā Nadwī's father, Sayyid 'Abdul Ḥayy al-Ḥasani (d. 1923) was a distinguished scholar who is best known for a monumental biographical dictionary of the Indian *'ulamā* in the Arabic language.[1] He was closely associated with the Nadwat-ul-'ulamā[2] (hereafter referred to as Nadwah), an institution for higher Islamic learning. From 1915 till his death in 1923, al-Ḥasani served as the administrator (*nāzim*) of Nadwah.

As a child, Maulānā Nadwī was sent to the village mosque school, where he studied the Qur'ān and learnt Arabic and Urdu. His father, Sayyid 'Abdul Ḥayy al-Ḥasani, an accomplished Islamic scholar in his own right, died when he was nine, and so he was brought up by his mother, a pious woman who had memorised the entire Qur'ān and was a poetess as well as a writer, a rare distinction for a woman of her times. A particularly important influence on him at this stage was his elder brother and mentor, Maulānā Sayyid 'Abdul 'Ali who later went on to train as a medical doctor at King George's Medical College, Lucknow, and then assumed the post of rector of Nadwah. From his brother Maulānā Nadwī learnt Arabic and studied books on the life of the Prophet (SAW) and developed a deep commitment to the cause of Islam. Maulānā Nadwī was admitted to Nadwah in 1929 where he studied Arabic language and literature under some illustrious teachers such as the Yemeni scholar, Shaykh Khalil Ansārī and the noted littérateur Taqī-al-dīn Hilāli of Morocco.

---

1. Sayyid Abul Ḥasan 'Ali Nadwī, *Hayāt-i-'Abdul Hayy*, Karachi: Majlis Nashriyāt-i-Islam, 1985. He was the author of the *Nuzhat-al-Khawāthir*, an eight-volume encyclopaedia containing biographical sketches of over five thousand Indian *'ulamā*. He headed the Nadwat-ul-'ulamā from 1915 till his death in 1923.

2. Established in 1898, the Nadwah sought to provide a harmonious blend of traditional Islamic and modern education. For a detailed historical account of the institution see Nadwī, Ishāq Jalis, *Tarikh Nadwat-ul-'ulamā*, Lucknow: Nadwah Office, 1984, vol. I. All graduates of Nadwat-ul-'ulamā carry the *nisba* (title) "Nadwī." In this study, however this *nisba* (when not accompanied by a scholar's full name) refers exclusively to Sayyid Abul Ḥasan 'Ali Nadwī.

Educational Background

In order to train as an *'ālim* (Islamic scholar) he was sent to the Nadwah for higher Islamic studies. Established in 1898, the Nadwah saw itself as a leading centre for the training of reformist *'ulamā*. It aimed at producing Islamic scholars who would be specialists in classical Islamic disciplines and contemporary knowledge and thus regain the intellectual initiative lost in the wake of colonial occupation. At the institution, Maulānā Nadwī was exposed to new trends in Islamic thought in other Muslim countries, gaining in the years that he spent there a mastery of the Arabic language. He also travelled to Lahore, where he studied the Qur'ān for a while under the illustrious scholar Maulānā Aḥmad 'Ali (d. 1962). In 1931, he went to Azamgarh to study with the noted Islamic scholar, Maulānā Sayyid Sulaymān Nadwī at the Dār-ul-Muṣannifin, established by the renowned Maulānā Shibli Nu'māni (d. 1914).[3] The next year he went to Deoband, where he studied Qur'ānic commentaries (*tafasīr*) under the noted Deobandi *'ālim*, Maulānā Sayyid Ḥussain Aḥmad Madani. He also met Muhammad Iqbal on two occasions,[4] whose poetry and critique of Western civilisation shaped his understanding and future role in contemporary Islamic thought. Alongside his specialised study of the Qur'ān and Islamic history, he began taking an interest in *taṣawwuf* (Sufism) as well.[5] A major turning point in Maulānā Nadwī's life came in 1934, when he was appointed to teach Arabic literature and Qur'ānic

3. Nadwī, 'Abdullāh Abbās, *Mīr-i-Kārwān*, New Delhi: Majlis-i-Ilmi, 1999, 31-38.

4. Sayyid Abul Ḥasan 'Ali Nadwī, *Glory of Iqbal*, Lucknow: Academy of Islamic Publications, 1987, 12-18.

5. For a detailed account of the influence of the Sūfī orders among the *'ulamā* fraternity, see Barbara Daly Metcalf, *Islamic Revival in British India*, Deoband, 1860-1900, Karachi: Royal Book Company 1989, 138-97.

commentary (*tafsīr*) at the Nadwah. At Nadwah, he implemented a comprehensive programme of action to achieve its objective: a well-structured educational system compatible with current expectations and needs.[6] He carried on with teaching at Nadwah even after he was appointed its rector in 1961 after the death of his brother, a post that he occupied till his death in 1999.

Reformatory Contributions

Maulānā Nadwī's scholarly contributions as envisaged by Nadwah's mission statement — to maintain an Islamic identity and to infuse the Arabic language with a dynamic spirit in the Indian context — was a deliberate attempt to expose the secular orientations of textbooks taught in the Arab world.[7] Maulānā Nadwī also compiled an anthology of Arabic prose (*mukhtārāt*) which won international acclaim for its selection of literary figures whom he considered to be authentic interpreters of Islamic identity. His *mukhtārāt* has served as a conduit for Maulānā Nadwī's twofold aims:

- to enlarge the sphere of Arabic literature and to include the notion of an "Islamic" *adab*[8] (literary theory) that is exemplified by the classical writings of traditionalists and jurists like Ibn Taymiyyah, and mystics like al-Ghaẓāli, and
- to articulate his vision of the revivalist (*tajdīdī*) movements which embody not only moral and spiritual conduct but also embrace eminent scholars who through their writings of literary value have

6. Muhammad Nafis Ḥasan, *Meri Tamām Sarguẓasht: Sayyid Abul Ḥasan 'Ali Nadwī*, Delhi, 2000, 32.
7. *Kārawān*, vol. I, 210.
8. M.A.M. Shukri, "Towards an Islamic Theory of Literature," Islamabad, *Islamic Studies* 31:4, 412-25.

added new dimensions to Islamic spirituality. The *Saviours of Islamic Spirit*[9] epitomises Maulānā Nadwī's effort to foster an Islamic identity and consciously promote his concept of Islamic authenticity. His other biographical writings[10] though not comprehensive as *Saviours of Islamic Spirit* also served to augment and enlarge the scope of *tajdīd*. To this end, Maulānā Nadwī's choice of *mujaddid*s and scholars of reformist persuasion are also drawn from the Indian soil who have given Indian Muslims a much stronger religious consciousness, a purer Islamic zeal, and a stronger commitment to Islam.[11] According to Maulānā Nadwī, the tradition of revivalism is uninterrupted and he insists that if we fail to see its continuity it is because Muslim historians have not done much to bring it out.[12] These writings are representative of Maulānā Nadwī's commitment to highlight to the Arab world the Indian Muslim's contribution to Islamic thought and their commitment to Islamic authenticity drawn solely from the Qur'ān and *sunnah*. This, Maulānā Nadwī states, means that any resurgent movement must be based on Islamic foundational texts, a paradigm that he developed for his own *tajdīdī* framework.

---

9. The *Saviours of Islamic Spirit* provides an alternative view of looking at Islamic history as a history of *'ulamā* and intellectuals instead of a chronicle of sultans and regimes, some noble and some ignoble.

10. See Nadwī's *Tadhkirah* (biography genre) series namely, *Sawānih Maulānā 'Abdul Qādir Raipuri*, which delineates Raipuri's formative influence on Nadwī's spiritual development.

11. Sayyid Abul Ḥasan 'Ali Nadwī, *Al-Islam wa-al Mustashriqun*, Lucknow: Nadwat-ul-'ulamā, 1983, 33-5.

12. Ibid., 36.

MUSLIM CORPORATE IDENTITY: MAULĀNĀ NADWĪ'S CONTRIBUTION

Maulānā Nadwī articulated his commitment to the Muslim corporate identity (*tashakkhus*) through his association with leading Muslim institutions sharing similar vision. The Dīnī Ta'līm Council was an authoritative representative of the Indian Muslim commitment to education. The Council under the chairmanship of Maulānā Nadwī vigorously campaigned for the incorporation of Islamic education at primary school level and consolidated its presence through a network of efficiently designed curricula.

The reconstruction of Muslim society in India was of primary concern for Maulānā Nadwī; his writings and lectures addressed issues and offered solutions in order to restore the dignity of Muslims exposed to the growing menace of Hindutva. Maulānā Nadwī upheld the supremacy of the Shari'ah and encouraged Muslims to engage constructively in supporting efforts aimed at preserving their corporate Islamic identity. The All India Muslim Personal Law Board under the chairmanship of Maulānā Nadwī received fresh impetus to resist the nefarious activities of hostile elements which sought to undermine this institution. Maulānā Nadwī played a leading role in strengthening its cause and enhancing its status. A noteworthy feature of Maulānā Nadwī's activities was that they transcended the national barriers; his writings are all-embracing and portray an international character. His thoughts have a direct bearing on the Muslim *ummah*; his emotional attachment carry an impassioned appeal and strikes a responsive note to Muslims living throughout the world.

Likewise religious bigotry and intolerance were alien to Maulānā Nadwī's personality. His *Payām-i-Insāniyat* (Message for Humanity) profiled Maulānā's endeavours to bring together well-wishers from divergent religious spectrums to work towards a common goal: respect for human life.[13] *Da'wah* activities were discernible in the early phase of Maulānā Nadwī's academic career. His perception and interpretation of *da'wah* were shaped by the illustrious Mujāhid, Sayyid Aḥmad Shahīd. Maulānā Nadwī had also established contact with Jamā'at-i-Islami but his attachment with the Tabligh Jamā'at and its founder, Maulānā Ilyās, was most profound. His reformatory endeavours were complemented by the *islāḥī* elements of the Tabligh Jamā'at as well as Sūfī activists. He interiorised these inner dimensions in his personal conduct.

Academic Profile

Apart from his scholarly output which won him accolades from Islamic scholars, both in the Subcontinent and the Arab world, Maulānā Nadwī was associated with several Indian as well as international Islamic organisations, a testimony of the respect he was accorded among Muslims across the world. His membership with the following institutions are indicative of his scholarly contributions:

- President: Dīnī Ta'līmī Council (Religious Education Council) — Uttar Pradesh, India.
- Member of the Standing Committee of Dar-ul-Musanniffīn (Research Institute) in Azamgarh, India.
- Member of the Consultative Committee (Majlis-i-Shurā) of Dār-ul-'ulūm, Deoband, India.
- Member: Board of Directors of Rābita al-Adab al-Islam al-Alami (World Federation of Islamic Literature), Amman, Jordan.
- Member: Standing Committee of Rābita al-Alam al-Islami (Muslim World League), Makkah, Saudi Arabia.

13. For a comprehensive discussion on these aspects, see Ali Sheikh Jameil, *Islamic Thought and Movement in the Subcontinent*, New Delhi: D.K. Printworld, 2010, 299-346.

- Member: Consultative Committee of Jāmi'ah al-Islamiyyah (Madinah University), Madinah, Saudi Arabia.
- Visiting Professor: Universities of Damascus, Madinah and Morocco.
- Chairman: Oxford Centre for Islamic Studies, England.

Awards

- In 1980 Maulānā Nadwī was awarded the King Faisal Prize for his Islamic services.
- He received a honorary PhD degree from the University of Kashmir in 1981.
- In 1988 he won the United Arab Emirates *Man of the Year Award*.
- The Sultan Hasan Bolkiah of Brunei International Prize for Islamic Scholarship (1999) was awarded to Maulānā Nadwī for his multi-volume *Saviours of Islamic Spirit*. The government organised an International conference in recognition of his Islamic services in 1996.[14]
- "Shah Waliallah Award" was given to him posthumously in 2000 by the Institute of Objective Studies, New Delhi, India.
- Posthumous Award by ISESCO, a research wing of Organisation of Islamic Countries (OIC) in Rabat, Morocco, 2000.

---

14. Details of the awards are discussed in Nadwī's multi-volume autobiography, *Kārwān-i-Ẓindagī*, vol. 3, 161-4, 216-34; vol. 6, 282-9. Cf. Abdullāh Abbās Nadwī, *Mīr-i-Kārwān*, New Delhi: Majlis-i-Ilmī, 1999, 316-26.

Islamic Resurgence: Definition and Scope

The term "Islamic resurgence" is typically used in the context of modern Islamic movements although they have pre-modern roots. In a pre-modern context, the terms *iṣlāḥ* and *tajdīd* were used to indicate the renewal of Islamic faith and practices. G.P. Makris has made an important remark that Islamic resurgence associated with *tajdīd* acts as a "bridge between the past and the present and to reconcile current realities with the stipulations of the Islamic vision."[15] In other words, there is an unbroken link in the *tajdīdī* tradition that manifests itself in various forms over the centuries in the Muslim world.

Islamic resurgence derived its source from the backwardness and stagnation in Muslim societies during the eighteenth and nineteenth centuries. In response to these periods of decline and stagnation, Islamic intellectuals and *mujaddid*s (reformers) encouraged "a renewed commitment to Islamic values and practices as the means to achieve development and progress."[16] The discourse of Islamic resurgence emphasised the primacy of the Qur'ān and *sunnah* in meeting the challenges spawned by the Muslim encounter with the West. However, it would be simplistic reading to suggest that a fundamentalist approach (*uṣuliyyah*) was envisaged by the reformers to meet the new challenges. Even if the call was for a restoration of the ideal past with the *ṣalf-al-ṣāliḥ* mediating between the past heritage and present realities, the historical process and geo-politics determined the varied forms of *tajdīd*.

---

15. G.P. Makris, *Islam in the Middle East: A Living Tradition*, Malden: Blackwell Publishing, 2007, 194.

16. John Esposito, Revival and Renewal in *Oxford Dictionary of Islam, Oxford Islamic Studies Onilne*; http://www.oxfordIslamic studies.com/articles, accessed on 24/04/09.

TIME-LINE OF ISLAMIC RESURGENCE

The time-line of *tajdīd* roughly commenced with Aḥmad bin Ḥanbal (d. 825), considered to be the influential figure of a *salafi* interpretation of Islam. Likewise as an articulator of *tajdīd*, Ibn Taymiyyah (d. 1328) is considered the ideologue of the Salafiyyah movement which has assumed considerable importance and aroused scholarly interest in the last few decades. Salafiyyah represented a return to the original sources of Islam and the established practices of the earliest representatives of Islam (*ṣalf-al-ṣāliḥ*).[17] The concept of *tajdīd* interwoven with Islamic resurgent tradition was a sustained effort to eradicate syncretic practices, deviant beliefs and erosion of its ethical values. The time-line of Islamic resurgence defined the parameters of Islamic discourse which were influenced by the dynamics of change.

Patterns of Muslim rule — caliphate and monarchical[18] — also provided variation among the resurgent movements. Two revivalists (*mujaddids*) may be mentioned to illustrate this point. Shaykh Aḥmad Sirhindī[19] (d. 1624) of the Indian sub-continent played an active role in restoring the primacy of the Qur'ān and *sunnah* by defining an Islamic society. His contribution on the uniqueness of Islam rejected efforts to

17. For a scholarly treatment of this term, see As'ad Abu Khalil, "Revival and Reform" in John Esposito, *The Oxford Encyclopedia of the Modern Islamic World*, Oxford: Oxford University Press, 1995, 431-34. Cf. Fazlur Rahman, *Revival and Reform in Islam*, Oxford: Oneworld, 2000, 1-29.

18. The resurgent element in the Caliphate and monarchy has elicited diverse opinions in scholarly studies: Two works for example reflect this trend: Abul A'la Mawdudi, *Khilafat wa Malukiyyat*, Lahore: Islamic Publications, 1966; Habibul Haq Nadvī, *The Dynamics of Islam*, Durban: Academia, 1982, 1-106.

19. Muhammad 'Abdul Haq Ansari, *Sufism and Shari'ah: A Study of Shaykh Aḥmad Sirhindi's Effort to Reform Sufism*, Leicester: The Islamic Foundation, 61-94.

formulate a syncretic religion of Islam and other Indian faiths. In political terms, Sirhindī emphasised the purity of Islam in a multi-religious society as India. In contrast, the revivalist of Nigeria, 'Uthmān don Fodio[20] (d. 1817) launched his movement to eliminate syncretism in both religion and politics and to establish an Islamic state based on the example of the Prophet (SAW). Although socio-political differences were unavoidable, the Islamic paradigm of *tajdīd* had a shared characteristic: Islamic authenticity. This term focused on emulation of the Prophetic model. Textual authority drawn from the lives of the *ṣalf-al-ṣāliḥ* served as the basis for the socio-political transformation of Muslim societies.

Islamic resurgence in retrospect constituted the bedrock of the *iṣlāḥ* and *tajdīd* tradition. It drew its inspiration from the earlier precursors of Islam and operated within a socio-political framework. The movement at large responded to the challenges of the day and established reformist trends in specific historical settings. Contextualisation therefore played a pivotal role in defining its character and mission. The polemics against Islamic resurgence by both Western and Muslim scholars stem from a set of prejudices one of which is fundamentalism. The images conjured up by this term have caused a rupture in understanding the development of *tajdīd* that is interwoven with any *iṣlāḥ*-based initiative. The historical continuity of *tajdīd* crystallising from Ibn Taymiyyah to the contemporary scene essentially stimulated a spirit of re-awakening among Muslims and an emphasis on the unbroken link with which the past converges with the present.

---

20. Abd al-Rahman Doi, *Shaikh Uthmān Dan Fodio: The Grand Mujahid and Mujaddid of Africa*, Pretoria: Al-Madinah Publishers, 1998, 91-102. Fodio's trenchant criticism of syncretism (*takhlit*) which retarded the growth of *tajdīd* is highlighted in this section of Doi's book.

ISLAMIC RESURGENCE: EARLIER REPRESENTATIVES

It would be worthwhile to discuss the implications of the term "resurgence" in a contemporary context. The term *nahḍah*[21] (reawakening) is closely associated with resurgence although the former is associated with a contemporary Arab revival.

Abu Rabi' has elaborated on the term *nahḍah* to show its political connotation. The reawakening was in response to a "total colonial hegemony over Egypt by the West" during the nineteenth century. Muslim intellectuals saw the need for a total revitalisation of Islam against the encroaching Western culture which posed not only a threat to the Arab world but to Islam as a religion. The theory of *nahḍah* implied that Islam was inherently rational and compatible with the scientific spirit of the West. The tacit endorsement of the West's supremacy created a discourse for Muslim intellectuals to re-define the role of Islam in a modern setting. It must be noted that *nahḍah* was rooted in an Arab soil and focused on the relationship between Islam and Arab nationalism. Maulānā Nadwī's important work *Islam and the World* (1973) contained a critique on the emergence of Arab nationalism particularly under the Nasserist regime.

The changing nature of *nahḍah* was expressed at three levels in Egypt. In the first phase of the *nahḍah,* Islam assumed a nationalistic meaning; the objective was to build a strong state competing with the West. The second phase of *nahḍah* saw Islam interpreted in pan-Islamic terms. The third phase of the *nahḍah* began roughly in the twentieth century and saw the emergence of intellectuals who interpreted Islam to be an individual relationship between man and God.

---

21. The term *nahḍah* (re-awakening) has been critically examined by Abu-Rabi' Ibrahim, *Contemporary Arab Thought: Studies in Post-1967 Arab Intellectual History,* London: Pluto Press, 2004, 57-62.

Islamic Fundamentalism

A parallel development to *nahḍah* was the rise of "Islamic fundamentalism" under the name of the Muslim Brotherhood movement (*Ikhwān-al-Muslimīn*). One of the major goals of the founder of the Ikhwān was to establish an Islamic state. The Ikhwān's programme attempted to show the primacy of the Qur'ān and *sunnah* in all walks of life. Its founder, Ḥasan al-Bannā envisaged the supremacy of Islamic culture against the pervasive influence of the West.

Islamic fundamentalism is derived from the Arabic word *aṣl* (root), plural: *usūl* (fundamentals) to describe religious ideologies seen as advocating a return to the "fundamentals" of Islam: Qur'ān and *sunnah*. Definitions of the term fundamentalism vary.[22] Bernard Lewis for example deems this term to be problematic by those who suggest that Islamic beliefs require all Muslims to be fundamentalists.[23] David Zeidan[24] is representative of this trend. In his article, "The Islamic Fundamentalist View of Life as a Perennial Battle", Zeidan argues that "all fundamentalists are separatists in the moral and behavioural spheres . . . by setting visible boundaries and demanding some degree of separation from worldly society and its corrupting influence, evidenced by norms of conduct, dress and behaviour."[25] This stereotypical

22. Islamic fundamentalism is seen as a negative term and this term has gained wide currency in journalistic circles and polemical literature. According to Martin E. Marty, fundamentalists look to religious precepts, doctrines and laws in creating and sanctioning the new order they seek to build. The approach is "reactive" as it attempts to find solutions from original sources in an altered, modified form.

23. Bernard Lewis, *Islam and the West*, New York: Oxford University Press, 1993.

24. David Zeidan, "The Islamic Fundamentalist Views of Life as a Perennial Battle", in *Meria Journal*, vol. 5, no. 4, 9.

25. Ibid., 11-30.

representation of Islamic fundamentalists by Zeidan as an ideology is the theme of his article.

Fundamentalism is a Western term embedded in Protestant ethics and has been randomly applied to Islamic resurgent movements. According to Makris, Protestant fundamentalism especially in the USA focuses on the strengthening of personal faith which "leads to a rebirth or restoration of the person through the radical reformulation of individual consciousness."[26] In other words, this form of fundamentalism emphasises on individual values and a private relationship with religion. Yet its fundamental difference with Islamic resurgence sets the two views apart. The very concept of *tajdīd* has been a recurring feature stimulated by political decline, theological, psychological and socio-economic crises and conflicting milieus. The cyclical period of *tajdīd* is opposed to the view that there existed a rupture in Islamic history and as a result, a re-reading of this tradition was essential to discover its true rationale. These theories are examined in Chapter 4.

Maulānā Nadwī's comments on the phenomenon of fundamentalism in Muslim countries is instructive. Islamic resurgent movements particularly in the Arab world have earned the appellation of "fundamentalists" or "extremists" on account of their call for a reform of Muslim society. Maulānā Nadwī laments the fact that Muslim regimes with questionable human rights record have launched propaganda campaigns to undermine their *iṣlāḥī* efforts.[27]

Islamic Resurgence: Assessment

No study in Islamic studies is complete without understanding the dynamics of change. The *tajdīd* tradition is integral to a

26. Makris, *Islam in the Middle East,* 195.

27. See *Kārwān-i-Ẓindagī,* vol. 5, 208-9.

coherent and systematic understanding of this phenomenon. It would be a daunting task to separate this term from the broader framework that is envisaged in this tradition. The study presupposes an understanding of this term in relation to the resurgent movements that have defined the twin concept of reform and revival. Islamic history is replete with the emergence of this trend which has given fresh impetus to an interpretive reading of the role of the *mujaddid*s.

It would be worthwhile to examine the scope of the *tajdīd* tradition as an element of reformulating the paradigm that is largely associated with it. Contemporary Islamic thought does not suggest a discourse that is monolithic; rather it aims to show its heterogeneous character. Islamic thought though a dominant feature varies from one country to another and reflects the distinctive characteristics that are built around it. For example, the Partition of India in 1947 brought into bold relief how religion was invoked to carve out an Islamic country which would symbolise the aspirations of Muslims in this region. Of course, the conflicting debates on what constituted Islamic authenticity continued to shape Muslim identity and paradoxically created a deep divide in the subcontinent provoking a wave of communal unrest and religious polarisation. On the other hand, Islamic discourse in Indonesia was rooted in a colonisation setting and had profound political implications. The resurgent movement in Indonesia was at variance with other Muslim countries which also experienced the throes of colonisation by the West. However, their respective responses reflected a set of circumstances peculiar to their historical settings.

Contemporary Islamic Thought

Linked with Islamic resurgence is the concept of "contemporary Islamic thought" which reflects a wide variety of intellectual currents dominating the contemporary Muslim world. The period under study — nineteenth and twentieth centuries — are linked with the dominant presence of the West in the Muslim world. There are four major intellectual movements that constitute contemporary Muslim intellectual life: (1) nationalism, (2) Islamism, (3) Westernisation, and (4) state ideology. These movements are set apart by a number of factors; hence it is problematic to refer to one homogeneous Islamic intellectual history. Rather there exist multiple identities that make up contemporary Islamic thought. For example, the Partition of India in 1947 and the subsequent creation of a nation-state in the name of Islam called Pakistan has a distinct contemporary intellectual history in South Asia. Likewise, the emergence of Indonesia as a nation-state with Islamic ethos carries the intellectual experience of Muslims in that particular country. These multiple intellectual developments reflect diverse cultural and political transformation which to a large extent has been exposed to Western imperialism.

The challenges facing Muslim countries since the nineteenth century were also influenced by the period of decolonisation. In fact, the diversity of intellectual trends expresses the various positions on *iṣlāḥ* and *tajdīd*. In the Arab world, the chief architect of the contemporary intellectual movement was Jamāluddīn Afghānī (d. 1898) whose pioneering efforts are generally associated with "Islamic modernism." Similarly South Asia witnessed the emergence of Syed Aḥmad Khan (d. 1898) whose contributions spawned several movements of diverse intellectual backgrounds. The main features of Islamic modernism included finding Islamic solutions to the challenges of the West and constructing new institutions in response to modernity. Thus Islamic modernism and modernity (which are analysed in Chapter 1) developed an Islamic discourse which embraced both Salafiyyah and the emergent trends associated with these concepts. The ambivalence was also brought about by the conflicts these concepts presented to "Islamic modernism" which adopted a new understanding of Islam. For these reformists (Islamic modernists), Islam was a natural, moral and social way of life, rather than a mystical or other-worldly spirituality. In promoting this Islamic paradigm, "Islamic modernism" adopted a modern idiom that has played a significant role in the twentieth-century Islam. Islamic modernism like the *nahḍah* trends shared distinctive features and responses to Islamic resurgence. In contrast "Islamic fundamentalism" which is interchangeably used for Islamism provided alternative views on *tajdīdī* expressions in a modern setting. This aspect is discussed in the next section.

Islamism: A General Overview

During the last two decades or so Islamism which has been defined as a particular form of political assertiveness with visible political traits has been vigorously scrutinised in the Western world. In this section I present the conceptual framework within which Islamists articulate their discourse of Islamic resurgence.

DEFINITION

Islamism came into prominence after the 1979 Iranian Revolution. Since then it has been described by a variety of terms such as Islamic fundamentalism, Islamic extremism or political Islam. All these terms are not suited to describe the phenomenon as they are emotionally loaded over-simplifications based on socio-political assumptions.

It would now be pertinent to present a general outline of Islamist discourse and its response by both Muslim and Western scholars in relation to modernity. The main policy of Islamism is to promote a vision of an Islamic polity through a call to Islam (*da'wah-al-Islamiyyah*). This approach endeavours to make Islam more visible in everyday life mainly through preaching, using an Islamic public awareness programme, co-ordinating social welfare activities and discussion of spiritual subjects and current affairs. Islamic issues assume institutional forms in advancing Islam as a *dīn* (way of life). The yearning for a "return" to an "authentic" Islamic culture by Islamists provides tangible expressions of the *iṣlāḥ/tajdīd* tradition.

ISLAMISM AND SALAFIYYAH: A COMPARISON

Equally problematic is to distinguish Islamism from Salafiyyah. The blurring of ideological boundaries becomes more pronounced in these resurgent movements' response to modernity and the conception of an Islamic order. Political strategies as well as socio-economic environments dictate the form and character of *tajdīd*. The Islamist discourse is articulated in a discursive tradition which is dynamic, fluid and ever-transforming within the parameters of an ongoing project of producing "orthodoxy" through the reinterpretation and re-evaluation of texts and practices.[28] Simply put, Islamist discourse cannot separate its present with its past antecedents.

ISLAMISM AND THE ISLAMIC ORDER: A COMPARISON

Another view suggests that the Islamist movement was in response to the West's incursion into the Muslim world. Thus its emergence was conceived as an Islamic alternative to Marxist socialism which Quṭb claimed was a kind of mirror image of Western ideology.[29] The Ikhwān in Egypt became the pioneer of the Islamist movement since it symbolised Muslim unity in opposition to the radical secular position of

28. See *Kārwān-i-Ẓindagī*, vol. 5, 20.

29. Ibrahim Abu Rabi', *Islam and the Search for a Social Order in Modern Egypt: An Intellectual Biography of Shaykh 'Abd-al-Halim Mahmud*, Ph.D thesis, Temple University, 1987, 10-11.

Ataturk who abolished the Caliphate in Turkey. The workings of Islamist groups in the Muslim world only confirm the variation that exists within them. It reflected the continuing process of decolonisation (during the centuries under study) and sought to define the destiny of the *ummah*.[30]

Still other Islamist groups are focused more specifically on the spiritual goals of Islam. The failure of the West to give a spiritual grounding, Islamists contend, is only realised in the Islamic framework which provides support for a truly ethical and moral society. Khurshid Aḥmad, a noted economist and intellectual of Pakistan, laments the fact that Western analyses of contemporary Islamic resurgence do not focus on the importance of the spiritual dimensions in explaining the strength of Islamist movements. The spiritual dimensions which are associated with an interpretive reading of the Qur'ān and *sunnah*, are reflected in the Salafiyyah worldview.[31] Therefore, Islamist movements represented by Maulānā Maudūdī and Quṭb in our study generally reinforce the strands of *tajdīd* discussed in this section. To be more specific, Maulānā Maudūdī is a central figure in the revival of Islam in recent decades. His interpretation of Islam has formed the foundation of contemporary Islamic thought.[32] Prolific and articulate, he has greatly influenced contemporary Muslim scholars throughout the world. Maulānā Maudūdī

---

30. For a critical discussion on this historical process see Esposito, *Makers of Contemporary Islam*, 3-22.

31. Khurshid Aḥmad, *Islam and the New World Order in Middle East Affairs*, 1:3, Spring/Summer 1993, 10-11.

32. On the impact of Maudūdī's thought on Islamic movements in the Muslim world, see John Esposito, *The Islamic Threat: Myth or Reality*, New York: Oxford University Press, 1992, 154-55; Sivan Emmanuel, *Radical Islam, Medieval Theology and Modern Politics*, New Haven: Yale University Press, 1985; Rahnema Ali (ed.), *Pioneers of Islamic Revival*, London: Zed Books, 1994, 98-120.

began to set his views on Islam and its place in Muslim life in 1932. He advocated complete obedience to Islamic law, (Ḥākimiyyah). Politics, according to Maulānā Maudūdī, was an integral and inseparable component of the Islamic faith, and this set down a political interpretation of Islam, in which religious piety was transformed into a structure of authority. The Jamā'at-i-Islami[33] of Pakistan of which he was a founder was established to transform Islam into an ideology which Maulānā Maudūdī referred to as *dīn* (literally, "religion"). His ideology showed modernist tendencies, as did his political outlook. Maulānā Maudūdī's discourse also revolved around the Hindu threat which decades later (Partition of India) crystallised into Hindu and Muslim hostilities. The establishment of Pakistan as an Islamic state, which Maulānā Maudūdī and his Jamā'at advocated, demanded a government inspired by the Shari'ah and which promised a utopian order that would give direction to Islamic social action.

Maulānā Maudūdī's vision was also the product of a discourse with the "other," the West. His trenchant criticism of the Western ideology which he arguably maintained was based on Jāhiliyyah (ignorance) was to be echoed by the Egyptian ideologue, Sayyid Quṭb (1906-66), of the Ikhwān-al-Muslimīn in his prolific writings. In a similar vein, Quṭb was influenced by Maulānā Nadwī's widely acclaimed *Islam and the World* (1976) in which a contextualised analysis of Jāhiliyyah was elaborated. It is interesting to note that their respective interpretation of this concept was not monolithic and a variation was discernible in its application to contemporary society. These concepts and their implication on the Islamist movements in the contemporary Muslim world are examined in Chapter 4.

33. For a biographical account of the Jamā'at-i-Islami and its vision of an Islamic state in Pakistan, see Seyyed Vali Reza Nasr, *The Vanguard of the Islamic Revolution*, Berkeley: University of California Press, 1994.

In contrast to Maulānā Maudūdī's ideological interpretation of Islam, Maulānā Wahiduddin Khan (b. 1925) of Delhi, India, is a leading *'ālim* who has sought to develop his own understanding of Islam and its place in the modern world.[34] As a member of the Indian Muslim minority, he has attempted to present Islam in terms that are intelligent to the modern mind, as well as make it possible for Muslims in India to create a balance between their Islamic identity and their loyalty to the state. Peace and dialogue are the dominant themes in his writings, a concern which he shares with Maulānā Nadwī. His views are best articulated in one of his important works, *Indian Muslims* (1977), in which he discusses the role of both Muslims and Hindus in a progressive India. According to Khan, this strategy is only possible if "dialogue could be held in all seriousness, in a spirit of accommodation and with a strict sense of justice, as a result of which Hindu-Muslim relations could very soon be normalised, and this in itself would immediately open up a whole new chapter in the history of modern India." Although Khan may have not established a movement like Maulānā Maudūdī, Quṭb and Maulānā Nadwī, he certainly does reflect an important voice among the Muslims of India today.

Maulānā Nadwī's paradigmatic shift to a more critical appraisal of an Islamic order in India must also be seen in terms of global events with special reference to the Muslim world. The shifting political landscapes in India and the unpredictable rise of Salafiyyah in Muslim countries created a specific discourse which engaged both *'ulamā* and other intellectuals. His participative role in mainstreaming Islamic activities defined his contribution to contemporary Islamic thought. The salient features that characterise Maulānā

34. Wahiduddin Khan, *Islam and Peace*, New Delhi: Maktaba al-Risala, 1999.

Nadwī's Islamic order reflect his concern for chalking out a conceptual framework that is practical in a Hindu-dominated society. Maulānā Nadwī's role in fostering a harmonious relationship has a chequered history; his autobiography sheds much light on this development. Parallel to his efforts was the establishment of the *Payām-i-Insāniyat* (Movement for Humanity) which is an attempt to give a tangible expression to the mission and vision of interfaith dialogue. (The movement is examined in Chapter 5.) The success of *Payām-i-Insāniyat* is inextricably linked with Maulānā Nadwī's charismatic personality, and by examining his writings during its formative period we can evaluate the crisis of Islamic identity to which Indian Muslims were exposed. Maulānā Nadwī also extends a critique to Islamist movements that adopt confrontational approaches in order to establish a society in India based on the Prophetic model. While Maulānā Nadwī shares much the same understanding of Islam as an all-comprehensive way of life, he differs from several Islamic movements on the crucial questions of strategy, seeing their approach as unrealistic in the Indian context where Muslims are a relatively small minority.

ISLAMISM: AN ASSESSMENT

The roots of Islamists' current ideological problem lies in the recent history of their Muslim societies. According to them colonialism consolidated its presence in Muslim nations through its Western ideas such as democracy, socialism and secularisation of society. This problematic assumption does not take into account the Islamists' assimilation of some Western ideas to bolster their *tajdīdī-iṣlāḥi* trajectory. Thus the Islamists' discourse does not operate in a vacuum and is also influenced by the historical process of modernity and globalisation which are largely of Western origin. Likewise Maulānā Nadwī also belonged to a hierarchy of *'ulamā* who played a significant role in presenting a reformist vision of

Islam. Their contributions to Islamic resurgence have been scrutinised in recent writings as shown in the next section.

'Ulamā: Custodians of Change or Conservatism

Maulānā Nadwī's influential role in the contemporary Islamic thought as both a traditional and intellectual scholar mirrors in some instance the active role of *'ulamā* in Islamic history. Briefly the *'ulamā* were not part of the political structure of the Caliphate; they acted as intellectuals who often provided critiques of existing conditions in the Muslim *ummah*. However, during the evolution of Muslim societies, the *'ulamā* emerged as part of the established structure of authority. Two conflicts emerged within this historical framework: *taqlīd* (imitation) versus *ijtihād* (independent judgement). These conflicting concepts developed over the centuries and provided categories of *'ulamā* formation. Conservative *'ulamā* who were a significant force within the Islamic community were associated with the tradition of *taqlīd*. In contrast *mujaddid*s were considered to be the upholders of *ijtihād* with a distinct worldview. During the nineteenth century the most active *'ulamā* were those within the *tajdīdī* tradition of Muslim intellectuals. However during the twentieth century major Islamic institutions and the *'ulamā* became a deciding conservative force. Political reasons were attributed to this loss of authority. In Egypt, the *'ulamā* lost their authoritative presence when Al-Azhar University in Cairo was nationalised by the State in 1961. This trend as concluded by Esposito brought fresh challenges from modernity to which the *'ulamā* responded by withdrawing into a defensive conservatism. This generalisation has been challenged by Muḥammad Qasim Zaman in his seminal study of the *'ulamā* fraternity, *The 'Ulamā in Contemporary Islam.*[35] The highly original work focuses largely

35. Muhammad Qasim Zaman, *The 'Ulamā in Contemporary Islam: Custodians of Change*, Princeton: Princeton University Press, 2002.

on *'ulamā* in South Asia and attempts to explain the religious transformations of the *'ulamā* in the modern world. Zaman examines the legal and political role of the *'ulamā* during the crucial period of Islamic resurgence and points to the conflictual relationships between the *'ulamā* and the Islamists. Implicit in the study is Zaman's evaluation of activist *'ulamā* like Maulānā Nadwī and nationalist *'ulamā* like Maulānā Ḥusain Aḥmad Madani (d. 1957) and their respective responses to modernity, nationalism and securalism.[36]

The importance of investigating the role of *'ulamā* in South Asia is also to show their link to the *turāth* (authenticity) which is a central theme in Maulānā Nadwī's writings. Representatives of Islamic authenticity are epitomised as a "network of transmission."[37] These networks articulate sources of authority from an Islamic perspective. In this context the study of Maulānā Nadwī's academic background is useful in reconstructing his multi-dimensional personality that enabled him to interact with intellectuals and movements of diverse religious backgrounds.

In conclusion, it may be stated that Maulānā Nadwī's contribution to an Islamic order should be placed in its historical context and in the evolution of modern India. Maulānā Nadwī is a traditionalist thinker whose understanding of Islam is characterised by his doctrinal orientation and a global vision of Islam both of which affirm the return to the original sources of Islam as a response to religious extremism and cultural chauvinism.

Purpose of Study

The plethora of writings in Islamic resurgence continue to

---

36. Muhammad Qasim Zaman, *The 'Ulamā in Contemporary Islam: Custodians of Change*, pp. 170-73.

37. Ibid., 161-70.

dominate contemporary Islamic thought. Two emergent trends provide the contrasting discourse on this movement. Again the orientations of writers specialising in this field suggest the multiple identities that make up this phenomenon. A random selection of writings, like Nazih Ayubi,[38] Oliver Roy[39] and Bassam Tibi[40] tend to focus on the fundamentalist character of Islamic resurgence and its impact on Islam's future relations with the West. The element of impasse or conflicting views are explicitly stated in their writings. Recent scholarly studies have re-examined the stereotypical assumptions that have shaped an understanding of the resurgent movements in the light of globalisation and have drawn new conclusions that are insightful and revealing. Works belonging to this trend are scholars like John Esposito,[41] Francis Robinson,[42] Abu Rabi',[43] etc.

A noteworthy contribution on the rapprochement between resurgent movements and the West is elaborated in recent studies by Francis Robinson. The "Clash of Civilisation"[44] discourse by Samuel Huntington is critically

38. See Nazih Ayubi, *Political Islam, Religion and Politics in the Arab World*, London: Routledge, 1982.

39. Olivier Roy, *Globalised Islam: The Search for a New Ummah*, London: C. Hursts Co., 2002.

40. Bassam Tibi, *Political Islam, World Politics and Europe*, London: Routledge, 2007.

41. John Esposito, *Voices of Resurgent Islam*, Oxford: Oxford University Press, 1983.

42. Francis Robinson, *Islam and Muslim History in South Asia*, New Delhi: Oxford University Press, 2001.

43. Abu Rabi' Ibrahim, *Intellectual Origins of Islamic Resurgence in the Modern Arab World*, New York: SUNY Press, 1996.

44. Huntington argues that in the post-Cold War era the prime distinction between people were less ideological and economic than cultural. World politics was being reconfigured along civilisational lines. As the process took place deep fault lines →

examined and an alternative view of this theory is offered. According to Robinson, Huntington's theory is drawn on the old polemics against Islam, Western fears of Islam and a strong dose of orientalism. In contrast to this hostile approach Robinson remarks

> . . . there is a long history of the Muslim and Christian civilisations drawing on each other, and this is a process which, whatever the rhetoric, still continues. There have been and still are, many bridges across the so-called fault lines between the two civilisations. Historians can help to make them better signposted and better used.[45]

This approach is represented in Maulānā Nadwī's conception of an Islamic order and to which the study attempts to contextualise in a contemporary setting.

The study will examine the interaction between Islamic resurgent movements and how they have shaped the discourse of an Islamic order. This term is interchangeably used for Islamic state and Islamic society in the study. The common strands that bind together *tajdīdī* movements are tangible expressions of an Islamic polity. In other words, they envision an Islamic paradigm associated with the Prophetic model followed by the Caliphate rule. The changing paradigms are invariably based on socio-political changes. However, the interconnectedness of a globalised society has thrown up new challenges that have no precedent in the past.[46] In a sense it is productive to view this phenomenon from the perspective of "identity politics." The term is

→ were emerging between the Muslim world and the West. Indeed it had "bloody borders" and represented the greatest challenge to world peace. Samuel Huntington, *The Clash of Civilisation and the Remaking of the World*, New York, 1996.

45. Robinson, *Islam and Muslim History in South Asia*, 42.

46. For the impact of globalisation in the Muslim World, see Abu Rabi', *Contemporary Arab Thought*, 185-201.

associated with individuals and resurgent movements articulating a collective identity in response to socio-political challenges within specific timelines. The notion of identity politics has had longer presence in both pre-colonial and colonial situations. Its relevance can be seen even in Maulānā Nadwī's interaction with his contemporaries for an Islamic order. More importantly, the "horizons of significance" tend to merge with politics, culture and society giving it a collective identity.[47] This trend is evident in Maulānā Nadwī's worldview where a minority (Muslim community) with a status has to operate in a contested discourse of secularism and democracy. The following comment by Homi Bhabha succinctly expresses the challenges faced by minorities (in our study, Indian Muslims) in order to define their Islamic identity.

> Social articulation of difference, from the minority perspective, is a complex, ongoing negotiation that seeks to authorise cultural hybridities that emerge in movements of historical transformation.[48]

While Maulānā Nadwī's Islamic order is expressed in a commitment to a very transparent course of action, the overlapping and sometimes antagonist identities cannot be ignored. It is "hybridities" that create space for new discourse, informed choices and understanding the "bigger picture" in a changed historical situation. Maulānā Nadwī's Islamic order as distinct from other formulations by his contemporaries is investigated to understand the dynamics of the Islamic tradition.

---

47. Shamil Jeppie, *Language, Identity, Modernity*, Pretoria: HSRC, 2007, 12-13.

48. Cited in Jeppie, *Language, Identity, Modernity*, 12.

CHAPTERISATION

The Introduction provides an overview on Islamic resurgence with focus on Maulānā Nadwī, the *'ulamā* and Islamists and transmitters of *tajdīd*.

Chapter 1 provides a detailed historical analysis on the phenomenon of the Islamic resurgent movements. Relevant concepts and terminologies are elaborated to demonstrate a link with the theme of the study.

Chapter 2 examines the sources of Islamic authenticity (which is interchangeably used for *turāth*) of an ideal past (*ṣalf-al-ṣāliḥ*) in relation to Islamic reformist thought. The literary genres, autobiography and its subgenres are scrutinised to highlight its link with the *tajdīdī* tradition.

Chapter 3 explores the networks of transmission that have contributed to Maulānā Nadwī's formulation of Islamic resurgences. The networks include historical figures, Maulānā Nadwī's contemporaries and Islamic institutions which are linked to Maulānā Nadwī's Islamic authenticity paradigm.

Chapter 4 is based on a comparative analysis of key concepts associated with an Islamic order which also focuses on the theme of the study. The theories of Jāhiliyyah and Ḥākimiyyah are examined in the writings of Quṭb, Maulānā Maudūdī and Maulānā Nadwī. Their respective orientations and critiques are elaborated for a coherent understanding of the conflicting viewpoints on these theories. Maulānā Nadwī's formulation of *dīn* is also examined against the backdrop of historical developments in post-Partition India.

Chapter 5 is a summative assessment of the Islamic order envisaged by Maulānā Nadwī and his contemporaries. The challenges Indian Muslims as a minority face from Hindutva ideology against the background of secularism and democracy are closely examined. The thematic links to the study in the chapter are systematically developed to illustrate the impact of Islamic resurgence on the Islamic order.

METHOD OF RESEARCH

The trends in Islamic resurgence offer a variety of challenges in terms of its dynamic character and interactive relationships with other Islamic movements. The aim of this study is to provide an understanding of the growth and development of the Islamic resurgent movements with reference to Maulānā Nadwī and his contemporaries, and other ideological relationships that shape contemporary Islamic thought with specific reference to the Islamic order. Maulānā Nadwī's major contribution is analysed to show that an Islamic order is not monolithic and is rooted in specific socio-political milieu. More importantly, the study seeks to show the contrasting worldviews expressed by his contemporaries in their interpretation of an Islamic polity and how they differ from his conceptual framework based in an Indian setting.

The multiple identities examined in the study show Islamic resurgence caught in a flux of historical processes. Therefore a straightforward chronology of events would have served no purpose for the study. I have tried to locate the resurgent trends in broader political and Islamic contexts. There is no certainty to the number of contexts one can place the movements in and I have therefore provided the historical settings in which they have operated. Thus this study has two broadly interconnected components:

Firstly an analytical approach combined with discursive tradition. Maulānā Nadwī by and large endorses this approach in his writings on Islamic resurgent movements which are relevant to our study. The methodology employed by Maulānā Nadwī in his *Saviours of Islamic Spirit* is explained in the following words:

> [F]or presenting the viewpoint of any particular person or a movement, his own writings or sayings have been relied upon. If they have been found inadequate, only then has recourse been taken from the writings or descriptions left by his friends, contemporaries and pupils. In the latter case more reliable and authentic sources have been preferred without placing undue reliance on those who were nearer to him in time; trustworthy material has been used whenever it could be found after careful verification of facts.[49]

This methodological approach is also expressed by the noted historian, E.H. Carr who maintained that the historian is necessarily selective and historical facts cannot be analysed independently of interpretation.[50] Maulānā Nadwī's *Saviours of Islamic Spirit* and *Islam and the World* accentuate an Islamic authenticity that is drawn from the lives of the *ṣalf-al-ṣāliḥ* and the later generations of scholars and sūfīs. The focus is on the historical continuity of its reformers whose contributions form a *tasalsul* (unbroken chain) in the *tajdīdī* tradition. The discursive tradition is also applicable to Quṭb's *magnum opus* "*Fī-Zilāl-al Qur'ān*" which elaborates on the *tajdīdī* efforts of the *ṣalf-al-ṣāliḥ*. It is evident that for Quṭb Islamic authenticity is expressed in the earliest generations of Muslims. Unlike Maulānā Nadwī, his *tajdīdī* views are restrictive and rigidly applied to an idealised society which has no traces of Jāhiliyyah. Like Maulānā Nadwī, Maulānā Maudūdī seeks to articulate an Islamic authenticity in a political context. Although the discursive tradition is not coherently expressed in Maulānā Maudūdī's *A Short History of the Revivalist Movements in Islam*, his analysis differs from both Maulānā Nadwī and Quṭb. Maulānā Maudūdī contends that apart from the *ṣalf-*

49. Nadwī, *Saviours of Islamic Spirit*, vol. I, xl.
50. Cited in Jameil Ali, "Mawlana Sayyid Abul Hasan 'Ali Nadwī's Reorientation of Islamic History", in *Hamdard Islamicus*, vol. XXX, no. 4, 86.

al-ṣāliḥ, later generations of reformers did not exert a profound influence on *tajdīd*. There was a rupture in the history of Islam and this lacuna often created an intellectual and moral crisis which Maulānā Maudūdī termed Jāhiliyyah. This aspect is examined in Chapter 4.

Secondly, the study of discursive tradition is a useful tool in interpreting the different responses by individuals in the *tajdīdī* tradition to Western civilisation in the Muslim world. According to Talat Asad, an Islamic discursive tradition "is simply a tradition of Muslim discourse that addresses itself to conceptions of the Islamic past and future, with reference to a particular Islamic practice in the present."[51] In other words, what is the correlation between traditional Islam (represented by its past) and its interaction with the present (challenges posed by West) to work out its future course of action in a globalised world?

Discursive tradition as Abdulkader Tayob has explained in *Islam in South Africa* can be appreciated in its varied historical contexts and discourses. The methodology in the study illustrates how Islamic trends and resurgent movements may be regarded as a discursive tradition that is linked to other Islamic practices, both past and present.[52] The practices in a wider sense may refer to political or ideological developments and their interconnectedness to specific time frames. Islamic resurgence mirrors such trends as it embodies a flux of events that can be located in historical settings.

Scope of Study: General Observations

- The term "resurgence" (resurgent: adjective) has

51. Talat Asad, *The Idea of an Anthropology of Islam*, Washington: Centre for Contemporary Arabic Studies, 1986, 14.

52. For a detailed discussion, see Abdul Kader Tayob, *Islamic Resurgence in South Africa,* Cape Town: UCT Press, 1995, 16-37.

multiple connotations: socio-political, religious, anti-statal in the Muslim world.

- Categories of Islamic resurgence include traditional and modernist understanding of *iṣlāḥ* and *tajdīd*.
- Islamic resurgence has been largely influenced in the beginning of the twentieth century by Salafiyyah in its divergent forms.
- The rise of Islamism has provided the contesting discourse of an Islamic order of which Maulānā Nadwī, Quṭb and Maulānā Maudūdī are leading representatives.
- *Tajdīd* has a broader implication in contemporary Islamic thought and functions against multiple factors which include Western democratic institutions.
- The formulation of an Islamic order is not monolithic and is adaptable to changed socio-political situation. This is evident in Maulānā Nadwī's vision of an Islamic order in an Indian setting. In contrast to this vision are other forms of an Islamic order which are based on a Divine-sovereignty (Ḥākimiyyah).
- Forms of religious extremism pose a challenge to movements pursuing balanced religious ideals. In this study, Hindutva espouses a radical interpretation of Hinduism and opposes interfaith dialogue, particularly with Islam.

SURVEY OF LITERATURE

The Arabic bibliography of Maulānā Nadwī's works lists 167 publications. The corpus of writings produced by Maulānā Nadwī can broadly speaking be categorised in the following genres:

- In the *sīrah* (biography) of the Prophet Muḥammad series, *Muḥammad Rasulullah* (1985) is considered to be an excellent contribution. Written originally in Arabic it has been translated into the major European languages.
- The *tadhkirah* (memoirs) genre which has been skillfully crafted in the Indo-Islamic culture has seen a plethora of *sawāniḥ* (biographies) on Muslim scholars, saints and Sūfīs. *Sawānih 'Abdul Qādir Rāipuri* (1981) is representative of Maulānā Nadwī's Sūfī's orientation.
- Indo-Islamic culture is a dominant theme in Maulānā Nadwī's writings. The motivation for such works is evident in his popular work *Muslims in India* (1976). "It is hoped that the book will be read with interest among the educated circles . . . and prove of some value in reducing the ignorance and the attitude of indifference which exists in sister-communities towards the Muslims."
- Maulānā Nadwī's projection of the *tajdīdī* (revivalist) movements is encapsulated in his widely-acclaimed *Saviours of Islamic Spirit* (1993). Written in four volumes, it represents Maulānā Nadwī's interpretation of Islamic history as a history of *'ulamā* and intellectuals instead of as a chronicle of sultans and regimes, some noble and some horrible.
- *Da'wah* paradigms: Some of the books published are discussed in Chapter 2 and outline the importance of *da'wah* in both societal and global contexts. *Islam and the West* (1985) illustrates Maulānā Nadwī's vision of *da'wah* in the West.
- Arabic literature has been Maulānā Nadwī's forte and he was the first Indian writer whose distinguished works were prescribed as reference works in a number

of Islamic universities. His *Mukhtārāt* (1980) which is an anthology of prose has carved out a niche for Maulānā Nadwī as an Arabic littérateur.

- *Da'wah* literature for the Arab world. Arab nationalism and commitment to Islam form the basis of Maulānā Nadwī's prolific writings. The books published are monographs, travelogues, compilation of lectures, etc. and, by and large, are impassioned appeals for the Arab world to "shoulder the responsibilities of the mission of Islam." *Baynal-ṣuratān wal haqiqat* (Between Appearance and Reality) is representative of this *da'wah* genre for the Arab audience.

The primary sources consulted for developing a coherent understanding of Maulānā Nadwī's contribution to the Islamic resurgence are the following works:

- *Islam and the World*
- *Saviours of Islamic Spirit*
- *Kārwān-i-Ẓindagī*

These writings share a common theme: *iṣlāḥ* and *tajdīd*. *Islam and the World* is considered Maulānā Nadwī's major work and has received critical acclaim for its reformist thrust. Maulānā Nadwī's formulation of Islamic resurgence is articulated in this work. Key concepts like Jāhilliyah and Islamic authenticity are developed and elaborated in the works mentioned hereunder.

The multi-volume *Saviours of Islamic Spirit*[53] provides a broader framework of *tajdīd* and includes several distinguished *mujaddids* from the Indian subcontinent. This work provides an alternative view of looking at Islamic history as a history of *'ulamā* and intellectuals whose respective contributions articulated Islamic

53. Nadwī, *Kārwān-i-Ẓindagī*, vols. 1-7, Lucknow: Majlis Nashriyāt-i-Islam, 2000.

authenticity. This theme developed by Maulānā Nadwī is examined in respect of his contributions to Islamic authenticity. A salient feature of *Saviours of Islamic Spirit* is *iṣlāḥ* which in Maulānā Nadwī's view is the basis for an Islamic order. This work is an internal critique of Maulānā Maudūdī and Quṭb's formulation of the Ḥākimiyyah doctrine. *Kārwān-i-Ẓindagī* provides meaningful insights to Maulānā Nadwī's literary career and pioneering contribution to contemporary Islamic thought. Details pertaining to his works examined in the study form a link to his understanding and interpretation of Islamic resurgence. These motivations and rationale are key elements to identify the thematic coverage in his other writings. The Islamic discourse embodies both narrative and analytical forms and traces significant events in Maulānā Nadwī's life. *Kārwān-i-Ẓindagī* portrays Maulānā Nadwī's versatility and also provides a repertoire of his activities with organisations with which he was associated and his pro-active role in shaping the destiny of Indian Muslims. A salient feature of his autobiography is the absence of embellished anecdotes which otherwise tend to mar personal narratives. The worldview of Maulānā Nadwī should become clear from the text which *Kārwān* seeks to present.

As the study focuses on Maulānā Nadwī and his contemporaries, it would be useful to outline the writings selected for a comparative analysis. Two major contemporaries Quṭb and Maulānā Maudūdī drawn from two Islamic countries, Egypt and Pakistan, are leading figures in the Islamic resurgence across the Muslim world. Maulānā Maudūdī's important work, *A Short History of the Revivalist Movements in Islam*[54] re-examines the traditional roles of *mujaddids* based on his own formulation of the Ḥākimiyyah

54. S. Abul A'la Maudūdī, *A Short History of the Revivalist Movement in Islam*, Lahore: Islamic Publications Ltd., 1972.

doctrine. Another work, *Four Basic Qur'ānic Terms* augments his theorisations on the concepts investigated in the study. In fact, Maudūdī's thesis on Ḥākimiyyah is elaborated in this book. Maulānā Nadwī's critique on Maudūdī's Ḥākimiyyah formulation is expressed in his *Appreciation and Interpretation of Religion in the Modern Age.*

Quṭb's *Milestones,* his last work, is considered the icon-text of his theories on Jāhiliyyah and Ḥākimiyyah. This writing in particular was viewed as a threat to the nationalist regimes in the Muslim world from Egypt to Iraq and is also viewed as a threat to the West. Quṭb's *Milestones* is an elaboration of his theories of Jāhiliyyah and Ḥākimiyyah which is an indictment on Muslim societies who in his view have deviated from the Islamic way of life (*dīn*). The polemical content has had far-reaching implications for Islamist groups pursuing a militant vision of Islamic resurgence.

To date, no detailed study has been published on the life and thought of Maulānā Nadwī in English. A recent work in German by Jan-Peter Hartung, *Viele Wege und ein Ziel: Leben und Wirken von Sayyid Abu-l-Ḥasan Ali al-Ḥasani Nadwī*[55] is a useful guide to understand the contributions of Maulānā Nadwī to contemporary Islamic thought. This book is an intellectual biography of the Maulānā Nadwī. The crucial question to be answered is why Maulānā Nadwī emerged as a transnationally influential personality and remained such beyond his own death. The book works with an innovative analytical framework that combines both social network and discourse analysis. Several other works however provide a comparative study between Maulānā Nadwī and his contemporaries on a single aspect of the Islamic resurgence. Two recent studies deserve mention. *The Political Thought of Sayyid Quṭb* by Sayyid

55. Jan-Peter Hartung, *Viele Wege und ein Ziel: Leben und Wirken von Sayyid Abu-l-Ḥasan Ali al-Ḥasani Nadwī,* Wurzburg: Ergon, 2004.

Khatab[56] explores the development of Jāhiliyyah until it became a mature confrontational theory. The book sheds light on Islamic radicalism and its intellectual origins by presenting new analysis of the intellectual legacy of Quṭb in *tajdīd* tradition. Chapter 5 in this book examines among other issues Maulānā Nadwī's influence on Quṭb's Jāhiliyyah doctrine. The primary source is Maulānā Nadwī's *Islam and the World.*

Aḥmad Mukarram's doctoral thesis focuses on Ḥākimiyyah in the writings of Maulānā Nadwī and Maulānā Maudūdī: *Some Aspects of Contemporary Islamic Thought: Guidance and Governance in the Works of Maulana Abul Ḥasan 'Ali Nadwī* and *Maulānā Abul Aa'la Maudūdī.*[57] The thesis investigates the divergent opinions on Ḥākimiyyah between these two scholars based on their respective intellectual orientations. As this work is not located in an Islamic resurgence framework, there is not much elaboration on the *tajdīdī* impact on Islamist thought. Another study on interfaith relations is Yoginder Sikand's *Muslims in India Since 1947: Islamic Perspectives on Interfaith Relations.*[58] A chapter is devoted to Maulānā Nadwī's contributions to the Muslim-minority issue. This work sets to highlight the multiple voices representing Indian Muslims' response to dialogue and conflict.

A peculiarity of magazines and journals written in Urdu is the "Special Number" issue. Several volumes reflecting Maulānā Nadwī's contributions in general have been published since 2000. The *Ta'meer-i-Hayāt*, an organ of Nadwah

56. Sayed Khatab, *The Political Thought of Sayyid Quṭb*, London: Routledge, 2006.

57. Mukarram Aḥmad, *Some Aspects of Contemporary Islamic Thought: Guidance and Governance in the Works of Maulana Abul Hasan Ali Nadwī and Maulana Abul Aala Maudūdī*, D. Phil. Thesis, Oxford University, 1993.

58. Yoginder Sikand, *Muslims in India Since 1947: Islamic Perspectives on Interfaith Relations*, London: Routledge, 2004.

published a *Mufakkir-ul-Islam* (Thinker of Islam) number.[59] The contributions are drawn from a wide spectrum of Islamic institutions and movements and the articles focus largely on the versatility of Maulānā Nadwī in contemporary Islamic thought. Only a few articles critically examine his contributions to Islamic resurgence.

Conclusion

The study seeks to provide a coherent and comprehensive understanding of Maulānā Nadwī's pioneering role in Islamic resurgence which continues to shape new discourses in the Muslim world. Implicit in the study is a re-evaluation of the function of an Islamic order based largely on Maulānā Nadwī's presentation of this concept. The formation of Islamic resurgent movements in the period under study is examined to locate their influence on Maulānā Nadwī and his contemporaries. More importantly, the relationship between Islamic resurgence and an Islamic order is investigated to locate its significance in the *dīn* paradigm envisaged by Maulānā Nadwī's contemporaries.

---

59. Shamsul Haq Nadwī (ed.), "Mufakkir-al-Islam Sayyid Abul Hasan Ali Nadwī" in *Tameer-i-Hayāt 'Ali Nadwī*, Lucknow, July-August, 2000.

1

Islamic Resurgence
Trends of Tajdīd in the Muslim World

DURING the past two centuries, Muslim societies have experienced significant transformation. Central to the phases of transformation has been the rise of Islamic resurgence[1] which has influenced contemporary Islamic thought. The resurgence (*nahḍah*) which is associated with the *iṣlāḥ* (reform) and *tajdīd* (revival) tradition emerged in the Arab world during the nineteenth century and spawned a number of Islamic movements pursuing their respective goals of Islamic resurgence.[2]

Tajdīd is the axis on which Islamic resurgence revolves. The study seeks to examine the dynamics of Islamic resurgence with special reference to Maulānā Nadwī and his contemporaries. As an influential scholar, Maulānā Nadwī's influence in the Muslim world has been significant. It is, however, in the contemporary Muslim thought especially in the current history of revivalism that Maulānā Nadwī occupies a unique position. This is evident in his interaction with Islamists who represent various strands of Salafiyyah and the *'ulamā* with distinct ideological perspectives. Of no less importance are the Muslim modernists whose

1. A detailed treatment examination of Islamic resurgence is found in Abu-Rabi', *Intellectual Origins of Islamic Resurgence in the Modern Arab World*, New York: Suny Press, 1996, 40-61.

2. Ibid.

interpretation of *tajdīd* sheds understanding on the variable trends of this concept within the Islamic resurgence framework.

Tajdīd (Revivalism): A Conceptual Framework

The Arabic terms *iḥyā'* (revival) and *tajdīd* (renewal) which are interchangeably used have their roots in an Islamic tradition of a *mujaddid* (renewer of faith). The appearance of a *mujaddid* is supported by the following *ḥadīth*:

> Allah will raise at the head of each century such a people for this *ummah* as will revive its religion for it.[3]

Two interpretations by Maulānā Maudūdī and Maulānā Nadwī to this *ḥadīth* reveal their respective ideological orientations. In his classical work, *A Short History of the Revivalist Movement in Islam*,[4] Maulānā Maudūdī elaborates on the function of the *mujaddid*. He states the *mujaddid* may imply a single person, a group of persons or even an organisation of people who "will exercise a dominant influence on the various branches of knowledge and trends of thought and life prevalent in their age."[5] As this study will seek to show Maulānā Maudūdī's focus on the concept Jāhiliyyah (ignorance) overlaps in his discussion on *tajdīd*. According to Maulānā Maudūdī, "no century (of the Muslim era) will remain devoid of such persons as will rise in the face of 'Ignorance' and endeavour to purge Islam of all kinds of impurities and enforce its system in the world in its original form and spirit." Jāhiliyyah has clear political overtones for Maulānā Maudūdī (which is critically analysed in Chapter 4).

---

3. Abu Dawood.
4. Abul A'la Maudūdī, *A Short History of the Revivalist Movement in Islam*, Lahore: Islamic Publications Ltd., 1972.
5. Ibid., 32.

Muslim scholarly interest in the *ḥadīth* on *tajdīd* in earlier writings has focused almost exclusively on personalities, i.e. on the identity of the *mujaddids*. Thus the *mujaddid*'s role has not been objectively discussed. The analysis by Seyyid Vali Reza Nasr on leader-intellectuals in contemporary Islamic thought is instructive. He observes:

> It is they who advanced the formative ideas, spoke to the concerns of various social groups, shaped public debates by selecting the ideas that would be included in them and those that would not, and relative individual and social experiences to lasting questions and concerns about freedom, justice, good, evil and salvation. It is they who initiated the process of interpretive reading of the Islamic faith with the aim of leading the struggle with Western thought, and help give it a role in rapidly changing Muslim social life. In short, they articulated the foundational ideas that are associated with contemporary Islamic thought, which uses social impulses to make a new discourse possible.[6]

The rise by Islamist movements in the twentieth century has contributed largely to scholarly studies on *mujaddids*. A coherent formulation on *tajdīd* in a socio-political context by contemporary works is in marked contrast with hagiographical accounts of traditional scholars.

Maulānā Nadwī's discussion on *tajdīd* is expressed in his multi-volume *Saviours of Islamic Spirit*.[7] The *iṣlāḥi* (reformist) tradition which is explored in the lives of *mujaddids* is a recurrent theme in Maulānā Nadwī's other writings[8] dealing with biographies on scholars largely drawn from the Indian subcontinent. According to Maulānā Nadwī, the *tajdīd*

---

6. Cited in Nasr, *Maudūdī and the Making of Islamic Revivalism.*
7. SAHA Nadwī, *Saviours of Islamic Spirit,* vol. I, Lucknow: Academy of Islamic Research and Publications, 1971.
8. See the following works:

   SAHA Nadwī, *Sirat-i-Sayyid Ahmad Shahid* (Karachi, 1987) and *The Life and Mission of Maulana Mohammad Ilyas,* Lucknow, 1979.

tradition is infused with the dynamic spirit of Islam. This tradition of struggle against un-Islam, the spirit to persevere and renovate the pristine teachings of the faith and the effort to infuse people with a revolutionary spirit to reassert the divine message are as old as Islam itself.[9]

The continuity of *tajdīd* implies that Islam has not suffered any rupture in terms of its reformatory endeavours during the past 1,400 years. Maulānā Nadwī admits the emergence of heretical movements[10] during these centuries which had threatened to stifle Islam. It was however the efforts of the *mujaddid*s that "defended Islam against philosophies and schools thought incompatible with it."[11]

A salient feature of Maulānā Nadwī's portrayal of the *mujaddids* is his reference to those *'ulamā* and Sūfīs whom Habib-ul-Haq Nadvi regard as political positivists.[12] This term is intended to highlight the *'ulamā*'s active role in the field of *jihād* and *ijtihād* and perhaps negate the image built around them as being state functionaries. This view is articulated in Maulānā Nadwī's widely-acclaimed *Islam and the World*.[13] Maulānā Nadwī says:

---

9. Nadwī, *Saviours of Islamic Spirit*, vol. I, 11.

10. The establishment of *Dīn-i-ilāhī*, a syncretism of Islam and Hinduism propagated by the Mughal Emperor Akbar, is one such example of a heretical movement. See Nadwī, *Saviours of Islamic Spirit*, vol. 3 for an analysis of this movement. The noted historian, Khaliq Aḥmad Nizami has studied this movement from a socio-political perspective. See Khaliq Aḥmad Nizami; *Akbar on Religion*, Delhi: Idarah-i-Adabiyat, 1989.

11. Nadwī, *Saviours of Islamic Spirits*, 3.

12. Syed Habib-al-Haq Nadvi, *Islamic Resurgent Movements in the Indo-Pak Subcontinent*, Durban: Academia, 1987, 37-38, 51-52.

13. The importance of Nadwī's *Islam and the World* in the Islamist circle is expressed in Abu Rabi' Ibrahim, *Intellectual Origins of Islamic Resurgence in the Modern Arab World*, New York: Suny Press, 1996, 18-21.

> The whole course of Islamic history is lighted up with the crusading endeavours of conscious, determined, brave hearted men, who, like the true successors of the prophets, faced the challenges of the time and restored, revived and kept on moving the *millat* (muslim community) by resorting to *jihād* and *ijtihād*. These two principles which embody the dynamism of Islam could never suffer a vacuum in its structure. They remained operative ceaselessly in the body of Islam as living factors, holding aloft the torch of religious endeavour in the midst of the severest tempests.[14]

It would be worthwhile to refer to Maulānā Nadwī's definitions of *jihād* and *ijtihād* to centextualise this twin concept to the *tajdīd* tradition. According to Maulānā Nadwī, *jihād* in Islamic terminology means to strive to one's utmost to achieve the noblest object on earth. Its overall aim is for the individual "to exert himself for the betterment of his fellow-beings and the establishment of Divine sovereignty over the world around him."[15] The *jihād* he advocated has a universal message for mankind and negates the militant tone found in the discourse of several Islamists, in particular Sayyid Quṭb. In Maulānā Nadwī's view *ijtihād* "is the ability to cope with the ever-changing pattern of life's requirements. It calls for a deep insight into the soul of Islam and a thorough knowledge of the basic principles of Islamic jurisprudence. It also includes the ability to harness the treasures of nature to the service of Islam. . . ."[16] Maulānā Nadwī seeks to illustrate the dynamism of the *shari'ah* in formulating responses to the challenges Muslims face in specific situations. Again the concept of *ijtihād* is linked to *tajdīd* and is integral to the evolution of Islamic jurisprudence. Maulānā Nadwī's implicit

---

14. Nadwī, *Islam and the World.*
15. Ibid., 92.
16. Ibid., 93-94.

advocacy of *ijtihād* states that it has been a historical phenomenon in Islamic resurgence.

This twin concept is reflected in the *tajdīdī* efforts of Ibn Taymiyyah (d. 1328)[17] who, by all accounts, is considered the precursor of the *salafi* and modern reformist movements beginning in the nineteenth century. It is clear that Maulānā Maudūdī refers to Ibn Taymiyyah to justify his own interpretation of *tajdīd* which negated rigidity (*jumu'*) on an intellectual level. Maulānā Nadwī's detailed account of Ibn Taymiyyah's contributions is a tacit endorsement of the latter's *tajdīdī* role. However, the *'ulamā* of Deoband leanings were by and large not appreciative of Ibn Taymiyyah. Even so, Maulānā Nadwī's position among the *'ulamā* of the subcontinent did allow for a review and conciliatory approach amongst the *'ulamā* towards Ibn Taymiyyah's writings. Thus Nadwah as an ardent admirer of Ibn Taymiyyah's intellectual legacy played a significant role in this regard.

IMPACT OF IBN TAYMIYYAH ON REVIVALIST TRENDS

A detailed study of Ibn Taymiyyah's voluminous writings shows that his aim was "to rediscover and intellectually reconstitute the early normative community of Islam which was based on the Qur'ān and Sunnah, as he saw it."[18] This comment by the noted scholar, Fazlur Rahman (d. 1988)

---

17. Nadwī has made an interesting remark on Ibn Taymiyyah's works in his *Saviours of Islamic Spirit*, vol. 2, 7. "Deviating from the beaten track of graceless and severe style, Ibn Taymiyyah's dress of thought is graced by literary allusions and quick wit; ease and lucidity of style and vigour and eloquence which possess an immediate appeal to readers."

18. Fazlur Rahman, *Revival and Reform in Islam*, 133-65. Fazlur Rahman devotes a chapter to Ibn Taymiyyah's intellectual legacy in terms of his theological and political doctrines. His reformist views on *salafi* and modern thought are clearly evident as discussed elsewhere in the chapter.

reiterates the intellectual contribution of Ibn Taymiyyah in the *tajdīdī* tradition. Two distinctive qualities stood him apart from the *'ulamā* establishment: firstly he was a forceful advocate of a reform of the administration in the spirit of the *shari'ah*. His insistence that the *shari'ah* be implemented in totality for good governance of Muslim states was in direct conflict to the practices of the Mamluk sultans ruling both Egypt and Syria. His political candour was met with spells of imprisonment which led to his death. Secondly, Ibn Taymiyyah claimed the right of *ijtihād* and used his independent judgement in re-articulating the general principles of the Qur'ān and the *sunnah*.[19] According to Maulānā Maudūdī, Ibn Taymiyyah was not only vocal in his criticism of *taqlīd* (rigid conformity) but understood *ijtihād* in the manner of the early religious doctors. This approach enabled him "to explain the Islamic beliefs and injunctions in their right perspective and with their true import."[20] In a similar vein, Maulānā Nadwī's biography on Ibn Taymiyyah sets out to trace his social milieu and his singular contribution to *tajdīd*. Maulānā Nadwī maintains that Ibn Taymiyyah stands out as the "greatest thinker and reformer in Islam whose influence extends to almost every reformative movement started since the eighth century, and particularly to those which gained impetus during the twelfth century of the Islamic era."[21]

IMPACT OF IBN TAYMIYYAH'S IDEAS IN THE SUBCONTINENT

Among the intellectual figures of the subcontinent, Shah Wali-allah (d. 1762) emerges as an original thinker in the religio-

19. Nadwī, *Saviours of Islamic Spirit*, vol. 2. These two qualities are elaborated by Serajul Haque in his chapter on "Theologico-Philosophical Thought" in M.M. Sharif, *A History of Muslim Philosophy*, vol. 2, Karachi: Royal Book Company, 1983, 796-819.

20. Maudūdī, *Revivalist Movement in Islam*, 64.

21. Nadwī, *Saviours of Islamic Spirit*, vol. 2, 142.

academic renaissance of the Muslims of South Asia. According to Muḥammad al-Ghazali, Shah Wali-allah was profoundly influenced by Ibn Taymiyyah who paid "rich tributes to the scholarship and his typical revolutionary orthodoxy."[22] Similarly, citing Ibn Taymiyyah in his *Saviours of Islamic Spirit*, Maulānā Nadwī attempts to show the parallels between the *tajdīdī* endeavours of both Ibn Taymiyyah and Shah Wali-allah.[23]

It is outside the scope of this study to examine in detail Ibn Taymiyyah's impact on the various Islamic movements, both orthodox and modernist, that drew their inspiration from this great reformer. Khaliq Nizami's insightful article, "The Impact of Ibn Taymiyyah on South Asia,"[24] is a summative assessment of his major influence in this region. Here mention may also be made of Ibn Taymiyyah's influence on Maulānā Nadwī. Several of his other writings[25] reflect his praise of Ibn Taymiyyah's intellectual contributions and this perhaps has led his critics to label him a *salafi*. Nizami's remark about Maulānā Nadwī's position in this regard is indicative of the latter's pragmatism on several contentious issues: "He (Maulānā Nadwī) propagated Ibn Taymiyyah's ideology without bringing it into clash with the religious psychology of the Muslims in South Asia."[26] However, Khurshid Aḥmad (b. 1932), an internationally recognised Islamic activist and senior member of the Jamā'at-i-Islami, in his review of

22. The impact of Ibn Taymiyyah on Shah Wali-allah's intellectual orientation is discussed in Muḥammad Ghazali, *The Socio-Political Thought of Shah Wali Allah*, Islamabad: Islamic Research Institute, 2001.

23. Nadwī, *Saviours of Islamic Spirit*, vol. 4, 94-96.

24. Khaliq Aḥmad Nizami, *On Islamic History and Culture*, Delhi: Idarah-i-Adabiyat-i-Delli, 1995, 76-113.

25. See Nadwī, *The Four Pillars of Islam* (1988) on Ibn Taymiyyah's impact on Nadwī's writings.

26. Nizami, *On Islamic Culture . . .*, 107.

Maulānā Nadwī's *Saviours of Islamic Spirit*, vol. 2, has made the following observation: "(Maulānā Nadwī) has provided a 'sanitised' approach on *taqlīd* (rigid conformity) and *taṣawwuf* of Ibn Taymiyyah's critique. On the contrary, his *fatwā* contains some trenchant comments on these concepts."[27]

It is thus clearly evident that sectarian bias and conflicting views define the boundaries of revivalist thought with regard to Ibn Taymiyyah's contributions which continue to dominate mainstream Islamic reformist movements.

The golden chain (*silsal-at-dhahab*) of *mujaddids* is largely drawn from Maulānā Nadwī's viewpoint that there has been no rupture in Islamic terms of *tajdīd*. Thus Ibn Taymiyyah and Wali-allah, drawn from two different periods of Islamic history are considered models for reformers. The impact of Wali-allah on Maulānā Nadwī's important writings that deal with *tajdīd* is evident. The intellectual legacy of Wali-allah is examined in *Saviours of Islamic Spirit*, vol. 4, and here Maulānā Nadwī makes appreciative comments on Wali-allah's reformulation of Islamic intellectual thought. The affinity of ideas on *taqlīd* by Wali-allah and Maulānā Nadwī is conspicuous as both articulate a paradigm of Islamic resurgence that is pragmatic and shaped by socio-political circumstances.

The emergence of *tajdīd* in the nineteenth and twentieth centuries is inextricably linked to a re-interpretation of Islamic sources to which Egypt and India were representatives of this trend.

ASSESSMENT

It is evident that Maulānā Nadwī follows a traditional approach to the *tajdīdī* concept which allows him to draw his

27. Khurshid Aḥmad, "Tārikh Da'wat wa Azimat", in Safir Akhtar (ed.), *Maulānā Sayyid Abul Hasan Ali Nadwī: Hayat wa ifkār ke chand Pehlu*, Islamabad: Idāra Tahqiqāt-i-Islam, 2002, 114-15.

personalities considered *mujaddids* from sources of Islamic authenticity. Maulānā Maudūdī's views on the *mujaddid* in contrast are more liberal and are in line with his theorisation of Ḥākimiyyah (divine sovereignty). His thesis of an Islamic state articulates his vision of *tajdīd* against the backdrop of Western concepts of democracy. The divergent views on *tajdīd* have spared a number of Islamic movements claiming to be representatives of the *tajdīdī* trend. It must be noted that their respective orientations on *tajdīd* have not provided a coherent presentation of the concept which supports our view that *tajdīd* is not monolithic and its diverse forms allow for adaptability and dynamism.

Genealogy of Tajdīd in the Nineteenth and Twentieth Centuries

The call for *tajdīd* emanated from the detection of symptoms of backwardness and stagnation by Islamic thinkers in the nineteenth century. However, it was the *tajdīdī* endeavours of Muḥammad Ibn 'Abd-al-Wahhāb, founder of the Wahhābiyah movement that served as a link between classical Islamic reformist thought represented by Ibn Taymiyyah and the *salafi* movements which emerged in the nineteenth century.

Albert Hourani in his classical work *Arabic Thought in the Liberal Age: 1798-1938*[28] projected nineteenth-century reformist thought in relation to the crisis faced by the Muslim states against the backdrop of the rise of Western civilisation. Egypt and India felt the impact of the West's ascendancy largely because of colonial rule. The responses from Muslim reformists[29] such as Muhammad 'Abduh and Rashid Rida in Egypt and Syed Aḥmad Khan in India highlighted the changing religious landscape in the Muslim world. They

28. Albert Hourani, *Arabic Thought in the Liberal Age 1798-1939*, Oxford: Oxford University Press, 1983.

29. Ibid., 103-92.

represented a cadre of scholars who advocated interaction with Western ideas and systems. Abu-Rabi' rightly remarks that the primary concerns of the Muslim intelligentsia in the nineteenth century must be examined in terms of contemporary Islamic thought. These reformers began to write down the general outlines of "Islamic modernism." The major features of Islamic modernism included the following:

- the revival of Islamic rational elements in the Islamic tradition,
- finding Islamic solutions to the challenges of the West, and
- constructing new academic and religious institutions to meet the challenges of modernity.[30]

It has been wrongly assumed that the reformist thought was formulated by intellectuals who drew their worldview from the Salafiyyah. The *'ulamā* who were the representatives of the centuries of Islamic tradition responded to Western challenges albeit with a different outlook.[31] In his study *The 'Ulamā in Contemporary Islam: Custodians of Change,* Zaman examines issues of religious authority exercised by the *'ulamā*. The Al-Azhar institution which represented Sunnī Islam for almost a thousand years was exposed to the strong current of the Western system. The leading scholars who responded to these challenges belonged to the *'ulamā* fraternity with its established tradition of religious autonomy, a salient feature of Al-Azhar.[32] Parallel to the Western incursion in the Muslim

---

30. Ibrahim Abu Rabi', *Contemporary Islamic Intellectual History: A Theoretical Perspective in Islamic Studies,* vol. 44: 4, 511-12.

31. This aspect is critically examined by Francis Robinson in several of his writings dealing with *'ulamā* in South Asia. For a detailed elaboration, see F. Robinson, *Islam, South Asia and the West,* New Delhi: Oxford University Press, 2007, 59-98.

32. Zaman, *The 'Ulamā in Contemporary Islam,* 144-50.

world was the emergence of pan-Islamism which played a leading role in providing an impetus to Islamic resurgence.

PAN-ISLAMISM

The term pan-Islamism denotes the intellectual trend towards unity that emerged among Muslim nations, beginning in the mid-nineteenth century and continuing through the twentieth century. According to Caesar Farah in his recent study, *Abdul Hamid and the Muslim World*, pan-Islamism represented both an instrument of Islamic solidarity and a prescription for both reform and defence.[33] Since the term was coined in the West it had two significant connotations: cultural and political hostility by Muslim nations as a result of colonial rule.[34] Afghānī is considered the pioneer of pan-Islamism, whose contributions have been analysed by Maulānā Nadwī in the *Introduction* of this study. Afghānī worked towards Islamic solidarity among Muslim nations and at the same time advocated a reform of Muslim society in the intellectual field.[35] Later reformers like his student 'Abduh pushed ahead with a reform that was clearly modern. In this context, the term Islamic modernism emerged which attempted to respond to the new challenges by the intrusive presence of colonialism. The solutions offered by the reformers for an Islamic resurgence were based on a critical examination of the decline of the Muslim *ummah* in a theme that dominated

---

33. Caesar Farah, *Abdul Hamid II and the Muslim World*, Istanbul: ISAR, 2008, 168.

34. SAHA Nadwī, *Western Civilisation: Islam and Muslims*, Lucknow: Academy of Islamic Research and Publications, 1974, 94. Nadwī noted that Afghānī could not realise his vision of pan-Islamism and also could not produce a new school of thought that could make a critical evaluation of Western civilisation. However, he succeeded in strengthening the Muslim intelligentsia's reverence for Islamic teachings and its universal message.

35. Ibid., 95.

Islamic discourse during the nineteenth and twentieth centuries. Thus the emergence of Islamic modernism was set against the background of political circumstances which aimed to remedy the malaise affecting the Muslim world.[36] It brought in its wake a critical reappraisal of the role of *ijtihād* in the reformulation of the intellectual reawakening in the Muslim *ummah*. This vision was a marked departure from the traditional interpretation of Islamic sources and the beginning of Salafiyyah with a strong reformist content. The paradox in the term "Islamic modernism" was ambiguous: return to the ideal past while adopting uncritically Western concepts for an intellectual renewal.

Islamic Modernism and Modernity: A Critique

It would be difficult to separate modernity from "Islamic modernism" as the latter incorporates features that betray an Islamic discourse. The recent debate on modernity has elicited several responses across the Muslim world. Khalid Adeeb contends that modernity "is a global condition that brings with it new forms of organisation of self and society, new forms of intellectual production and new ways of imagining the world."[37] Abul-Faḍl on the other hand says that by modernity the "standards of acculturation to the times were those set by the West"[38] and the paradigms adopted in the name of national development programmes by the Third World were influenced by Western culture. The West according to Abul-Faḍl is going through a process of re-thinking in terms of its own heritage and it is doing so "in a relative openness to its own past as well as to the cultural

36. For a detailed discussion on the growth and development of pan-Islamism, see Farah, *Abdul Hamid II*, 164-224.

37. Adeeb Khalid, *The Politics of Muslim Cultural Reform: Jadidism in Central Asia*, Berkeley: University of California Press, 1999, 2.

38. Mona Abul-Faḍl, *Where East Meets West*, Herdon: IIIT, 1992, 26.

experience of others."[39] This implies the West has a decisive influence in terms of cultural appropriation and Muslim countries have assimilated these values which often are in contradiction of their Islamic heritage.

Khalid's definition of modernity does not hint at the West's hegemony. His emphasis on its global phenomenon may be contextualised in his study of the *jadīdī* movement in the early twentieth century in Central Asia. The term *jadīd* (new) refers to the class of intellectuals (*ẓiyālilar*) who campaigned for a reform of the Central Asian society from cultural accretions.[40] The transformations of *jadīdism* embraced changes to interpret the role of Islam in society. The new knowledge brought in print[41] and led to a new understanding of the world. Furthermore the dominant discourse of contemporary Europe was used for measuring the utility of ideas and practices in Muslim society.[42] Progressive Islam in the discourse of *jadīdism* challenged the practices of religious scholars (*'ulamā*) in their interpretation of Islam. The *jadīd*s claimed the sources of Islam were open to anyone with the requisite Islamic knowledge.

A variant interpretation of modernity is found in the writings of the noted scholar, Fazlur Rahman (d. 1988). His critique on revival and reform[43] represents a modernist reading

39. Mona Abul-Faḍl, *Where East Meets West*, Herdon: IIIT, 1992, 29.

40. Khalid, *The Politics of Muslim Cultural Reform*, 92-93.

41. See Robinson's *Islam in South Asia* — a detailed study of the print/ press in transforming Muslim societies.

42. Adeeb Khalid, *The Politics of Muslim Cultural Reform*, 281.

43. For a detailed analysis of Fazlur Rahman's interpretation of *Reform and Revival* see his *Revival and Reform in Islam*, Oxford: Oneworld Publications, 2000. The introduction by Ebrahim Moosa who edited the posthumous work of Fazlur Rahman reinforces the latter's vision of an intellectual reformulation of contemporary Islamic thought euphemistically termed as re-thinking Islam, p. 6.

of this twin term. It is in this context that his exposition of modernity must be understood. In his *Islam and Modernity: Transformation of an Intellectual Tradition*[44] Fazlur Rahman states that the revivalists' main aim is to arrest the process of secularisation and de-Islamisation of Muslim societies. Secularisation is "the removal of religious values from all aspects of society except that defined as specifically religious."[45] Their underlying assumption is: the same Islam which empowered the early Islamic community is also capable of empowering modern Islamic societies. In contrast to this view, Fazlur Rahman argues that the revival of Muslim societies is rooted in the intellectual legacy of Islam. Therefore it is inconsequential to abandon various Western institutions and behaviours to sustain the revivalist spirit. As an alternative, Fazlur Rahman presents his Islamic methodology which is an attempt to equip the Muslim with intellectual tools[46] to promote a creative understanding of Islamic thought which is not tradition-bound. It is therefore not surprising that based on this thesis, the revivalist movement in the twentieth century, the Jamā'at-i-Islami of Pakistan is criticised by Fazlur Rahman for its failure to distinguish between modernism and modernity.[47]

A scholar who endorses modernity fully is Bassam Tibi.

---

44. Fazlur Rahman, *Islam and Modernity: Transformation of an Intellectual Tradition*, Chicago: University of Chicago Press, 1982. The major themes discussed in this book are found in their formative stages in his *Major Themes in the Qur'ān* (1979), *Islam* (1967) and numerous articles published in leading journals. Cf. Fazlur Rahman, "Islamic Modernism: Its Scope, Method and Alternative" in *International Journal of Middle East Studies*, vol. 1, 1970, 1:329.

45. Tamarra Sonn, "Fazlur Rahman's Islamic Methodology", in *The Muslim World*, vol. 81, July-October, 1991, 3-4: 226.

46. Rahman, *Islam and Modernity*, 8-10.

47. For an elaboration of this dichotomy see Basit Koshul in Fazlur Rahman's "Islam and Modernity Revisited" in *Islamic Studies*, vol. 33, 1994, 403-18.

He has published several works[48] related to Islam and modernity. In Tibi's view, science and knowledge both of which measure the West's progress embody a set of cultural values. He castigates the resurgent voices of Islam as being fundamentalists for adopting modern science and technology of the West and rejecting its "cultural underpinnings."[49] In contrast to Tibi's endorsement of modernity is Parvez Manzoor, a trenchant critic of this concept. His main contentions against modernity are based on the following points:

- the doctrine of progress is paradoxical, and
- the concept of reason extends beyond the confines of modernity.[50]

This comment is elaborated by Shamil Jeppie in *Language, Identity, Modernity*. He states that "Islamic modernism" has both "intellectually enabling attributes and inherent contradictions and limitations."[51] According to Jeppie the modernist's penchant for the "cause of Muslim decline" tends to dwell on the absence of the scientific spirit in Muslim countries against Western hegemony. They ignore the complex effects and consequences of the colonial power in the past and imperialism in the present.[52] Modernity is largely associated with Islamic modernism. The views expressed by Muslim

48. For a listing of these works, see Basam Tibi, "Culture and Knowledge: The Politics of Islamisation of Knowledge and a Postmodern Project: The Fundamentalist claim to De-Westernisation", in *Theory, Culture and Society*, 12/1, 1995, 24.

49. Cited in Aslam Farouk-All, "Islamic Discourse after Modernity and Postmodernity", in Abu Rabiʿ Ibrahim (ed.), *The Blackwell Companion to Contemporary Islamic Thought*, Blackwell, 2006, 290.

50. Parvez Manzoor, "Islam and the Crisis of Modernity", http://www.algonet.se/-pmanzoor.

51. Shamil Jeppie, *Language, Identity, Modernity: The Arabic Study Circle of Durban*, Cape Town: HSRC, 2007, 10.

52. Ibid., 11.

scholars show the problematic relationship between modernity and Islamic modernism. Modernity embraces features of globalisation which in turn shapes an Islamic discourse on *tajdīd*. In contrast, Islamic modernism challenges core ideological issues in the light of Western civilisation. This distinction is important to understand how these concepts are perceived in relation to Islamic resurgence.

We now turn to "Islamic modernism" to examine its influence in the Muslim world. The study also seeks to show that "Islamic modernism" has its roots in the *tajdīdī* tradition; however its expression is largely Western in character with norms reflecting the rapidity of social change.

Voices of Islamic Modernism

"Islamic modernism" believes in the sovereignty of reason and repudiates every authority that cannot stand the test of reason. The modernist Muslim reformers and scholars emphasise the need for radical reformation in Muslim society. They maintain that the Muslim is "an efficacious agent in controlling his destiny."[53] They are preoccupied with a social order which envisages a rejection of Sūfī theology which they consider deterministic and *taqlīd* (a blind adherence to authority) as rigid. According to the reformers the attempt to go back to pristine Islam can succeed only if the "chains of medievalism are broken."[54] Medievalism, according to them, represents a traditional interpretation of Islam ignoring its intellectual and scientific legacy.

The binary opposites of modernism and medievalism clearly sets out the parameters of Islamic discourse. According to Siddiqi, reformers in the early twentieth century included

53. Mazheruddin Siddiqui, *Modern Reformist Thought in the Muslim World*, Islamabad: Islamic Research Institute, 1982, 36.

54. Ibid., 37.

intellectuals like Muḥammad 'Abduh (d. 1905), Rashid Riḍā (d. 1935), Sir Syed Aḥmad Khan (d. 1898),[55] Shibli Nu'māni (d. 1914), Muḥammad Iqbal (d. 1938), 'Ubaidullah Sindhi (d. 1944) and Maulānā Abul Kalām Āzād (d. 1957). Their intellectual contributions have given birth to new concepts, ideas and theories which have changed traditional ways of thinking. These reformers belong to diverse religious backgrounds from both Egypt and the Indian subcontinent.[56]

Muḥammad 'Abduh, a traditional *'ālim* from Al-Azhar, changed the curriculum of the university to make it compatible with modern institutions.[57] Shibli, a noted scholar who was exposed to modern educational trends at Aligarh Muslim University, attempted to reconstruct the Nadwat-ul-'ulamā (Lucknow) along modern lines.[58] In his *Reconstruction of*

---

55. Syed Aḥmad Khan's contribution to revivalist thought has given rise to a plethora of writings often reflecting his controversial role. See JMS Baljon, *The Reforms and Religious Ideas of Sir Sayyid Ahmad Khan*, Lahore, 1970; Haider Hussain, *Syed Ahmed Khan: Pioneer of Muslim Resurgence,* Lahore, 1970; Aziz Aḥmad, *Islamic Modernism in India and Pakistan, 1857-1964*, London: Oxford University Press, 1967. Cf. Nadwī, *Western Civilisation and Muslims,* 74-75 for a balanced account of Sir Syed's contribution to the educational upliftment of Indian Muslims and the successful role played by Aligarh Muslim University in the demand for a separate Muslim homeland, i.e. Pakistan. Sir Syed Aḥmad Khan established the Aligarh Muslim University through which he proceeded to interpret the Islamic faith and the Qur'ān in the light of materialistic thought.

56. Cf. Mazheruddin Siddiqi, *Modern Reformist Thought in the Muslim World,* 41-112.

57. Ibid., 223. Cf. Albert Hourani, *Arabic Thought in the Liberal Age, 1798-1939*, 136-50.

58. Ibid., 224. For an elaboration of Shibli's rationalist theology see Mehr Afroz Murad, *Intellectual Modernism of Shibli Nu'māni*, Lahore: Institute of Islamic Culture, 1976, 1-56.

Religious Thought in Islam[59] Iqbal pointed out the role of modern knowledge in the re-statement of Muslim theology. Likewise, Sindhī, a product of Dār-ul-'ulūm, Deoband, influenced by his years of exile in Russia and Europe, propagated a reconstruction of Islamic theology based on socialist lines.[60] Similarly, Āzād, an illustrious *mufassir* (commentator of the Qur'ān) sought to synthesise Islam and other faiths in a political setting.[61]

It is clear from the above discussion that "Islamic modernism" does not share a uniform and monolithic form. Rather political circumstances dictated the nature and scope of its reformist trends. The examination of the role of the Islamist and Salafiyyah in the *tajdīdī* tradition reveals a similar dimension. The polemics again "Islamic modernism" is best represented by Maryam Jameelah (b. 1934) whose writings advocate a literalist adherence to Islam.[62] Her trenchant criticisms of Western civilisation are summed up in her widely-read book *Western Civilisation Condemned by Itself*.[63] The polemical contents are based on selective quotations from original

59. Ibid. Cf. Iqbal Muḥammad, *The Reconstruction of Religious Thought in Islam*, Lahore: Sh. Muḥammad Ashraf, 1971, 146-80.

60. For a detailed account of his life and thought, see Shaik Muḥammad Hajjan, *Maulana Ubaid Allah Sindhi: A Revolutionary Scholar*, Islamabad: NIHCR, 1986.

61. Ian Henderson Douglas, *Abul Kalam Azad: An Intellectual and Religious Biography*, Delhi: Oxford University Press, 1993, 269-73. Cf. Lini S. May, *The Evolution of Indo-Muslim Thought after 1857*, Lahore: Sh. Muḥammad Ashraf, 1970, 185-201.

62. Esposito considers Jameelah to be one of the makers of Contemporary Islam. On her contribution, see Esposito, *Makers of Contemporary Islam*, 54-67.

63. Maryam Jameelah, *Western Civilisation Condemned by Itself*, Lahore: Yusuf Khan, 1970. The introduction of her writings shares a common theme: condemnation of Western civilisation. This theme is also echoed in her *Islam and Modernism* (1975), vii-xiii.

sources of both Greek and Roman civilisations and are aimed at exposing the inherent weaknesses of Western civilisation. Her views have been articulated by either Islamists in their condemnation of Western civilisation. Maulānā Nadwī too has expressed his admiration of her writings.[64] In a similar vein, Jameelah is critical of Muslim reformers who support a modernist interpretation of Islam. According to Jameelah "modernism is a militant revolt against religious and all the spiritual values it represents."[65] Thus several reformers whose contributions have been highlighted in the chapter are subjected to her tirade in her *Islam and Modernism*.[66]

The salient feature of "Islamic modernism," according to Akbar Ahmed, is to locate this concept in a historical context. In his *Postmodernism and Islam*, Ahmed states the modernists wished to come to terms with European colonialism. They sought "synthesis and ideally looked for harmony between their own position and that of the Europeans."[67]

The dynamic spirit of Islamic modernism according to Ebrahim Moosa has died down. This view is elucidated in a collection of interviews with Muslim intellectuals in the twenty-first century by Farish Noor in his *New Voices of Islam*.[68]

---

64. In his autobiography, *Kārwān-i-Ẓindagī*, vol. 2, 269, Nadwī makes a pertinent remark, "We became aquainted with each other through our respective writings. Many of her views shared by me as well."

65. Maryan Jameelah, *Islam and Modernism*, Lahore: Yusuf Khan, 1975, 16.

66. In this work Āzād is described as a champion of nationalism and secularism in Muslim India while Muḥammad 'Abduh pioneered his vision of the compatibility of Islam and Western civilisation. Jameelah, *Islam and Modernism*, 77-87; 147-54.

67. Akbar S. Ahmed, *Postmodernism and Islam: Predicament and Promise*, London: Routledge, 1992, 29.

68. Farish A. Noor, *New Voices of Islam*, Leiden: ISIM, 2002.

Moosa expresses his concern about the "rupture and crisis"[69] which is the message facing Muslim intellectuals today. The discourse which developed with Islamic modernists did not maintain a continuity. According to Moosa there have been several reasons for this rupture:

> It must be remembered that these Muslim thinkers were themselves located between two traditions: Islamic conservatism and secular modernity. In their attempt to modernise and reform Islam, many of these reformist thinkers ended up internalising the values of the modernist project. So it is hardly surprising for us to read how people like Al-Afghānī, 'Abduh and Maudūdī were concerned about economic development, material progress and catching up with the Western world.

Moosa's remark implies that these reformers are a product of a distinct political setting and grounded in a colonial discourse.

The Islamic modernists of the nineteenth century were thus a hybrid constituency and they were liminal figures both in Western secular and conservative Islamic circles. The conservative *'ulamā* opposed them because they were seen as too "Western-oriented" while the secular Westerners saw them as apologists for Islam. Today, those who want to defend the Islamic modernist project are at a loss over how to defend some of the ideas and positions held by these modernist thinkers. As a result much of what they said and wrote has been taken at face value, and the impulse towards critical thinking and self-reflection has been sidelined.[70] It is largely for this reason that Salafiyyah as a movement has been considered a reactionary movement that negates the dynamic character of Islamic culture and considered as antithesis of Islamic modernism. This aspect is examined in the next section.

---

69. Farish A. Noor, *New Voices of Islam*, Leiden: ISIM, 2002, p. 1.

70. Ibid., 24.

Growth and Development of Salafiyyah

In his assessment of the Salafiyyah, Abu Rabi' in his major study *Contemporary Arab Thought*[71] has outlined the historical character of the movement. The Salafiyyah has its roots in the Prophetic model exemplified by the practices of the Rightly Guided caliphs. The contemporary *salafi* trends have gone through "a number of challenges and mutations"[72] although it has not lost sight of its vision of Islamic identity and authenticity which clearly define its orientation.

The world Salafiyyah is derived from the Arabic root *salaf,* "to precede."[73] The Qur'ān uses the word to refer to the "past"[74] in specific historical settings. The authoritative Arabic lexicons[75] refer to the *salaf* as the virtuous precursors (*al-salaf al-ṣāliḥ*). In reformist parlance, the *salafi* is one who draws only from the sources of the Qur'ān and *sunnah* for religious rulings.

The term Salafiyyah is often used interchangeably with *iṣlāḥ* (reform) and *tajdīd* (renewal)[76] which are the fundamental concepts to Islam's worldview. Salafiyyah is also equated with Islamists movements of the twentieth century[77] with specific

71. Ibrahim Abu Rabi', *Contemporary Arab Thought in Post-1967 Arab Intellectual History*, London: Pluto Press, 2004.

72. Ibid., cf. Ibrahim Abu Rabi', "Contemporary Islamic Intellectual History: A Theoretical Perspective", in *Islamic Studies*, vol. 44, no. 4, winter 2005, 511-12.

73. Rohi Baalbaki, *Al-Mawrid: A Modern Arabic-English Dictionary*, Beirut: Dar el Ilm 1993, 641.

74. "Say to unbelievers, If they now desist (from unbelief), their past (*salaf*) would be forgiven them" (8:38); Yusuf Ali, *The Holy Qur'ān: English Translation of the Meanings and Commentary*, Medina, 1990, 480.

75. For example, *Al-Qamus*, Beirut, 1966.

76. John L. Esposito, *The Oxford Encyclopedia of the Modern Islamic World*, Oxford: Oxford University Press, 1995, vol. 3, 463.

77. Divergent opinions have been expressed on the influence of the Islamist movements in contemporary Islamic thought. See the →

socio-political markers. For some scholars however the term connotes reaction and rigidity because of the movements' strict adherence to the Qur'ān and *sunnah* and its exaltation of the formative period of its Islamic legacy.

FORMS OF SALAFIYYAH

It is important to identify the types of Salafiyyah throughout Islamic history both classical and modern. Too often stereotypical representations prejudice a coherent understanding of this movement. The voices of resurgent Islam have their unmistakable imprints in the initial phase of the movement albeit in changed circumstances.[78]

CLASSICAL SALAFIYYAH

The first type of Salafiyyah is best represented by Aḥmad bin Ḥanbal[79] of the third Islamic century and Aḥmad bin Taymiyyah[80] of the eighth Islamic century. As an articulator of classical Salafiyyah, Ibn Ḥanbal emphasised the primacy

---

→ following works:

John L. Esposito, *Islam: The Straight Path*, New York, 1991; Malcolm H. Kerr, *Islamic Reform: The Political and Legal Theories of Muhammad Abduh and Rashid Rida*, Berkeley, 1966; Olivier Roy, *Globalised Islam: The Search for a New Ummahi*, London, 2002.

78. For a thorough study on the evolution and intellectual components of the Salafiyyah, see Muḥammad Sa'id Ramaḍan Buti, *Al-Salafiyyah: Madhab zamaniyah muharakah, la madhab Islam*, Damascus, 1988.

79. On Ibn Ḥanbal's contribution to Salafiyyah, see Abdul Hakim Al-Matroudi, *The Hanbali School of Law and Ibn Taymiyyah*, Oxford, Routledge, 2005, cf. Mawjood, Salahuddin Ali Abdul, *The Biography of Imam Ahmad bin Hanbal*, Riyadh: Darussalam, 2006.

80. For a biographical account on Ibn Taymiyyah and his ideas on popular religious practices, see Muḥammad Umar Memon, *Ibn Taymiyyah's Struggle against Popular Religion*, The Hague, 1976. Cf. Qamaruddin Khan, *The Political Thought of Ibn Taymiyyah*, Islamabad: Islamic Research Institute, 1973.

of the revealed text over reason. In line with major Sunnī schools of thoughts, Ibn Ḥanbal held the Qur'ān and the *sunnah* to be authoritative sources for understanding Islam. The consensus (*ijmā'*)[81] of the pious precursors (*ṣalf-al-ṣāliḥ*) exemplified the twin sources of Islam.

The Salafiyyah approach evolved over the centuries to address new issues confronting the Muslim community. It was Ibn Taymiyyah who consolidated the classical Salafiyyah doctrines. His approach focused on the creed of *tawhīd,* proving the compatibility of reason and revelation and rejection of innovation (*bid'ah*) and syncretism introduced by Sūfī orders.[82] In his initial reformatory phase, Ibn Taymiyyah worked within the Ḥanbali school of thought but as a result of political and social changes in Muslim societies he departed from it in certain respects. Although the Salafiyyah has been criticised for not advocating an overt rational position as Fahmi Jad'ān argues,[83] it has embodied the potential for reform and renewal particularly at times of degeneration in the Muslim community. In support of this statement Maulānā Nadwī cites Ibn Ḥanbal's strict adherence to the Sunnī position on the uncreated nature of the Qur'ān in his multi-volume *Saviours of Islamic Spirit.*[84] The Inquisition (*miḥnah*)[85] which was instituted by the Abbāsid Caliphate could not deter Ibn Ḥanbal from withdrawing his standpoint on this issue. According to Maulānā Nadwī "the undaunted courage and steadfastness of Aḥmad Ibn Ḥanbal

81. A comprehensive study on *Ijmā'* has been published by Islamic Research Institute, Islamabad. See Aḥmad Ḥasan, *The Doctrine of Ijmā' in Islam,* Islamabad, 1980.

82. Abu Rabi', *Contemporary Arabic Thought*, 65.

83. Ibid.

84. Nadwī, *Saviours of Islamic Spirit,* vol. I, 78-84.

85. Ibid., 78-84.

gave a death-blow to a sacrilege which had exposed the faith to a great danger."[86]

Similarly Ibn Taymiyyah's contribution redefined the dynamic spirit of the *sunnah* which boldly challenged *taqlīd* and advocated *ijtihād*. This approach served as a nexus for later reformers to formulate their respective readings of Salafiyyah.[87]

PRE-MODERN SALAFIYYAH

In the eighteenth century several revivalist movements emerged to address the social and moral decay of the Muslim community (*ummah*). In this historical context the Wahhābiyyah is the most important. Its founder Muḥammad Ibn Abdul Wahhāb (d. 1792)[88] was inspired by the teachings of Ibn Ḥanbal and Ibn Taymiyyah to purify the Arabian peninsula from shirk-laden practices and build an Islamic state modelled on that established by the Prophet Muḥammad (SAW). The Wahhābiyyah influenced other movements such as the Sanusiyyah[89] and Mahdiyyah[90] in North Africa which had strong sūfī tendencies.

Similar movements emerged in the Muslim community which were indirectly inspired by the Wahhābiyyah. The popular reformist movement led by 'Uthmān Dan Fodio (d.

---

86. Nadwī, *Saviours of Islamic Spirit*, vol. I, 85.
87. See Esposito, *Makers of Contemporary Islam*, 54.
88. For a biographical account on Shaykh Muḥammad bin 'Abdul Wahhāb, see Aḥmad Abdol Ghafour Attar, *Muḥammad Ibn Abdul Wahhab*, Makkah, 1982; Emad Eldin Shahin, "Salafiyyah" in *The Oxford Encyclopedia of the Modern Islamic World*, Oxford: Oxford University Press, 1995, vol. 3, 463-68.
89. On the Sanusiyyah, See Nichola A. Ziadel, *Sanusiyah: A Study of a Revivalist Movement in Islam*, London: EJ Brill, 1983.
90. The Sūfī aspect of these reformers is clearly evident in Nadwī's writings. Cf. Nadwī, *The Life of Caliph Ali*, Lucknow, 1991, 252-55.

1817) of Nigeria[91] made a strong impact in West Africa. Likewise Shah Wali-allah (d. 1762) of India[92] provided an intellectual framework for his revivalist mission whose traces are to be found in both reformist and modernist movements in the subcontinent.

Shah Wali-allah was a contemporary of Shaykh 'Abdul Wahhāb. Both these reformers were unequivocal in their condemnation of innovation (*bid'ah*) and a strict adherence to the Prophetic model. However, Maulānā Nadwī states that the range of Shah Wali-allah's intellectual and reformative endeavour was much wider "for it covered the areas of regeneration of Islamic branches of learning as well as Islamic thought, elucidation of the wisdom underlying the injunctions of the *shari'ah* . . . harmonization of reason and religious thought and co-ordination of different juristic thoughts."[93] Likewise in his defence of Sayyid Aḥmad Barelwi (d. 1831)[94] whose movement earned the epithet of "Wahhābī" by his detractors, Maulānā Nadwī refutes this claim. In his *A Misunderstood Reformer*[95] Maulānā Nadwī laments the fact that

91. Abd al-Rahman Doi, *Uthmān Dan Fodio: The Grand Mujahid and Mujaddid of Africa*, Pretoria: Daral Salam Islamic Research Centre, 1998.

92. The studies on Shah Wali-allah reflect his versatile genius and his significant contribution to Islamic thought in South Asia. The following works delineate his contribution: Mahmood Aḥmad Ghazi, *Islamic Renaissance in South Asia 1707-1867*, Islamabad: Islamic Research Institute, 2007; Ishtiaq, Hussain Qureshi, *Ulema in Politics*, Karachi: Ma'arif Press, 1972; Nadwī, *Saviours of Islamic Spirit*, vol. 4, Lucknow, 1993.

93. Nadwī, *Saviours of Islamic Spirit*.

94. The Sayyid occupies a unique position among revivalist movements. See Nadwī, *Tarikh Da'wat-i-wa Azimat*, vol. I/2, Karachi: Majlis Nashriyāt-i-Islam, 1987; Muhiuddin Aḥmad, *Sayyid Ahmad Shahid*, Lucknow: Academy of Islamic Research and Publications, 1975.

95. Nadwī, *A Misunderstood Reformer*, Lucknow, 1978.

several Arab writers[96] based on the secondary sources and orientalist prejudices have regarded the Sayyid as a Wahhābi. On the contrary, Maulānā Nadwī notes, the call given by the Sayyid was to "reinstate the *shari'ah* in the Muslim society for integrating the *ummah* with the whole of practical and conceptual structure of Islam."[97]

Maulānā Maudūdī, a contemporary of Maulānā Nadwī, refers to the Sayyid's movement as "complementary to the revivalist work of Shah Wali-allah."[98] The opinion expressed by Maulānā Maudūdī is to show the Sayyid's appreciation by scholars of diverse opinions.[99] However, Maulānā Maudūdī's critique of the Sayyid's contribution to *tajdīd* is consistent with his liberal views on the features of Islamic resurgence. This aspect is discussed in Chapter 3.

MODERN SALAFIYYAH

The modern Salafiyyah was established by Afghānī and 'Abduh in Egypt at the turn of the twentieth century. It focused on the need to rid the *ummah* of *taqlīd* (blind imitation) and *jumūd* (stagnation), to restore Islam in its pure form and to reform the political and cultural conditions in the Muslim world.[100] A notable feature of the modern Salafiyyah was its

96. Nadwī, *A Misunderstood Reformer*, Lucknow, 1978, 45-46.
97. Ibid., 12.
98. Sayyid Abul A'lā Maudūdī, *A Short History of the Revivalist Movement in Islam*, Lahore: Islamic Publications Ltd., 1972, 104.
99. Maulānā Maudūdī's interpretation of revivalist trends is examined in subsequent chapters.
100. Details on the historical development of the modern Salafiyyah can be seen in Nikki R. Keddie, *An Islamic Response to Imperialism*, Berkeley, 1983, 65. Afghānī advocated a progressive notion of the evolution of the human knowledge. This implied a ready acceptance of rational sciences which are the salient features of Western civilisation.

emphasis on Islam's intellectual legacy and diverse modernist nature which paradoxically showed an anomaly in its vision.

The Salafiyyah in its formative stages attempted to revitalise Islam and to bridge the gap between historical Islam and modernity. Abu Rabiʿ rightly refers to the movement as "colonial Salafiyyah"[101] in terms of the challenges posed by Western colonialism. The writings of Afghānī and ʿAbduh as well as other reformers like Rashīd Riḍā[102] addressed issues that made up the core ideological foundation of the movement. Yet, the vision of the movement assumed different expression and emphasis. In Algeria, for example, ʿAbdul Ḥamid Ibn Bādis (d. 1940)[103] focused his reform efforts on the establishment of education to combat the assimilisationist policy of the French colonialists. According to Bādis, national identity and Islam were not incompatible and thus he played a pioneering role in Algeria's independence.[104]

A comparative analysis of the modern Salafiyyah by Maulānā Nadwī suggests the ambivalent responses of Muslim scholars. In his major work, *Western Civilisation, Islam and Muslims*,[105] Maulānā Nadwī strikes a balance in his critique of

---

101. Abu Rabiʿ, *Contemporary Arab Thought*, 67.

102. Albert Hourani, *Arabic Thought in the Liberal Age* 1798-1939, London, 1962. Chapters on Afghānī, ʿAbduh and Rashid Riḍā provide a detailed background and analysis of their lives and views.

103. There exists a lacuna of writings on Ibn Badīs in English. For a detailed comparison of Ibn Badīs' thoughts and movement with Afghānī and ʿAbduh, see Uthmān Fathi, *ʿAbd al-Hamid Ibn Badīs: Rāʾid, al barakah al Islamiyah fi al-jazāʾir al-muʿāsirah* (Kuwait, 1987), cf. Manzoor Alam, *100 Great Muslim Leaders of the 20th Century*, New Delhi: Insitute of Objective Studies, 2005, 191-97.

104. Esposito, *The Oxford Encyclopedia of the Modern Islamic World*, vol. 3, 466-67.

105. Nadwī, *Western Civilisation, Islam and Muslims*, Lucknow, 1974.

Afghānī. Political activities shut out for Afghānī the opportunity to make a positive contribution to the reconstruction of Islamic life and society. However, his strength lay "in reviving and strengthening for Islam and a living faith in the soundness and universality of its message."[106]

With regard to 'Abduh, Maulānā Nadwī acknowledges his valuabe services to the cause of Islam. Even so, Maulānā Nadwī states that 'Abduh was among the pioneers of the modernist movement in the Arab world. According to Maulānā Nadwī "he ('Abduh) gave a powerful call for the reinterpretation of Islam in order to make it conform to the requirements of the twentieth-century society."[107] 'Abduh was thus regarded as a forerunner of Western thought[108] in the Arab world. Maulānā Nadwī's critique of 'Abduh is not shared by his contemporary scholars. Āzād, for example, built his pan-Islamic vision on the thoughts of Afghānī and 'Abduh.[109] The *Al-Manar* group led by 'Abduh's successor, Rashīd Riḍā had a direct impact on his religious thinking. Paradoxically Āzād juxtaposed his modernist trends of Islamic thought with Indian nationalism which suggested his abandonment of his early pan-Islamic policy.[110]

For a different view altogether on the Islamist construction of the *ṣalf-al-ṣāliḥ* is Asma Afsaruddin's recent study, *The First*

106. Nadwī, *Western Civilisation, Islam and Muslims*, Lucknow, 1974, 96.

107. Ibid., 95.

108. The chapter "Movement for Modernisation and Westernisation" in *Western Civilisation* . . . also examines other modernist reformers in the Muslim world.

109. Cited in Francis Robinson, *Islam and Muslim History in South Asia*, Oxford: Oxford University Press, 2001, 284-85.

110. The following books give a synoptic view of his transition from a Pan-Islamist to a nationalist. Qureshi, *Ulema in Politics*, 365-68; L.S. May, *The Evolution of Indo-Muslim Thoughts after 1857*, 185-95; Abul Kalam Āzād, *India Wins Freedom*, Orient, 1967.

Muslims.[111] The author argues that the Islamic modernists are in fact much closer to the *ṣalf-al-ṣāliḥ* in their worldview and may rightly be called "fundamentalists." The Islamic modernists focus on "retrieving the fundamentals of their religious tradition and the most historically relevant information regarding the *salaf*, shorn of the late interpretations and constructions which have generated on occasion skewed codes of conduct and legislation.[112] In her critique of Islamists, Afsaruddin maintains that they have a highly politicised version of Islam which in essence is a contemporary response to the political supremacy of the modern West. The interpretations and "constructions" imply that the Islamists have deviated from the authentic version of Islam.

The analysis of the *ṣalf-al-ṣāliḥ* presented by Afsaruddin is a radical departure from the traditional understanding of their term. Our assessment of Islamic modernists points out to their rationalisation of the Islamic tradition. Furthermore, their worldview is informed by scientific spirit which has its roots in Western civilisation. In retrospect, Islamic modernists believe *tajdīd* to be compatible with their rational understanding of Islam, a view shared by Afsaruddin. Also the *sunnah* is not considered to be legally binding and their eclectic understanding of it is much in evidence.

INFLUENCE OF SALAFIYYAH ON MODERN ISLAMIC MOVEMENTS

The teachings of Salafiyyah continued to influence later generations of Muslim activists. Two major movements emerged during the 1930s which shared many of the ideas of

---

111. A critical assessment of the *ṣalf-al-ṣāliḥ* is provided in order to deconstruct the conventional reading of this term. Asma Afsaruddin, *The First Muslims: History and Memory*, Oxford: Oneworld, 2008, 148-99.

112. Ibid., 197.

the Salafiyyah. The Ikhwān-al-Muslimīn established by Hasan al-Bannā (d. 1949) in Egypt[113] whose movements ideologue was Sayyid Quṭb (d. 1966)[114] and in South Asia, Maulānā Sayyid Abul 'Ali Maudūdī (d. 1979)[115] founder of the Jamā'at-i-Islami. Both these movements upheld the primacy of Islamic teachings to future progress and were convinced of its adaptability to modern life. According to Esposito these movements were sceptical of the West and while accepting modernity they believed in the self-sufficiency of Islam as the basis of society and state.[116] The Ikhwān and the Jamā'at advocated *tajdīd* along the lines of the early precursors (*ṣalf-al-ṣāliḥ*) which emphasised the centrality of the Qur'ān and *sunnah*.[117] The puritanical approach may imply a rigidity on the movements' vision to restore Islam's universal appeal. A detailed analysis however reveals interesting insights into these movements' *modus operandi*.

For our study purpose we will examine Quṭb's

---

113. For a biographical sketch on al-Bannā see Richard P. Mitcheel, *The Society of Muslim Brothers*, London, 1969; Ishaq Musa al Husayni, *al-Ikhwān al-Muslimun kubra al-barakat al-Islamia al-ḥadīthā*, Beirut, 1955. cf. Nadwī, *Kārwān-i-Ẓindagī*, vol. 1, 378-82.

114. Sayyid Quṭb's importance in the Ikhwān has been discussed in various writings. A comprehensive study by Sayed Khatab, *The Power of Sovereignty*, London: Routledge, 2006 is one of the latest additions to the ever-growing interest on Quṭb's ideological contribution to *salafi* thought.

115. See Seyyid Vali Reza Nasr, *Maudūdī and the Making of Islamic Revivalism*, Oxford: Oxford University Press, 1996.

116. John Esposito, *Islam: The Straight Path*, New York, 1991, 152-60.

117. An insightful introduction to the Islamic movement can be seen in Maudūdī's, *The Moral Foundations of the Islamic Movement*, Lahore, 1976. An exhaustive introduction to this book is provided by Khurram Murad. See Abul Al'ā Maudūdī, *The Islamic Movement: Dynamics of Values, Power and Change*, Leicester: The Islamic Foundation, 1984, 5-69.

relationship with Western values. A parallel development during the twentieth century was the rise of Islamist phenomenon which shaped ideas of reformers like Quṭb. One can consider Islamism as a natural outgrowth of the nineteenth-century Salafiyyah especially in the Arab world. In Abu Rabi's view Islamism "is both an indigenous response to triumphant imperialism and the deep sense of political and intellectual malaise enveloping Arab society . . . after the abolition of the Ottoman caliphate in 1923."[118] Islamism responded to challenges posed by modernity which envisaged reform and progress as its salient features. However, the Islamist notion of progress is embedded in the centrality of the Islamic intellectual tradition and a return to its pristine past.[119] Quṭb's writings are indicative of this trend. Islam's pristine past which a Muslim society must emulate is advocated in his *Milestones*[120] and *Social Justice in Islam*.[121]

Islamist literature is replete with references to the "decline and defeat" of Christianity as a result of secularism. The Islamist critique of Christianity is based on the notion that the separation of religion and the state has had disastrous consequences for Christianity. Secularism, in other words, is antithetical to Islam. In his *Milestones* Quṭb directs his criticism against Muslim societies that "openly declare their secularism and negate all their relationships with the religion (Islam)."[122] I attempt to show Maulānā Nadwī's critique of the West. Maulānā Nadwī's approach to the West is based on the following premises:

---

118. Abu Rabi', "Contemporary Islamic Intellecutal History", in *Islamic Studies*, vol. 44, 513.
119. Abu Rabi', *Contemporary Arab Thought*, 69-70.
120. Sayyid Quṭb, *Milestones*, IIFSO, 1977.
121. Sayyid Quṭb, *Social Justice in Islam*, tr. John B. Hardie, New York: Islamic Publications International, 2000.
122. Quṭb, *Milestones*, 154.

The West still harbours a malevolence towards Islam for historical and ideological reasons. Firstly, the bitter memories of the Crusades between Islam and Christendom have defined the West's attitude towards Islam. Secondly, the protracted conflict between the Ottoman Empire and the European nations had created a wide gulf for a meaningful dialogue between Islam and the West. Lastly, Maulānā Nadwī argues that Islam possesses the unique philosophy of life that transcends racial and geographical barriers to stem the tide of the universal ascendancy of the West.[123]

The above critique of the West by Maulānā Nadwī does not imply that he is hostile towards the West. Rather Maulānā Nadwī points out to the ambivalence of Muslim countries towards the West. Muslim response to Western culture is examined in Maulānā Nadwī's *Western Civilisation, Islam and Muslims*. Unlike the *salafi*s and to some extent the Islamists who attribute Muslim failure to the West's pervasive influence, Maulānā Nadwī is pragmatic enough to state that Muslims can only maintain their universal status as the "Best of Nations" (*khair-ul-ummat*) if they can "[make] the full use of the physical sciences and technology of the West by learning them wholeheartedly and then subordinating them by means of their own intelligence and industry to the lofty purposes which the last of the Holy Prophets has bequeathed to them. . . ." In this regard Maulānā Nadwī is candid to say that the West has all the resources of the world but lacks a sense of purpose. Muslims, on the other hand, are endowed with the soundest of aims and ideals but are backward materially. Thus Maulānā Nadwī maintains that Muslim leadership in the world can only be achieved if a balance between the two extremes of the West and Muslim countries can be maintained.

---

123. Abdul Kader Choughley, *Da'wah, Peace and Dialogue in the Writings of Sayyid Abul Hasan Ali Nadwī, 1913-1999*, published MA Thesis, University of Johannesburg, 2004.

Maulānā Nadwī's critique of the West has important implications for his Islamic resurgence conceptualisation. In a contemporary context Maulānā Nadwī acknowledges the powerful presence of the West in terms of its technological advancement from which Muslims are not immune. However, he laments the fact that imitation of the West *in toto* has debilitated the Muslim temperament which integrates worldly pursuits in a spiritual framework. Thus according to Maulānā Nadwī Islamic resurgence must take cognisance of the contesting realities that inform the conflictual relationship between Islam and the West. This assessment by Maulānā Nadwī is in marked contrast to the *salafi*s, *'ulamā* and Islamists whose diatribe against the "Godless West" does not take into account globalisation and the spread of democracy albeit in limited ways, in Muslim countries. Maulānā Nadwī's engagement with democratic structures (examined in Chapter 5) enabled him to present his vision of an Islamic order in India where Muslims constitute a minority.

Two points are important in understanding the trends of Islamist thought. The unprecedented assault on Sufism occurred during the past century by *salafi*s. In an incisive study on the conflictual relationship between Sūfīs, *salafi*s and Ikhwān in Syria[124] Itzchak Weismann has made an interesting comment. The Salafiyyah and Islamist were motivated by a *Western rationalist outlook* (emphasis added) which they appropriated through an ideology of a return to original Islam against Sūfī traditions which they regarded as stagnation. However this thesis is contradicted by Abu Rabi' who contends that the movement developed as a result against a background of historical events. Therefore the current trend does not suggest that the Salafiyyah presented

124. Itzchak Weismann, "The Politics of Popular Religion: Sufis, Salafis and the Muslim Brother in 20th century", in *International Journal of Middle Eastern Studies 37*, 2005, 53-54.

a comprehensive view on the role of Islam in the modern and contemporary West.[125]

READINGS OF SALAFIYYAH

The variant terms to describe the Salafiyyah reflect a set of prejudices against the movement. Olivier Roy, for example, classifies the Islamists as *neo-fundamentalists*. In *Globalised Islam: The Search for a New Ummah*,[126] Roy has coined this term to denote Islamic movements which adapt to changing geographical and political landscapes. By this he means that neo-fundamentalism deals with a Westernisation that is now at the core and no longer at the frontiers of Islam.[127] In its response to Westernisation, they developed their own tenets of which two deserve mention for our study purpose. Neo-fundamentalists argue there is nothing positive to be borrowed from the West and reject the concept of an "Islamic ideology." They emphasise a literalist interpretation of Islam. Unlike the Islamists who espouse an Islamic political order, neo-fundamentalists tend to accept it without giving any legitimacy.[128] According to Roy, they are more adapted to living in the West than Islamists.[129] Neo-fundamentalists may wear different religious outfits in articulating their Islamic authenticity. The Tabligh Jamā'at, Wahhābis and Ikhwān are considered to be representatives of this phenomenon. Roy's failure to distinguish between categories of Islamists and neo-fundamentalists is evident in the above discussion. More importantly, his stereotypical representation of the Islamic movements does give the impression that they have a uniform vision. Our study attempts

125. Abu Rabi', *Contemporary Arab Thought*, 69.

126. Olivier Roy, *Globalised Islam: The Search for a New Ummah*, London: C. Hurst & Co., 2002.

127. Ibid., 234.

128. Ibid., 243-46.

129. Ibid., 247.

to show the non-monolithic expressions of Islamic resurgent movements.

In a recent study on the Salafiyyah, Leonard Shulze[130] has remarked that Maulānā Nadwī was a *salafi* with strong affiliation to the Wahhābi regime in Saudi Arabia. This designation is a misnomer as Maulānā Nadwī's traditional scholarship and ties with Sūfī traditions are in conflict with the Wahhābi ideology. Shulze himself acknowledges Maulānā Nadwī's independent standpoint:

> He (Maulānā Nadwī) was known on the one hand as a strict advocate of free scholarship and hence considered a worthy fellow combatant in the eyes of the Salafiyyah; but on the other hand, he had a generally positive relationship with the Islamic mystical tradition, with whom he often openly sided. The fact this could hardly be reconciled with the ideals of classical Salafiyyah did not bother him. On the contrary, his positive recourse to mysticism served his aim of establishing a new basis for the independent position of Islamic scholarship.[131]

The Salafiyyah in South Asia had witnessed an earlier movement *Ahl-i-ḥadīth*[132] which shared similar characteristics with it. However the *Ahl-i-ḥadīth* movement was engaged in sectarian debates largely with the Deobandis who strictly followed the Ḥanafi school of thought.[133] A parallel

130. Leonard Shulze, *A Modern History of the Islamic World.*

131. Ibid., 173.

132. The Ahl-i-ḥadīth constitute the major reference material for the legal literature of the law schools, bastion of orthodoxy and conservatism. See Reetz Dietrich, *Islam in the Public Sphere: Religious Groups in India 1900-1947*, Oxford: Oxford University Press, 2006, 123-48.

133. Barbara Metcalf in her seminal study, *Islamic Revival in British India: Deoband, 1860-1900*, Karachi: Royal Book Co., 1982 has described the sectarian polemics between the Deobandis and Ahl-i-ḥadīth. See her chapter: Alternative Tendencies within Sunni Islam: The Alh-i-hadīs and the Barelwis, 264-314.

development also emerged during this period — "Islamic modernists." Sir Syed Aḥmad Khan, the pioneer of Islamic modernism in the Indian subcontinent, attempted to remove the shackles of *taqlīd* while advocating a rationalist approach to the tenets of Islam.[134] His commentary of the Qur'ān[135] reveals new interpretive readings of Islamic thought and in a way reflects "a unity of thought" with other contemporary scholars. Muḥammad 'Abduh of Egypt is one such example whose modernist approach[136] was symptomatic of the conflicting trends emerging in the Muslim world in the nineteenth century. However, reformist developments in the twentieth century drew their inspiration from the Egyptian reformers who served as transmitters[137] for the Muslim world. According to Zaki Badawi, these reformist movements represented "a form of synthesis of trends within the *ummah*."[138]

"Sayyid Abu al-A'la Maulānā Maudūdī (1903-79) was one of the most influential and prolific of contemporary Muslim thinkers. His interpretation of Islam has contributed greatly to the articulation of Islamic revivalist thought and has influenced Muslim thinkers and activists from Morocco to Indonesia. His impact is evident in the exegesis of Sayyid Quṭb, as well as in the ideas and actions of Algerian, Iranian, Malaysian and Sudanese activists." The *Oxford Encyclopedia of the Modern Islamic World* begins its article on Maulānā Maudūdī

134. Hafeez Malik, *Sir Sayyid Ahmad Khan and Muslim Modernisation in India and Pakistan*, Karachi: Royal Book Co., 1988, 21-58.

135. Sir Syed Aḥmad Khan, *Tafsir-al-Qur'ān*, Lahore, n.d. For a critique on this tafsir, see Doi, *The Sciences of the Qur'ān*, 358-85.

136. Zaki Badawi, *The Reformers of Egypt*, London: The Muslim Institute, 1978; Albert Hourani, *Arabic Thought in the Liberal Age 1798-1939*, London, 131-59.

137. Abu Rabi' Ismail, *Intellectual Origins of Islamic Resurgence in the Modern Arab World*, 62-84.

138. Zaki Badawi, *The Reformers of Egypt*, 16; cf. Nadwī, *Western Civilisation, Islam and Muslims*, 91-122.

with the above words.[139] In South Asia where Maudūdī's idea undertook shape, his influence has even been more pronounced. His early writings which include *Towards Understanding Islam and Jihād in Islam* developed his *salafi* orientation. His articulation of *tajdīd* can be seen in his *A Short History of the Revivalist Movement in Islam.* Maulānā Maudūdī observes:

> It is not necessary for a single person to be a revivalist (*mujaddid*) for the whole Muslim world . . . . It is not necessary also that the person involved in such a work is to be given the title "revivalist." Such a title can deservedly be given only to those persons who have accomplished a great and shining feat for the revival of Islam.[140]

This opinion on *tajdīd* sets him apart from the traditional approach which seeks to bestow an aura of infallibility to the reformers. In his evaluation of the reformers' contribution to Islamic thought, Maulānā Maudūdī is at times unsparing in his criticism of them. This attitude partly explains the hostility he received from the *'ulamā* who challenged his religious credentials. Interestingly it is Maulānā Maudūdī's self-study of the sources of Islamic and Western culture[141] that equipped him with intellectual tools to make a profound contribution to the *tajdīdī* traditions. It is in this context that he viewed the *'ulamā* and the Islamic modernists with scepticism. Maulānā Maudūdī reproached the conservatives for their "exacting formalism and excessive eagerness to emphasise the legal minutiae. He blamed them for their unwillingness to comprehend the principles and essential features of the new civilisation of the West . . . and to fit these new instruments of

139. J. Esposito (ed.), *The Oxford Encyclopedia of the Modern Islamic World*, Oxford: Oxford University Press, 1995, vol. 3, 71.
140. Maudūdī, *A Short History of the Revivalist Movement*, 33.
141. For details, see Maudūdī Nasr, *The Making of Islamic Revivalism*, 16-19.

progress in keeping with the principles of Islam."[142] On the other hand, he was scathing in his criticism of the Islamic modernists who uncritically adopted every idea and institution that emanated from modern Europe. They claimed the West was associated with progress and happiness and felt convinced that those laws were compatible with Islam. In Maulānā Maudūdī's views these Muslims were clearly in retreat:

> Their minds and souls have passed under the sway of the West. Their thinking is being moulded by Western ideas and their intellectual powers are developing in accordance with the principles of Western thought.[143]

However, the critical appraisal of the Western civilisation did not imply as Maulānā Maudūdī argued severing all links with the West. In his formulation of contemporary Islamic thought there were unmistakable imprints of Western thought.[144]

Maryam Jameelah, an erstwhile admirer of Maulānā Maudūdī[145] has reviewed his major works in order to

142. Cited in Abdul Rashid Moten, "The Legacy of Allama Maudūdī", in Ibrahim Abu-Rabi' (ed.), *The Blackwell Companion to Contemporary Islamic Thought*, Blackwell Publishing Ltd., 2006, 189.

143. Abul-Al'ā Maudūdī, *The Sick Nations of the Modern Age*, Lahore: Islamic Publications Ltd., 1966, 11.

144. The detailed introduction by Khurram Murad to Maudūdī's *The Islamic Movement* is a synopsis of the West's influence on Maudūdī's reformulation of contemporary Islamic thought. Cf. Khurshid Aḥmad's remarks on Maudūdī's analysis of modernity: "He (Maudūdī) has tried to meet the new intellectual challenge of the West and has presented Islam in the language of today . . . he has not only presented the teachings of Islam in a clear, precise, cogent and convincing way but he has also interpreted them for our times." Abul-Al'ā Maudūdī, *Islamic Law and Constitution*, Lahore: Islamic Publications, 1976, 34-35.

145. In her *Who is Maudūdī: The Great Mujaddid*, Jameelah lavishes praises on Maulānā Maudūdī's extraordinary contribution to revivalism. Her admiration for Maudūdī is captured in the following lines: →

understand the impact of modernisation on his thoughts. Jameelah contends through extensive quotations from his important writings how Maulānā Maudūdī was affected by modernity in his all-out efforts to integrate it into present-day revivalism.[146] Maulānā Nadwī though critical of some views of Maulānā Maudūdī (which are examined in Chapter 4) expresses his admiration with regard to the latter's critique of Western civilisation. Maulānā Nadwī writes:

> Resistance to Western thinking and values was growing in its own way when in the first half of this century the articles of Maulānā Saiyyid Abul 'Ala Maudūdī published in this esteemed journal *Tarjumānul Qur'ān* from Hyderabad, which were written not in any defensive but in an aggressive way against Western civilisation and philosophy of life, attracted the attention of the educated Muslims. Those articles had confronted the movement of modernity bred by Western education and had opposed rank nationalism. He also wrote powerful and well-reasoned articles on Islamic *Shariat* and Laws which had become the target of attack like usury, *purdāh, jihād,* sacrifice, slavery, *ḥadīth* and *sunnah.* Through those articles, which later on appeared in the shape of bound volumes, and his other books and treatise, he moulded the thinking of recipients of modern education and restored in them confidence in Islamic values and thinking and rescued them from any sense of inferiority or defeatism. That was sterling work indeed which must be acknowledged and because of it many men of letters gave him the title of "Spokesman of Islam."[147]

→ "Combined with his broad knowledge, is an unsurpassed mental balance. . . . His thinking as revealed in his writings and speeches, also reveals his mental balance, a perfect equilibrium between realism and idealism, never overoptimistic or excessively pessimistic." Jameelah, *Who is Maudūdī: The Great Mujaddid,* 66.

146. Maryam Jameelah, "Modern Ideas and Concepts in the Works of Maudūdī" in *Islamic Studies,* vol. 42, no. 2, Summer 2003, 347-52.

147. Abul Ḥasan Ali Nadwi, *Appreciation and Interpretation of Religion in the Modern Age,* Lucknow: Academy of Islamic Research and Publications, 1982, 20-1.

Leonard Binder notes in his *Islamic Liberalism: A Critique of Development Ideologies* that both Maulānā Maudūdī and Quṭb share the conviction that Islam

> is engaged in a *kulturkampf* with Western imperialism, and ultimately the purpose or consequence of modernisation . . . is to complete the colonisation of the Muslim world by means of a moral and cultural colonisation. (Thus) the reassertion of Islam is a rejection of Western dominance, of Western culture, and of the identity which the West would impose upon Muslims.[148]

In retrospect, Maulānā Maudūdī's prolific writings have influenced a generation of intellectuals whose own contributions have also helped shape the current Islamic discourse on revivalism. In contemporary Islamist thinking many leading figures praise Maulānā Maudūdī's contribution. For example, the Tunisian leader of the banned Nahḍah movement, Rashīd al-Ghannushi,[149] emphasised Maulānā Maudūdī's remarkable intellectual capability in "theorisation and in organisation of his mass movement."[150] No less an important figure in Islamic resurgence, is the distinguished scholar-economist, Khurshid Aḥmad of Pakistan.[151] A versatile author and translator of several of Maulānā Maudūdī's works, Aḥmad has emerged as a spokesperson for the Jamā'at-i-Islami[152] founded by Maulānā Maudūdī in 1941. Like his

---

148. Leonard Binder, *Islamic Liberalism : A Critique of Development Ideologies*, Chicago: The University of Chicago Press, 1988, 175.

149. On Rashid Ghannoushi, see J. Esposito and J. Voll, *Makers of Contemporary Islam*, Oxford: Oxford University Press, 2001, 91-117.

150. Cited in Fathi Osman, "Maulānā Maudūdī's Contribution to the Development of Modern Islamic Thinking in the Arabic-Speaking World", *The Muslim World*, vol. 93, 2005, no. 3 & 4, 479.

151. For biographical details on Khurshid Aḥmad, see Esposito, *Makers of Contemporary Islam*, 39-53.

152. The establishment of the Jama'āt-i-Islami and its input on Islamist activism is examined in the next chapter.

mentor Maulānā Maudūdī, Aḥmad has critically reviewed the history of confrontation between Islam and the West and the impact of European colonialism in the Muslim world. In contrast to the radical militants, Aḥmad has not called for a total rejection of the West. Rather he has emphasised the need for better relations in order to redefine the co-existence and interaction of Islam with the West.[153] Aḥmad writes:

> If the only practical ground of co-operation is the assimilation of the Western culture and rejection of Islam as we understand it, then there is no ground for any meeting. But if the co-operation is to be achieved on equal footing then it is most welcomed.[154]

A closer study of Aḥmad's contributions to the Islamic resurgence shows his pragmatism of Muslim relations with the West. In fact, the Islamic Foundation established in Leicester (England) has over the years published works that are aimed to promote a better understanding between Islam and the West. It must be borne in mind that Aḥmad unlike his mentor has spent a major portion of his academic life in Europe[155] and this is a plausible explanation for his conciliatory approach to the West. Again the Islamic Foundation has published important writings of Maulānā Nadwī whose theme is "Islam and the West."[156]

A contemporary of Khurshid Aḥmad is Habib-ul-Haq

---

153. Esposito, *Makers of Contemporary Islam,* 45.

154. Khurshid Aḥmad, *The Religion of Islam,* Lahore: Islamic Publications, 1967, 61.

155. Esposito, op. cit., 45-46.

156. Mention may be made of the following books written by Nadwī and published by Islamic Foundation:
    - *Muslims in the West: The Message and Mission* (1983)
    - *Da'wah in the West: The Qur'ānic Paradigm* (1992)
    - *The Role and Responsibilities of Muslims in the West* (1993)

Nadvi (d. 1998).[157] His major publications which focus on Islamic resurgence particularly in South Asia show traces of Maulānā Nadwī's influence. Like Maulānā Nadwī, Habib-ul-Haq Nadvi examines Islamic fundamentalism against the rich background of *mujaddids* whose contributions have been discussed in the multi-volume *Saviours of Islamic Spirit*. In *Islamic Fundamentalism: A Theology of Liberation and Renaissance,* Habib-ul Nadvi echoes Maulānā Nadwī's presentation of the revivalists who by and large are *'ulamā* and *mashā'ikh* (spiritual guides). This emphasis is evident in the following quotation:

> Causes of the decline of the Muslim intellectual and creative scholarship in the contemporary world need to be probed and the innovative *geniuses* (emphasis added) need to be revived . . .. The commonwealth of Islam can be saved from any further decline and brain drain politics of the West if it follows the dictates of the Qur'ān which has promised the *ummah* for its sublime rise, provided it is endowed with faith (*imān*) and knowledge (*'ilm*).[158]

The innovative geniuses have been briefly discussed by Habib-ul Haq Nadvi through the fourteen centuries in his *The Dynamics of Islam*.[159] They are reformers who were motivated by the call of a return to the pristine Islam (*al-'awda-al Islam)*.[160] This credo is central to all reformatory endeavours. Maulānā Nadwī's works on *iṣlāḥ* and *tajdīd* have largely influenced Habib-ul Haq Nadvi's interpretation of Islamic resurgence.

---

157. To date there has been no study on the contribution of Habib-ul-Haq to contemporary Islamic thought. Nadwī makes a brief mention of Habib-ul-Haq Nadvi's writings which generally deal with Islamic resurgence and on contemporary issues. See Nadwī, *Kārwān-i-Ẓindagī,* vol. 7, 73-4.

158. Nadvi, *Islamic Fundamentalism*, 54.

159. Syed Habib-ul-Haq Nadvi, *The Dynamics of Islam,* Durban: Academia, 1982, 1-106.

160. Ibid.

ASSESSMENT

Salafiyyah spawned over the last two centuries has offered interesting insights on what constitutes an authoritative understanding of *tajdīd*. Its advocacy of a "return to the ideal Islamic past" is based on Islam's comprehensiveness (*shumuliyat*). Yet Salafiyyah has been constrained to re-define *tajdīd* in response to modernity and globalisation, trends which are decisively of Western origin. This approach supports our thesis that the "mutation" of *tajdīd* is linked with socio-political realities and implicitly dictates the patterns of Islamic discourse. The stereotypical representation of the Salafiyyah as a reactionary movement must be re-examined in respect of its growth and development of this phenomenon. The "return of the past" theme resonates in the discourse of the *'ulamā* group of which Maulānā Nadwī is considered a leading representative.

'Ulamā in South Asia

As mentioned elsewhere in the chapter, the modern Salafiyyah/Islamist[161] maintained a conflictual relationship with the *'ulamā*. In this regard Francis Robinson has remarked in one of his important works on South Asian Muslims, *Islam, South Asia and the West,*[162] that *'ulamā* as transmitters and interpreters of Islam have come to be challenged by scholars outside the *madrasa* system. Writings of Islamists like Quṭb and Maulānā Maudūdī have become prime sources of understanding Islam[163] and enjoy strong support among student organisations which they often dominate. Against

161. This description is meant to show that modern Salafiyyah and Islamist are not separate entitities; they are interchangeable terms functioning in specific historical context and social milieus.

162. Robins, Francis, *Islam, South Asia and the West*, Oxford: Oxford University Press, 2007.

163. Ibid., 55. For a fuller treatment on this subject by Robinson, op. cit., see Chapter 5, Knowledge, Its Transmission and the Making of Muslim Societies, 19-58.

this background, the role of the *'ulamā* and their contribution to the resurgent movement with particular reference to the Indian subcontinent is examined.

The status and the function of the *'ulamā* in the Muslim community have seldom been properly understood by scholars. The plethora of writing either tend to extol the role of the *'ulamā*[164] or to discredit them as conservatives.[165] Two significant works, *Islamic Revival in British India*[166] and *The 'Ulamā in Contemporary Islam*[167] have attempted to provide an objective study on the position of the *'ulamā* in the Muslim society and in this study, in the Indian subcontinent.

Before embarking on our discussion it is necessary to outline the nature and impact of a reformist trend that focused on "this-worldly" Islam.[168] The nineteenth and twentieth

---

164. Biographical accounts in Urdu on the *'ulamā* by and large fit into this categorisation. The iconic status given to them by their biographers has precluded an objective assessment of their contributions to the *tajdīdī* traditions. 'Abdullāh 'Abbās Nadwī observes:

 "Biographical accounts on *'ulamā* and *mashā'ikh* are generally of two types. One genre tends to glorify the *shaykh* and the exaggerated veneration of his personality gives the impression that his status may be equal to a prophet. This embellished style identifies qualities and attributes which implicitly suggest his *ismat* (infallibility)." 'Abbās Nadwī, *Mīr-i-Kārwān*, New Delhi: Majlis-i-Ilmi, 1999, 16-17. In a similar vein, Maulānā Maudūdī's criticism of his contemporary *'ulamā* raised a storm of protest in Deobandi circles. Cf. Maudūdī, *A Short History of the Revivalist Movement in Islam.*

165. Islamists and modernists in particular tend to undermine the role of *'ulamā* as interpreters of Islam.

166. Barbara Daly Metcalf, *Islamic Revival in British India: Deoband 1860-1900*, Karachi, 1982.

167. Muḥammad Qasim Zaman, *'Ulamā in Contemporary Islam: Custodians of Change*, Princeton: Princeton University Press, 2002.

168. Francis Robinson, *Islam and Muslim History in South Asia*, New Delhi: Oxford University Press, 2001, 107.

centuries in the subcontinent saw a growing attack on intercessionary Sūfīsm which was blamed for Islam's backwardness. As such it was the *'ulamā* who played a key role in maintaining an Islamic identity that was free from a cult-laden Islam. Robinson has rightfully noted in his *Islam: South Asia and the West* that the *'ulamā* as scholars "have reflected upon the significance of the central messages of Islam for their time, as teachers they have transmitted these messages and skills to make them socially useful to the coming generations."[169] Ishtiaq Qureshi in his study, *Ulema in Politics*[170] while critical of the *'ulamā*'s conservatism, has conceded that they have preserved the heritage of Islam.[171] The positive contribution of the *'ulamā* in shaping Muslim societies cannot be overlooked. This theme is echoed in Metcalf's *Islamic Revival* in which she describes the period 1800-1950 as a turning point both in terms of the loss of political power for Muslims and the entrenchment of colonial rule.[172] It was the *'ulamā* who showed great creativity in developing new ideas and in fashioning new institutional frameworks.[173]

---

169. Francis Robinson, *Islam, South Asia and the West*, New Delhi, 2007, 59.

170. Ishtiaq Hussain Qureshi, *Ulema in Politics*, Karachi: Ma'aref Ltd., 1974. This work by the learned author has pro-Pakistani leanings and is therefore critical of *'ulamā* who opposed the creation of Pakistan.

171. Ibid., Chapter 1 is a critical appraisal of the role of the *'ulamā* in the Muslim society.

172. Metcalf has described the role of the *'ulamā* in both the eighteenth and nineteenth centuries. The chapters are aptly titled: *'Ulamā in Transition* to show the *'ulamā*'s response to the challenges spawned by Western civilisation. On the British colonial rule, see Marshall Hodgson, *The Venture of Islam*, vol. 3, Chicago, 1974; Aziz Aḥmad, *An Intellectual History of Islamic India*, Edinburgh, 1969 and Muḥammad Mujeeb, *The Indian Muslims*, London, 1967.

173. Ibid., 87-111, cf. Reetz, *Islam in the Public Sphere*, 63 Deoband institutionalised Islamic education for a wide, if not mass audience, in contrast to traditional home-based instruction.

The Deoband *madrasa* (Dār-ul-'ulūm) played a pivotal role in formulating a reformed understanding of Islam. Metcalf outlines the social milieu[174] that shaped the vision of the Dār-ul-'ulūm to demonstrate its link with Shah Wali-allah tradition.[175] Mahmood Ghazi in his important study on Shah Wali-allah, *Islamic Renaissance in South Asia 1707-1867* has shown how the Dār-ul-'ulūm patterned its curriculum within the Wali-allah tradition[176] which stressed on *tajdīd*. Their vision illustrated the strands of reformist thought that was shared by a large number of Islamic institutions in the subcontinent.

DĀR-UL-'ULŪM DEOBAND: TRANSMITTERS OF REFORMIST ISLAM

The founders of this important movement were indirect descendants from the Wali-allah tradition. Maulānā Muḥammad Qasim Nanautawi,[177] founder of the Dār-ul-'ulūm Deoband, had participated in the first war of Independence of 1857[178] against British rule. The failure of the uprising in

174. Mahmood Aḥmad Ghazi, *Islamic Renaissance in South Asia: 1707-1867: The Role of Shah Wali-Allah and His Successors*, Islamabad: Islamic Research Institute, 2002, 138-97.

175. Shāh Wali-allah (1703-63) who was perhaps the greatest Muslim scholar that South Asia ever produced has left a deep impact on subsequent generations. He is considered a link between medieval and Modern Muslim thought in the region where he was the initiator of modern Islamic renaissance. See *Al-Furqān Special Number on Shah Wali-allah*, 1941, 370-75.

176. Mahmood Aḥmad Ghazi, *Islamic Renaissance in South Asia: 1707-1867: The Role of Shah Wali-Allah and His Successors*, Islamabad: Islamic Research Institute, 2002, 232-37. Cf. Metcalf, *Islamic Revival*, 107-9.

177. On the history of Dār-ul-'ulūm Deoband, see Sayyid Mahbub Razwī, *Tārikh dar-ul-Ulum Deoband*, Deoband 1992. The study includes the life and thought of Maulānā Qāsim Nanautwi, 102-22.

178. The word "Mutiny" has been disputed by several scholars who insist that the uprising should be rephrased as the First War of Independence against British colonial rule. See Ghazi, *Islamic Renaissance*, 205-19.

which *jihād* was emphasised made it clear for Muslims that resistance had to be of a different kind. Thus the establishment of the Dār-ul-'ulūm was partly politically motivated. Zaman, following the political strand of Deoband institution, disagrees with Metcalf's elaboration on the social milieu which is drawn largely from the biographies of the first generation of Deobandi *'ulamā*. This approach, Zaman argues, blurs out the Deobandi *'ulamā*'s thoughts and discourses[179] which are important to understand their contribution to Islamic reformist thought. Thus Zaman offers a greater political insight on the *'ulamā*'s contribution in his major study, *The 'Ulamā in Contemporary Islam*.[180] Masooda Bano in the article, "Beyond Politics: The Reality of a Deobandi Madrasah in Pakistan"[181] contends that Zaman's work is too concerned with the public and political aspects of the operation of the Deobandi *'ulamā*. According to Bano, the Deoband movement aimed to train *'ulamā* who would be dedicated to a reformed Islam within the *tajdīdī* traditions.[182]

Deobandi *'ulamā* and their associates like Nadwat-ul-*'ulamā*, Ahl-i-Ḥadīth did not make a break from a scriptural understanding of Islam. They made sustained efforts to consolidate textually-anchored Islamic law and practices among Muslim masses. However, as Robinson noted, the period under review (1800-1950) represented a creative phase[183] for the *'ulamā*. Context was important to the development of new ideas. It was thus towards the end of the nineteenth

179. Zaman, *The 'Ulamā in Contemporary Islam*, 12-3.

180. Ibid., 144-80, cf. Jamal Malik, *Colonisation of Islam; Dissolution of Traditional Institutions in Pakistan*, New Delhi: Manohar, 1996, 192-93.

181. Masooda Bano, "Beyond Politics: The Reality of a Deobandi Madrasa in Pakistan", in *Journal of Islamic Studies I*, 2006, Oxford Centre for Islamic Studies, 3.

182. Ibid., 6-7.

183. Robinson, *Islam, South Asia*, 62-66.

century the *'ulamā* came to realise the full impact of British power equated with Western civilisation in the world. They saw how the West's influence marginalised their beliefs, law and culture and also gave rise to a new class of modernist Muslims. The *'ulamā* as transmitters and interpreters of the Islamic tradition[184] attempted to face these challenges posed by the West. For example, it was the Nadwah which promoted the idea that "English language should acquire a position in the Islamic curriculum and there might be some serious engagement with Western thought."[185] It must be noted that this approach was not a source of new religious understanding and practice. Indeed in time, it became a vehicle for reformist views.

Ironically not all the *'ulamā* groups shared Nadwah's viewpoint. Barelwi *'ulamā* led by the founder, Aḥmad Raḍā Khan of Bareilly (d. 1921)[186] resisted the movement of revival and reform. Instead they justified a custom-laden Islam which was closely tied to the Sūfī world of shrines — intercessionary Sūfīsm[187] which reformist *'ulamā* fought against. Thus it was inevitable that polemics would dominate the discourse between these oppositional *'ulamā* groups.[188] The ideological contestations among the *'ulamā* provided opportunities to glimpse the evolving facets of Islamic reformist thought and religious authority in South Asia.

---

184. Robinson, *Islam, South Asia,* 68.

185. Ibid.

186. Usha Sanyal, *Devotional Islam and Politics in British India: Ahmad Riza Khan Barelwi and His Movement 1870-1920,* Delhi: Oxford University Press, 1996.

187. For a brief account on the Barelwi group's justification of intecessionary Sūfīsm, see Reetz, *Islam in the Public Sphere,* 124-28. Cf. Sanyal, *Devotional Islam,* 134-35.

188. The polemical literature against the Deobandi *'ulamā* by Riḍā Khan and his associates can be seen in Habib-ul-Haq Nadvi's, *Islamic Resurgent Movements,* 99-122.

THE 'ULAMĀ AS GUARDIANS OF COMMUNITY BEHAVIOUR

A salient feature of the *'ulamā*'s religious authority was their development of their constituencies in the Muslim society. This leverage allowed them "to police the boundaries of behaviour."[189] In other words, the *'ulamā* produced biographical and *malfuzāt* (conversations by Sūfīs) literature[190] to benchmark what they considered to be appropriate conduct of Islamic behaviour. The scripturalist and prescriptive nature of the method created sectarian bias with other rival groups. It was however in the twentieth century that the *'ulamā*'s presence was felt in the public sphere.[191] They became advocates of Islamic causes on a broader spectrum. The Tabligh Jamā'at for example (which is discussed in Chapter 3) was an offshoot of the Deobandi's pro-active role in the Muslim society.

'ULAMĀ IN THE POLITICAL ARENA

The establishment of the Jami'at-ul-'ulamā Hind (JUH) in 1920[192] added a new dimension to the role of the *'ulamā* as political activists. The JUH had a voice and a political programme in Indian politics. It was however after the

---

189. Robinson, *Islam, South Asia,* 76.

190. The *malfuzāt* genre is unique to the Indian subcontinent. The "table talk" was employed by the Indian Sūfīs in transmitting their teachings to their devotees. For an insightful understanding of this genre, see Nizami Khaliq Aḥmad, *On Sources and Source Material,* vol. 2, Delhi: Idarah-i-Adabiyat-i-Delli, 1995, 40-73.

191. For an elaboration on the public sphere and Islam see Dietrich Reetz, *Islam in the Public Sphere,* 11-51.

192. *Jamiat-ul-Ulema-i-Hind: A Brief History*, Meerut, 1963. A critique of the JUH reveals two important points:
    - anti-Pakistan rhetoric tends to blur out the historical context of the Partition of India-Pakistan in 1947.
    - tirades against JUH most notably its pro-Congress position towards the establishment of Pakistan.

→

Partition of India in 1947 that JUH abandoned politics to concentrate on the spiritual, moral and educational upliftment of the Muslim community. It continued to maintain its link with the Indian National Congress[193] party which espoused secularism and nationalism for a multi-cultural society like India. In contrast the establishment of the *'ulamā* body, the Jami'at-ul-'ulamā Islam (JUI)[194] maintained a stronger political presence in the nascent Pakistan. The JUI's Deobandi orientation was evident in the large network of *madrasas* linked to its *alma mater* in India. Its political influence in challenging state powers since its inception underscored its religio-political activism.[195] A vocal critic of Indian politics, it rejected secularism as an expression of Western and Indian hegemony designed to subdue the Islamic forces in Pakistan.[196] This approach gradually set the two Jami'ats apart

→ Cf. Ziya-ul-Hasan Faruqi, *The Deoband School and the Demand for Pakistan*, Lahore, n.d., 67-91 and Ayesha Jalal, *Self and Sovereignty*, Routledge, 2000. The author is unsparing in her criticism of the JUH and the *'ulamā* fraternity, 376-7, 414, 417.

193. On the Indian National Congress, see Bipan Chandra, *Indian National Movement: The Long-Term Dynamics*, Delhi: Vikas, 1988.

194. Mushirul Hasan, *Legacy of a Divided Nation: India's Muslim Since Independence*, London: Hurst & Company, 1997. Parardoxically, it was a splinter group of the Deobandi *'ulamā* who formed the JUI. The religious orientation played a pivotal role by scholars sympathetic to the creation of Pakistan. See Qureshi, *Ulema in Politics*, 307-38.

195. The *madrasa* (Islamic school) in Pakistan has been much debated especially in the aftermath of 11 September 2001. *Schooling Islam*, Princeton, 2007, offers new perspectives into the *madrasa* system in specific Muslim countries. On the tradition and authority in Deobandi *madrasas* of South Asia, see Muḥammad Qasim Zaman, *Schooling Islam*, 61-86. The reform of *madrasas* is perceived as essential by the United States to counter the spread of radical ideologies especially in Pakistan. See Angel Rabasa et al., *The Muslim World after 9/11*, RAND Corporation, 2004, 275-78.

196. Reetz, *Islam in the Public Sphere*, 39.

in their vision of an Islamic society. Maulānā Nadwī, for example, supported the JUH's stand in encouraging Indian Muslims to use democratic structures to ensure their corporate Muslim identity. The rationale of such an approach by Maulānā Nadwī and his Indian contemporaries is examined in Chapter 5.

'ULAMĀ IN THE TAJDĪDĪ TRADITION

The foregoing pages have outlined categories of reformist movements and their respective contributions to the *tajdīdī* tradition. A close examination of these movements illustrates their divergent responses to Islamic resurgence. A combination of factors, historical and political, shaped these movements' intellectual contributions. The Islamist position is a case in point. Although the Islamists draw on their understanding of Islam from the foundational texts their articulation is different from the *'ulamā*. According to Zaman, the *'ulamā*'s understanding of the foundational texts is linked to a "historically articulated interpretive tradition."[197] In other words, there is a continuity in a traditional understanding of Islam. Thus this form of discourse is distinctive to the culture of *'ulamā*. This does not imply that the *'ulamā* remained immune from the massive transformations that modernity forced on to their institutions and discourse. Rather they appropriated specific forms in reaching out to the Muslim masses. The adoption of print[198] was the first stage in the democratisation of knowledge. The *'ulamā* used the print to make sources of knowledge accessible to the Muslim community. Not surprisingly this new freedom of access to

---

197. Muḥammad Qasim Zaman, *The Scope and Limits of Islamic Cosmopolitanism and the Discursive Language of the 'Ulamā*, 93.

198. Robinson has made a major study on the impact of print as a new transmitter of Islamic knowledge. Robinson, *Islam and Muslim History in South Asia*, 66-104.

Islamic knowledge challenged the authoritative interpretations of the *'ulamā*.[199] The writings of Islamists[200] as a corollary provided important sources of contemporary understanding of Islamic reformist thought whose influence continues to this day.

Maulānā Nadwī, on the other hand, is unique among the modern *'ulamā* in his ability to address a broad and diverse Muslim audience. It is precisely the language of discourse that has earned him popularity among scholars and institutions with diverse orientations. Maulānā Nadwī's career highlights the possibility of a sustained intellectual engagement with *'ulamā*, Islamists and modernists. It is this interaction that shows that the firmness of boundaries between them is largely overdrawn.[201] Maulānā Nadwī's own career suggests some of the ways in which *'ulamā* and Islamists came together in the course of the twentieth century. To illustrate this point: the concept of Jāhiliyyah which refers to the "age of ignorance" (dealt with in subsequent chapters) has been a salient feature in Quṭb's writings. Maulānā Nadwī too is credited to have developed his own reading of this concept which was introduced in the Arab-Islamist circle. In fact, Quṭb wrote a foreword to Maulānā Nadwī's best-known book, *Islam and the World*[202] which explains the latter's cordial relations with many Arab Islamists. These caveats are reminders that classifications like the *'ulamā* and Islamists are not by and large monolithic and these groups may have significant commonalities with their respective worldview. Maulānā Nadwī may be considered a forerunner in this emergent trend.

---

199. Robinson, *Islam amd Muslim History in South Asia*, 53-55.

200. The writings of Maudūdī and Quṭb, for example, have been translated into the major languages of the world.

201. Zaman, *The Scope and Limits of Islamic Cosmopolitanism*, 95.

202. Nadwī, *Islam and the World*, 1-6.

Conclusion

The phenomenon of Islamic resurgence in the last two centuries is rooted in the *tajdīdī* tradition. Reform and revival served as identity markers in the chequered history of *tajdīd*. Context played a significant role in determining the flux of events associated with the reformatory movements. The changing and transformative character of Islamic resurgence has been conspicuous during the nineteenth and twentieth centuries. It possessed the dynamism to reconfigure as a response to socio-political circumstances.

Maulānā Nadwī's understanding of *tajdīd* is an example of its dynamic character. According to him, Islamic resurgence functions in an Islamic authenticity framework without ignoring existing realities facing the Muslims. The Islamist vision of Islamic resurgence lacks a coherent presentation in view of their conflicting views on a pristine Islam and the challenges posed by the West. There is no reference to a rapprochement or at least a tacit endorsement of the challenges that shape their understanding of Islamic resurgence. Islamic modernists have reformulated their understanding of *tajdīd* on scientific and rational grounds. Their views offer useful insights to the progressive spirit that characterised the scientific and intellectual legacy of Islam.

At the same time its rhetorical slogans have assumed new challenges. The intellectual discourse shaped reformist vision and carried it through for centuries. The impact of Ibn Taymiyyah is a case in point. Another noteworthy feature of the movements (especially from the nineteenth century onwards) was its emphasis on "back to original Islam" (*al 'awda ilal Islam*)[203] — an implicit reference to the Islam practised by the *ṣalf-al-ṣāliḥ*. Quṭb and Maulānā Maudūdī's views are representative of this trend. Their responses to modernity

203. On this slogan see Nadvi, *The Dynamics of Islam*, 1-3.

and Western civilisation in a sense epitomised their predicament and ambivalence towards this phenomenon. The political dimension of the resurgent movements receives brief mention as it falls outside the scope of this study. However, a recent study by Nina Voges, *The Development of Islamic Resurgent Movements in Egypt*[204] provides a detailed account of the various movements that shaped the current debate on Islamic resurgence. Of significant interest is her analysis on the growth and development of the Ikhwān in Egypt which spawned a number of Islamic movements with various political agendas. The study is useful in drawing parallels with other contemporary Islamic movements across the Muslim world in their pursuit of an Islamic order.

---

204. Nina Voges, *The Development of Islamic Resurgent Movements in Egypt*, published PhD dissertation, University of Johannesburg, 2006.

2

Islamic Resurgence
A Genre Perspective

Literary Sources: Motivation

As discussed in the Introduction, contemporary Islamic thought is located in specific historical and political settings; thus the contributions of Maulānā Nadwī and his contemporaries reflect a variety of responses shaped by their respective understanding of Islamic resurgence. In our examination of Maulānā Nadwī's writings, literary sources underpin the theme of Islamic resurgence. In this context a literary approach on selected genres provides important perspectives on the dynamics of *tajdīd*.

LITERARY SOURCES FOR ISLAMIC RESURGENCE: AN OVERVIEW

A brief survey of Maulānā Nadwī's important writings reveals the trends of *tajdīd* expressed in various historical settings. Of particular importance are the works relating to his autobiographical and biographical accounts in terms of his formulation of *tajdīd*. These two genres embody Maulānā Nadwī's Islamic resurgence paradigm and offer useful insights into their thematic significance.

Islamic history possesses a rich treasure of these two genres which spanning over 1,000 years have covered the concepts of *iṣlāḥ* and *tajdīd*. Their forms have varied over the centuries on account of socio-political developments affecting the Muslim world. Chase Robinson has rightly remarked in his *Islamic Historiography* that the Islamic conquests of the early seventh century ushered in quite an exceptional period of cultural synthesis.[1] The plethora of works in the various Islamic sciences and arts also saw the emergence of literary genres particularly autobiography and biography in the Muslim world. These genres had a significant impact on the early development of *tajdīd*.[2] Maulānā Nadwī remarks that these genres were a projection of an Islamic ideal anchored in the Qur'ān and *sunnah*. For example, the biography of Aḥmad bin Ḥanbal epitomised the conflict between Islamic authenticity against the rationalist tendencies promoted by the Mu'tazilah sect who were supported by the 'Abbāsid rulers of the time. The Inquisition (*miḥna*)[3] to which Ḥanbal was subjected by the 'Abbāsid rulers because of his opposition to the created nature of the Qur'ān advanced by the Mu'tazilah is one example of how in its nascent stages *tajdīd* assumed significance as a distinctive form of protest against doctrinal expressions that were contrary to the established practices of Islam.

Maulānā Nadwī portrayed Ḥanbal as a foundational figure of traditional Islam whose achievement "lay in his fearless championship of the true content of the faith against the most powerful empire of the time."[4] *The Saviours of Islamic Spirit* also covers biographical accounts of classical reformers operating in an *iṣlāḥ-tajdīd* framework. The selection of these figures mirrors Maulānā Nadwī's conceptualisation of Islamic resurgence: Islamic personalities who have "relentlessly fought against the forces of corruption, defended the Islamic

1. Chase Robinson, *Islamic Historiography,* Cambridge: Cambridge University Press, 2003, 18.
2. Ibid., 63-64.
3. For a detailed description of the Inquisition, see Nadwī, *Saviours of Islamic Spirit,* vol. I, 80-86.
4. Ibid., 86.

precepts and teachings and rejuvenated the spirit of Islamic revival besides making valuable contributions to the intellectual and academic treasure of their people."[5] The theme of Islamic authenticity (discussed in Chapter 3) in Maulānā Nadwī's view is inseparable from *tajdīd.* This is clearly shown in his treatment of al-Ghazāli (d. 1111), an illustrious reformer of eleventh century whose writings on *taṣawwuf* and *tajdīd* have attracted scholarly studies from diverse intellectual backgrounds.[6] There emerges a consistent pattern in Maulānā Nadwī's *Saviours of Islamic Spirit* of scholars and intellectuals who are representatives of Islamic authenticity as envisaged by him. In the Indian subcontinent, for example, the Chishtiyyah Order[7] which originated in Afghanistan, achieved fame only in India. Its spiritual ideologue, Nizāmuddin Auliyā (d. 1325) was one of the most charismatic Sūfī personalities in the Indian subcontinent.[8] He idealised in his personality the universal message of love and peace which according to Maulānā Nadwī epitomised *da'wah,*[9] a theme elaborated in his *Payām-i-Insāniyat.* The choice of a Sūfī reformer drawn from the Indian soil during Muslim rule in India is significant to understand Maulānā Nadwī's articulation of Islamic resurgence, which, though embedded in Islamic traditions, is adaptable to changing landscapes.

---

5. Nadwī, *Saviours of Islamic Spirit,* vol. I, xx.
6. Ibid., 123-50.
7. On the Chishtiyyah Order, see Khaliq Aḥmad Nizami, *The Life and Times of Shaikh Nizamuddin Auliya,* Delhi: Idarah-i-Adabiyat-i-Delli, 1991; Sayyid Athar Abbas Rizvi, "The Chishtiyyah" in Seyyed Hossein Nasr (ed.), *Islamic Spirituality,* vol. 2, New York: Crossroad, 1991, 127-43.
8. Nadwī, *Saviours of the Islamic Spirit,* vol. I, 147-253.
9. Ibid., 249.

The "excellent humanitarian ideals in the society of Sūfīs"[10] as Maulānā Nadwī explains in *Muslims in India* provided him with a leverage to develop his understanding of *tajdīd*. In a particular sense, the *Saviours of Islamic Spirit* gives a systematic formulation of Maulānā Nadwī's Islamic resurgence paradigm which is elaborated in his other important works.[11]

FORMS OF LITERARY SOURCES: MAULĀNĀ NADWĪ'S FORMULATION OF ISLAMIC RESURGENCE

This chapter seeks to examine literary genres, autobiography as well as biography and its sub-genres, with specific relevance to the concept of *iṣlāḥ* and *tajdīd*. The motivation for including a literary approach against the backdrop of a comparative analysis (which is a salient feature of the study) is to show how such writings articulate on a personal level reformist ideals. As Barbara Metcalf has noted in her recent study *Islamic Contestations*[12] autobiographical writings focus mainly on issues of self-presentation and provide templates for the narrator's self-enriching experiences drawn from anecdotal accounts and personal reminiscences. In both Arabic and Urdu writings these characteristics are given prominence. The significance of this genre in Islamic reformist thought is also to be found in the writings of earlier scholars which are discussed in Maulānā Nadwī's *Saviours of Islamic Spirit*.[13]

A brief overview of the autobiography genre is given elsewhere in the chapter. The aim is to investigate the premise

10. Nadwī, *Muslims in India*, 65.

11. Mention may be made of *Islam and the World*, 160-78.

12. Barbara Metcalf, *Islamic Contestations: Essays on Muslims in India and Pakistan*, New Delhi: Oxford University Press, 2004, 18.

13. The first volume of *Saviours of Islamic Spirit* contains important details on Nadwī's motivation for selecting reformers and intellectuals who have left behind autobiographical writings in the *tajdīdī* tradition.

that Maulānā Nadwī's autobiography *Kārwān-i-Ẓindagī* covers two important elements of the genre: self-analysis and authenticity. The study seeks to show how these elements are reflected in his worldview of the *tajdīd* tradition. Likewise, a study of the autobiographical accounts by predecessors and contemporaries of Maulānā Nadwī will show contrasting landscapes of Islamic resurgence and how they provide a broader framework to analyse their respective contributions to contemporary Islamic thought. The multiple levels of contestations are also evident in the sub-genre, biography. Here again Maulānā Nadwī seeks to explore issues that are central to his understanding of *iṣlāḥ* and his interpretive reading of Islamic authenticity. In a sense his biographical writings, especially of his contemporaries,[14] have a niche market — an unbroken link to the *tajdīd* tradition. Implicit in his biographical writings are an internal critique of those contemporaries whose interpretations of Islamic resurgence are either politicised or apologetic.[15] Maulānā Nadwī thus expresses himself in the first person focusing on himself (autobiography) and the lives of others (biography) whose literary heritage is often autobiographical writings. These writings are critically examined by Maulānā Nadwī.

Maulānā Nadwī's influence in the Arab world is significant. His Arabic works, in particular his *Islam and the World,* have

---

14. Reference may be made to Nadwī's biographical account on the founder of the Tabligh Jamā'at (hereafter TJ), Maulānā Muḥammad Ilyas to understand his conceptual framework of *islāḥ* and *tajdīd*. A detailed explanation of Nadwī's involvement with the TJ appears in Chapter 3. See SAHA M. Nadwī, *Life and Mission of Maulāna Mohammad Ilyas*, Lucknow: Academy of Islamic Research and Publications, 1979.

15. For an elaboration on Nadwī's assessment, see Nadwī, *Western Civilisation and Muslims*, 33-154.

received critical acclaim.[16] An important aspect of his Arabic writings is *iṣlāḥ* which is intended to remind the Arabs of their commitment to Islam. Maulānā Nadwī wrote some important biographical accounts on distinguished Arab intellectuals to show that *tajdīd* tradition is a global Islamic phenomenon which has not suffered any rupture[17] in the whole course of Islamic history. The choice of Arabic is deliberate: Maulānā Nadwī wishes to remind Arabs that Indian Muslims represented by Maulānā Nadwī's international stature have also made important contributions to Islamic resurgence. A careful reading of *Saviours of Islamic Spirit* reveals Maulānā Nadwī's thoughts on this aspect. The Indian Muslims' link to the Arab world is an attempt to reveal the former's commitment to an Islamic authenticity over the centuries.

In order to elucidate the autobiography and biography as genre, a brief survey of the Arabic literature is examined to locate Maulānā Nadwī's literary contributions against contemporary Arab littérateurs. For the purpose of our study, the autobiographical and biographical writings' thematic significance to the Islamic resurgence will be investigated.

---

16. According to *Ta'meer-i-Hayāt* more than 100 editions of *Islam and the World* in Arabic have been published between 1951-99. See *Ta'meer-i-Hayāt*, Special Number. Habibul-Haq Nadvi states that the success of this major work of Nadwī is attributed to its reformist content. For a summative assessment on this book, see Sayyid Habibul Haq Nadvi, *The Dynamics of Islam*, Durban, Academia, 1982, 61-2.

17. This observation is noted in *Saviours of Islamic Spirit*, vol. I:

"... [T]he revivalist movement on intellectual history of the Muslim peoples encompassing the academic and speculative achievements of all those savants who have left an indelible mark on the world of Islam. In fact, there is no gap at all in the intellectual history of Islam; it is only in the presentation of the history of its peoples, which needs urgently to be filled in." (p. x)

This approach is evident in *Kārwān-i-Ẓindagī* and *Western Civilisation, Islam and Muslims* which are a critique of Islamic modernists and their critical assessment of *iṣlāḥ* and *tajdīd.*[18] Implicit in the latter work is Maulānā Nadwī's critical assessment of Arab writers' responses to Islamic resurgence in their autobiographical writings which are discussed elsewhere in the chapter.

In his formulation of *tajdīd* Maulānā Nadwī traces biographical writings of scholars representing the classical period of Islamic history and contemporary period. It reinforces Maulānā Nadwī's assertion of the continuity of *tajdīd* drawn from the primary sources of the Qur'ān and *sunnah*. The theme of self-presentation[19] is given prominence in *Saviours of Islamic Spirit* just as much as Maulānā Nadwī's biographical accounts of *mujaddid*s focus on specific socio-political milieus.[20] In a similar vein, *mujaddid*s of the earlier periods are juxtaposed to demonstrate the continuity (*tasalsul*) of *tajdīd*. This is evident in a writing peculiar to Urdu literature: *obituarals*. Written in three volumes *Purān-i-Chirāgh*[21] includes scholars, intellectuals and *'ulamā* of diverse backgrounds who

---

18. Nadwī, *Western Civilisation . . .*, 91-129.

19. Nadwī argues that the assessment of any character, in our study, *mujaddid*s cannot be done out of its own context of time as this approach is likely to diminish their true achievements and contributions. Here Nadwī obliquely criticises works which ignore the intellectual, cultural and spiritual temperament of the time in their evaluation. Nadwī, *Saviours of Islamic Spirit*, vol. I, xii-xiii.

20. These genres have played a significant role in delineating the contesting discourse of Islamic resurgence. They are expressed in various forms and reveal how the personalities under study have used these genres to formulate their vision of *iṣlāḥi* and *tajdīd*.

21. SAHA Nadwī, *Purān-i-Chiragh*, vol. 1-3, Karachi: Majlis Nashriyat-i-Islam, 1994.

in Maulānā Nadwī's estimation have contributed to the *iṣlāḥ* tradition. This work sets to present an impressionistic account of important personalities who are representative of Maulānā Nadwī's conceptual framework of *tajdīd*. It is a useful reference work which also elaborates on Maulānā Nadwī's understanding of Islamic resurgence.

The literary approach found in Maulānā Nadwī's autobiographical and biographical writings accentuate a worldview of scholarly tradition and different expressions of reformist thought through which he develops his understanding of *tajdīd*. This aspect is discussed in the chapter.

Growth and Development of Autobiography and Biography in the Arab World: A Synopsis

The following section briefly examines the autobiographical literature in the Arab world. The forms of biographical writings and their influence on Maulānā Nadwī's writings are discussed. These sub-genres focus on the Islamic authenticity and how they manifest themselves as important links to the *tajdīdī* tradition. However, some general remarks on autobiography as a genre will help the reader understand its contextual significance in Arabic literature.

AUTOBIOGRAPHY: DEFINITION

Bruss in her important study, *Autobiographical Acts* has delineated the salient features of the autobiography genre. The primary characteristic is to identify an author-narrator as a "real person" in the text.[22] The autobiographer is both the source of the subject matter and the structure represented in the text.[23] The genre focuses largely on self-analysis and plays an important role in defining truth-revealing episodes explored in the

22. Elizabeth Bruss, *Autobiographical Acts*, Baltimore: John Hopkins University Press, 1976, 5-6.

23. Ibid.

autobiography.[24] It is its anecdotal character that contains elements of subjectivity with a distinctive literary bias.[25]

The narratives or self-portraiture gives rise to the formation of ideas which are revealed through retrospection.[26] The autobiography records details of contemporary life that are too small or too ordinary to have been found worth recording in any official source. The text in the genre involves a reader who maintains a twofold purpose:

- an intimate picture of the central character (narrator) and
- identity of the subject matter and narrator who is truthful.

Gerard[27] maintains that identity proceeds from the use of the first person pronoun *I* which builds a nexus between the reader and narrator. Such an approach lends credence to narration, helps create a sense of intimacy and establishes the aura of authenticity.[28]

The above characteristics are also present in autobiographies dealing with important Muslim scholars in the twentieth century. Before we examine the impact of autobiography on Islamic resurgence, a brief discussion on the growth and development of Arabic literature will be useful to locate its *tajdīdī* importance.

---

24. This aspect has been discussed in detail by the French philosopher Rousseau in his *Confession;* see Robert Elbaz, *The Changing Nature of the Self: A Critical Study of the Autobiographical Discourse*, London: Croom-Helm Ltd., 1988, 2-3.

25. Elizabeth Bruss, *Autobiographical Acts;* John C. Hawley, *The Post-Colonial Crescent; Islam's Impact on Contemporary Literature*, 1998, 122.

26. John Sturrock, *The Language of Autobiography: Studies in the First Person Singular*, Cambridge: Cambridge University Press, 1993, 6.

27. Genette Gerard, *Figures III*, Paris: Editions du Sevil, 1972, 253.

28. Fedwa Malti-Douglas, *Autobiography and Blindness: Al-Ayyam of Ṭahā Ḥusayn*, Princeton: Princeton University Press, 1988, 93-94.

AUTOBIOGRAPHICAL & BIOGRAPHICAL WRITINGS IN ARABIC LITERATURE

Although Arabic literature began during the Jāhiliyyah (pre-Islamic) period, Islam had a profound influence on its development.[29] The Qur'ān revealed to Prophet Muḥammad (SAW) was a literary work and shaped centuries-long *turāth* (textual traditions) of the Arab-Islamic world.

The multinational empire[30] spanning from Spain to Afghanistan during the Islamic conquests created an efflorescence of Islamic literature. *Adab*[31] (literature) as a genre dominated the Arabic prose corpus and spawned a number of forms of literary texts that continued to be read and appreciated. The *maqāmah*,[32] the anecdotal literature genre, is a classical example of the major influence on the emergent patterns of literature. It would be useful to examine the influence of two sub-genres, *ṭabaqāt* and *tarjamah*, in defining *turāth* (Islamic authenticity) which is a salient feature of Maulānā Nadwī's Islamic resurgence paradigm.

BIOGRAPHICAL LITERATURE

ṬABAQĀT (BIOGRAPHICAL DICTIONARY)

Literature flourished in the Islamic East and the Islamic West. The hybrid literary population of these regions gave birth to a variety of literary forms of which mystical and philosophical narrative played an important role. The medieval

29. For a detailed account of Jāhiliyyah literature see R.A. Nicholson, *A Literary History of the Arabs*, Delhi: Adam Publications, 1996.

30. See the following: Sayyid Amir Ali, *A Short History of the Saracens*, New Delhi: Kitab Bhavan, 1981; T.W. Arnold, *The Preachings of Islam*, Lahore: Sh. Muḥammad Ashraf, 1979; S.M. Imamuddin, *A Political History of the Muslims*, vol. 2-3, Dacca: Najmahsons, 1977.

31. The evolution of *adab* as a literary genre has been succinctly analysed in *Encyclopaedia of Islam* (1st edn.), 175-76.

32. R.A. Nicholson, *A Literary History of the Arabs*, 328-36.

autobiographical form co-existed with a well-developed indigenous Arabo-Islamic form, the biography. The genesis of biographical dictionary (*ṭabaqāt*)[33] has been linked to *ḥadīth* with special focus on its *isnād* (chain of transmission).[34] The elements of Islamic authenticity which characterised the salient features of the autobiography formed the core biographical compendia. George Makdisi's[35] seminal study of the *ṭabaqāt* describes the rich legacy of Islamic culture this literary genre sustained over centuries in various Islamic regions which included cities with a strong Islamo-Persian tradition.[36]

In examining the *ṭabaqāt*, al-Qādri notes that the genre served "as a cultural and intellectual phenomenon in classical Islamic civilisation."[37] It also provided variant forms or sub-genres — *tārīkh* (history of politics) to Sūfī biographies — an expression which was given validity, legitimacy and even

33. Several works on Islamic history and historiography discuss biographical dictionaries. See HAR Gibb, "Tā'rikh" in *Encyclopaedia of Islam* (1st edn.), supplement, 233-45; T. Khalidi, "Islamic Biographical Dictionaries: A Preliminary Assessment", *Muslim World*, 63, 1973, 53-65.

34. The *Kitāb al-ṭabaqāt al-Kubrā* by ibn Sa'd (d. *c*. 845) illustrates how the earliest surviving biographical dictionary relied on the *isnād* system for an authentic representation of the early period of Islam. It is an eight-volume work with over 4250 entries recording the biographies of the companions of the Prophet Muḥammad then the followers of the Companions, then their Followers, then of the Muslim women who played a role in early Islamic society and Islamic learning.

35. George Makdisi, *The Rise of Colleges: Institutions of Learning in Islam and the West*, Edinburgh: Edinburgh University Press, 1981.

36. For a brief survey on the Islamo-Persian tradition see Lewishohn, *Classical Persian Sufism: From its Origins to Rumi*, London: Khaniqah Nimatullahi Publications, 1993.

37. Wadad Al-Qādrī, "Biographical Dictionaries: Inner Structure and Cultural Significance" in George N. Atiyeh (ed.) *The Book in the Islamic World*, Albany: State University of New York, 1995, 111.

roots in the very foundation of Islam.[38] Maulānā Nadwī in particular employed these forms of genres to articulate his vision of *tajdīd*.

TARJAMAH: COMPILATION OF BIOGRAPHICAL SKETCHES

Belonging to the autobiography genre is the *tarjamah*. According to Eickelman, the traditional Islamic *tarjamah* is generally written in third person, even if autobiographical. The components include a genealogy, an account of formal education and Qur'ānic memorisation, a list of teachers (often including close relatives, which indicates family support for religious learners), the books and subjects studied and selections from the subject's poetry, aphorisms and other contributions to learning.[39]

The *tarjamah* was a standard reference on Islamic scholars and their contributions. Even the Indo-Persian tradition of autobiography writing showed unmistakable traces of the *tarjamah*'s distinctive characteristics.[40] A more developed form of this genre was the *tadhkirah*, a biographical memoir. The texts in the *tadhkirah* were didactic in content; the lessons gleaned from the portrayal of the protagonists was a complete curriculum (*niṣāb*) of an enlightened lesson (*sabaq*) in dying for Allah and in living for Allah. The pedagogic potential of such memoirs is self-explanatory. Maulānā Nadwī too was influenced by this genre: his *tadhkirah* on the noted Sūfī

38. Wadad Al-Qādrī, "Biographical Dictionaries: Inner Structure and Cultural Significance" in George N. Atiyeh (ed.) *The Book in the Islamic World*, 107-10.

39. D.F. Eickelman, "Traditional Islamic Learning and Ideas of the Person in the Twentieth Century", in Martin Kramer (ed.), *Middle Eastern Lives: The Practices of Biography and Self-Narrative*, Syracuse, 1991, 39.

40. B. Metcalf, *Islamic Contestations, Essays of Muslims in India and Pakistan*, New Delhi: Oxford University Press, 2004, 71.

reformist, Fazlur Raḥmān Ganj-Murādabādi[41] reaffirms his definition of Islamic authenticity in the *tajdīdī* tradition. The memoir's reformist content again points to Maulānā Nadwī's choice of scholars and intellectuals who are considered authentic representatives of Islamic resurgence.

AUTOBIOGRAPHY IN THE ARAB WORLD

Dwight Reynolds has examined the elements of Arabic autobiography in his *Interpreting the Self.*[42] Based on Western representations of the autobiography, Reynolds shows that Arabic autobiography as "self-conscious, self-authored texts"[43] mirrors elements that we as twenty-first century readers can readily identify with. These are the portrayal of the inner self that traces the emotional life of the author, his or her private behaviour and the disclosures of motivations and reactions and evaluation of the author's personality. According to Reynolds these facets are termed as "self-revelatory experiences." In other words, the autobiography reflects a retrospective examination of the course of his/her life and "even a sense of imparting some of the hard-learned lessons of that life to posterity."[44]

For our study, the autobiographical writings of Maulānā Nadwī and his contemporaries will be located in a specific religio-political setting to understand the currents of Islamic resurgence that swept across the Muslim world during the twentieth century. The motivation for such writings illustrates how the contours of reformist thought map out the patterns

---

41. B. Metcalf, *Islamic Contestations, Essays of Muslims in India and Pakistan,* 71, see SAHA Nadwī, *Tadhkirah Maulānā Fazlur Rahman Ganj-Muradabadi,* Karachi: Majlis Nashriyāt-i-Islam, 1985.

42. Dwight Reynolds, *Interpreting the Self: Autobiography in the Literary Arab Tradition,* Berkeley: University of California Press, 2001.

43. Ibid., 74.

44. Ibid.

of Islamic resurgence in its various forms. The retrospective examination of the course of events in the narrator's life helps the readers to draw their own conclusions on contemporary Islamic thought.

Maulānā Nadwī's theme of Islamic authenticity is also articulated in his assessment of autobiographical works drawn from the classical Islamic period. Baghdād, the metropolis of Islam, attracted a phalanx of Islamic scholars who left behind significant autobiographies. Of particular importance is the autobiography of Abu Ḥāmid al-Ghazāli[45] (d. 1111), *Al-Munqidh min al-ḍalāl* (Deliverance from Error).[46] The *Munqidh* does not focus exclusively on autobiographical details *per se* but relates to the "experiences and personal perspectives of the author (which) constantly occupy the forefront of the work."[47] The *Munqidh,* Ebrahim Moosa maintains, is a spiritual testimony[48] rather than an autobiography of Ghazāli. The spiritual content is a dominant theme in this work: the concept of "self" and "identity" which linked to his spiritual journey are explored. According to Moosa, Ghazāli provides his readers with "snapshots" of the most significant moments that were burned on to his memory.[49] Maulānā Nadwī too refers to Ghazāli's "internal conflict and disquietude, the Promethean quest"[50]

45. For his life and discussion on his crisis, see among others, W. Watt, *Muslim Intellectual: A Study of Al-Ghazāli,* Edinburgh, 1963.

46. Translated into English by W. Montgomery Watt, *The Faith and Practice of Al-Ghazāli,* Lahore: Sh. Muḥammad Ashraf, 1981.

47. Eric L. Ornsby, "The Taste of Truth: The Structure of Experience in Al-Ghazāli's al-Munqidh min al-ḍalālah", in Wael Hallaq (ed.), *Islamic Studies: Presented to Charles Adam,* Leiden: E.J. Brill, 1991, 141.

48. Moosa, Ebrahim, *Ghazāli and the Poetics of Imagination,* Chapel Hill: University of North Carolina Press, 2005, 85-89.

49. Ibid., 88.

50. SAHA Nadwī, *Saviours of Islamic Spirit,* vol. 1, Lucknow: Academy of Islamic Research and Publications, 1971, 113.

which steered him to a different path with the ebb and flow of his intellectual career poignantly recorded in his *Munqidh*. Ghazāli's influence on Maulānā Nadwī's writings is best expressed in the latter's multi-volume *Saviours of Islamic Spirit*. In Ghazāli's critique of Muslim society, Maulānā Nadwī echoes similar comments which are rooted in an Indian social milieu.[51] The revivalist theme[52] as set out in Ghazāli's major writings deserves greater scrutiny in future study in order to evaluate Maulānā Nadwī's contribution to this field.

The autobiographical compendia which developed in the twentieth century co-existed with the political and cultural processes in the Arab world. The profound influence of the West was discernible in new literary genres, the novel and the short story. Reference may be made to Allen's *The Arabic Novel*[53] to get a synoptic overview of the radical changes that took place in the Arab world.

In the following sections the study will focus on authors whose autobiographies reflect a specific intellectual ethos. To contextualise the autobiography genre and its relevance to Maulānā Nadwī's intellectual contributions, two important autobiographies are discussed below. Although appearing

51. The following works by Nadwī elaborate on the theme of reconstruction of Muslim society.
   - *The New Menace and its Answer* (n.d.)
   - *The Fifteenth Century* (n.d.)
   - *Live to lead: A call to Indian Muslims* (n.d.)
   - *Reconstruction of Indian Society. What Muslims Can Do?* (n.d.)

52. The *tajdīd* and *iṣlāḥ* trends have succinctly been discussed in John Esposito et al., *Makers of Contemporary Islam*, 10-20; Ali Rahnema (ed.), *Pioneers of Islamic Revivalism*, London: Zed Books Ltd., 1994, 4-10; John Esposito (ed.), *Oxford Encyclopedia of the Modern Islamic World*, vol. 3, 242; Sayyid Habibul Haq Nadvi, *Islamic Resurgent Movements in the Indo-Pak Subcontinent*, Durban: Academia, 1987, 37-43.

53. Roger Allen, *The Arabic Novel: An Historical and Critical Introduction*, Syracuse: New York Press, 1982.

from two distinctive religious orientations[54] they are nevertheless representative of the emergent trends of contemporary Islamic thought. The reformist and modernist spirit articulated in their respective writings mirror the crises of confidence that, by and large, affected the Arab world. Egypt, in particular, embodied these two trends which were to have a profound influence in the Muslim world.

MUDHĀKARĀT: ḤASAN AL-BANNĀ

Maulānā Nadwī's chequered relationship with the Ikhwān-ul-Muslimīn (The Muslim Brotherhood)[55] can best be appreciated in the writings of its founder, Ḥasan al-Bannā (d. 1949).[56] Written a few years before his assassination in 1949, his *Mudhākarāt* (Memoirs)[57] reveals the intimate side of his life and outlines his intellectual and religious development. In a reflective but straightforward style al-Bannā "offers a clear portrait of a troubled self — a self that is torn between its passion for things Islamic and irritation at things un-Islamic."[58] In a sense al-Bannā makes references to the multiple forces

---

54. For a detailed analysis of this trend towards modernisation, see SAHA Nadwī, *Western Civilisation, Islam and Muslims*, Lucknow: Academy of Islamic Research and Publications, 1974, 10-31.

55. See the following: A.Z. Al-Abidin, *The Political Thought of Ḥasan al-Banna in Islamic Studies*, vol. 28:3, 219-37; I. Bello, *The Society of Muslim Brethren: An Ideological Study in Islamic Studies*, vol. 20:2, 1981; R.P. Mitchell, *The Society of Muslim Brothers*, New York, 1993.

56. I.M. Husaini, *The Muslim Brethren: The Greatest of Modern Islamic Movements*, Beirut: Khayāt's College Book Co-operative, 1956; Richard P. Mitchell, *The Society of the Muslim Brothers*, London, 1969.

57. Ḥasan Al-Bannā, *Mudhakarāt al-da'wah wa'l dā'iya*, Beirut, 1970. The *Memoirs* are translated partially into English: N.M. Shaikh, *Memoirs of Ḥasan al-Bannā Shaheed*, Karachi: International Islamic Publishers, 1981.

58. Abu Rabi' Ibrahim M., *Intellectual Origins . . .*, 66.

that affected him as a youth which afterwards shaped his goals and mission in the establishment of the Ikhwān.

The Introduction[59] to the *mudhakkarāt* written by Maulānā Nadwī illustrates his profound respect for al-Bannā. In a similar vein, Maulānā Nadwī maintained a close affinity with the Ikhwān and in many respects influenced the *da'wah* programme of the movement. Maulānā Nadwī's pioneering work *Islam and the World* written originally in Arabic was a standard reference work[60] for the Ikhwān with special reference to its interpretation of revival and reform (*tajdīd wa iṣlāḥ*). Maulānā Nadwī noted that "these scholars have relentlessly fought against the forces of corruption, defended the Islamic precepts and teachings and rejuvenated the spirit of Islamic revival besides making valuable contributions to the intellectual and academic treasure of their people."[61] Bannā's contributions were illustrative of the caravan of Islamic *da'wah* personalities (*dā'iyān-i-Islam*) which was never devoid of them during any period or era of Islamic history.[62] Again the theme of Islamic authenticity is shown in Maulānā Nadwī's appreciation of al-Bannā's *tajdīdī* contributions. Al-Bannā, in Maulānā Nadwī's words, "invited humanity to the unique position of the Muslim *ummah*."[63] This position, as Abu

59. A new edition of *Mudhākarāt* was published in Beirut (1997). Nadwī's insightful introduction sheds much light on his admiration for al-Bannā. Commenting on al-Bannā's contributions, Nadwī remarks: "He (al-Bannā) prepared a new generation and was a mentor to a whole nation. He was the founder of an intellectual and moral school of thought. Even educated individuals and those who hold ranking positions were not immune from the influence of his intellectual orientation," *Purān-i-Chirāgh*, vol. 3, 20.

60. SAHA Nadwī, *Kārwān-i-Ẓindagī*, vol. I, 376.

61. SAHA Nadwī, *Saviours of Islamic Spirit*, vol. I.

62. SAHA Nadwī, *Purān-i-Chirāgh*, vol. 3, 16.

63. Nadwī, *Puran-i-Chirāgh*, vol. 3, 15.

Rabi' noted, was an internal critique of the Muslim society by al-Bannā. Muslim decline made the Western penetration of all aspects of Muslim life and culture possible.[64] The focus on *iṣlāḥ* was al-Bannā's primary concern, a concern shared by Maulānā Nadwī too. However al-Bannā's position had not remained unchanged as political events in Egypt marginalised his vision of Islamic resurgence and instead gave rise to a number of readings of this concept against the background of the emergent Salafiyyah movement.[65]

AL-AYYĀM: ṬĀHA ḤUSAYN

The widely acclaimed autobiography of Ṭāha Ḥusayn (d. 1971)[66] *Al-Ayyām*, the complete text published between 1926 and 1967, is a landmark in the development of modern Arabic prose. *Al-Ayyām* was written during a tumultuous period in Egyptian history and had its distinctive cultural and literary context. The imperialistic policy of the West had a profound impact on its economic autonomy and cultural integrity. The cultural challenges of modernity, and Western leadership, spawned a generation of Egyptian scholars whose intellectual upbringing bore unmistakable imprints of the West. Ṭāha Ḥusayn, the blind intellectual played a pioneering role in highlighting the role of Europe on Egyptian culture. His education in Sorbonne (France) created a fundamental "ambivalent cultural identification"[67] in his narrative. The central character remains nameless in the first two volumes only to surface with a name in the third volume. Ḥusayn's

64. Ibrahim Abu Rabi', *Islam and the Search for a Social Order in Modern Egypt: An Intellectual Biography of Shaykh Mahmud Abd al-Halim Mahmud*, Published PhD, Temple University, 1987, 61-62.

65. Ibid., 51-74.

66. For a brief introduction to Taha Ḥusayn's life and works see: Albert Hourani, *Arabic Thought in the Liberal Age*.

67. Fedwa Malti-Douglas, *Blindness and Autobiography: Al-Ayyām of Tahā Husayn*, Princeton University Press, 1988, 7.

use of the synchronic and diachronic narratives in his autobiography reveals complexities and tension[68] of his world, an ambivalence that is embedded in his critique of Islamic culture.[69] Ḥusayn's representation of Islamic reformist thought falls in the category of Islamic modernism. Maulānā Nadwī laments the fact that Ḥusayn's intellectual stature did not contribute positively towards the "rejuvenation of Islamic thought."[70] On the contrary his advocacy of Western civilisation created an identity crisis for Egyptian Muslims in terms of Islamic authenticity. Islamic resurgence for Ṭahā Ḥusayn and other Arab reformers was associated with modernisation in which the success of the Arab world lay.[71]

While recognising Ḥusayn's literary production for its "simplicity, chastity and classical elegance"[72] Maulānā Nadwī is critical of those writings of Ḥusayn which bear the mark of Western orientalism[73] and a penchant for the new and original (*jadīd*). The rhetoric of polemics[74] in the assessment of Ḥusayn's contribution to Islamic modernism is notably absent in *Western Civilisation, Islam and Muslims* by Maulānā Nadwī.

---

68. Fedwa Malti-Douglas, *Blindness and Autobiography: Al-Ayyām of Ṭahā Ḥusayn*, Princeton University Press, 1988, 179.

69. Ḥusayn's *Shi'ral-Islam al Jāhili* (On pre-Islamic poetry) and *Mustaqbal-us-thaqāfat fi Misr* (The Future of Culture in Egypt) express his Western leanings. However, his *'Ali Hamish al Sīrah* and *Wa'd Hawā* (Truth Promised) delineate his reaffirmation of the Islamic *turāth*, a marked contrast to his earlier writings.

70. Nadwī, *Western Civilisation . . .*, 109.

71. Ibid.

72. Sayyid Abul Ḥasan Ali Nadwī, *Western Civilisation, Islam and Muslims*, Lucknow: Academy of Islamic Research and Publications 1974, 107.

73. Ibid.

74. Nadwī's critique on Ḥusayn bears a general pattern of critique and evaluation which is evident in his other writings too. For an elaboration on this topic see Atiq Aḥmad Qāsim, *Hadhrat* →

ASSESSMENT

One of the major international developments in the Muslim world is the *tajdīd* process taking place. The Islamist movements of which the Ikhwān is a notable example, have used Islamic literature to advocate their interpretation of Islam as a way of life (*dīn*). The Arabic literary discourse has been influenced by the Islamist movements and it is hardly surprising that the autobiography genre is embedded in a strong Islamic setting.[75] One of the major figures of the Islamist movement, Shaykh 'Abd al-Hamīd Kishk of Egypt (d. 1933) wrote his autobiography *Qiṣṣat Ayyāmi*[76] (Story of My Days) in which he chronicles not only his religious development but also his saga as a visually handicapped young man. The chronicles are intended to be life-enriching experiences for readers and a reminder of their commitment to Islam as a way of life (*dīn*). It must be noted that the projection of *dīn* by Kishk and other Islamists carries a conceptual vagueness and becomes more problematic when a political connotation is emphasised. This is clearly evident in Maulānā Maudūdī's and Quṭb's presentation of *dīn* as a comprehensive way of life which is dealt in Chapter 4.

Present-day Arabic literature is a complex discourse that embraces the cultural elements from both the Arabo-Islamic

→ *Maulānā Sayyid Abul Ḥasan Aliā Nadwī ka Tanqidi Uslub;* 'Abdul Qayyum Haqqāni, *Tadhkira wa Sawānih Mufakhir-ul-Islam hadhrat Maulānā Sayyid Abul Ḥasan Ali Nadwī: Al-Qasim Special Issue*, Nawshera: Al-Qāsim, 2002, 249-72. This approach is echoed in his *Qadianism: A Critical Study*, Lucknow, 1974: "The writer has not considered himself bound by his polemical tradition. This book (Qadianism) has been written with historical sobriety rather than the bigoted zeal of a debater," p. v.

75. John Esposito (ed.), *The Oxford Encyclopedia of the Modern Islamic World*, vol. I, 102.

76. 'Abd al-Hamid Kishk, *Qiṣṣat Ayyāmi: Mudhakkarāt al-Shaykh Kishk*, Cairo, 1986.

legacy and the equally rich Western tradition. Maulānā Nadwī's writings in Arabic emphasise on Islamic authenticity and present a critique of the Arab world in terms of surrender to Western culture. However, his Urdu writings largely reflect his concern for the Indian Muslims' commitment to Islamic norms and teachings which link them to the primary sources of Islam. The *turāth* motif is interwoven in his biographical writings of scholars and Sūfīs whom he considers to be ideal representatives of *iṣlāḥ* and *tajdīd*.

Biographical Literature in Indo-Persian Tradition

The influence of the Persianite tradition to autobiographical writing in the Indo-Pak subcontinent has followed a somewhat consistent pattern over the centuries. The *manāqib* (eulogy) element is embedded in this genre; the material presented does not follow a chronological order and there is no sequential development of persona. Rather the focus is on episodes and anecdotes to illustrate a moral understanding of the persona.[77]

The above description also applies to autobiographies of *'ulamā* nurtured in Islamic institutions with reformist leanings during the nineteenth and twentieth centuries. Dār-ul-'ulūm, Deoband, a premier Islamic institution which is based on the *tajdīd* and *iṣlāḥ* traditions, had produced a number of *'ulamā* whose contributions are widely acclaimed in the Muslim world. The autobiographies of two scholars from this institution will be examined in the study. Moreover, they were contemporaries of Maulānā Nadwī and their respective influences on his multi-faceted personality are also evaluated.

AAP BITI: MAULĀNĀ MUḤAMMAD SHAYKH ZAKARIYYAH (D. 1982)

The title of the autobiography *Aap Biti* is an ordinary word

77. Barbara D. Metcalf, *Islamic Contestations*, 72.

for one's own life story. Metcalf refers to the book as "a rich source for the history of the reformist, quietest Islam that has been so pervasive in the Muslim religious life in the Indian colonial and post-colonial periods."[78]

The *Aap Biti*[79] does not follow a given chronological sequence; rather the text is presented around personalities with whom the author has interacted. A close reading of the autobiography suggests that the *Aap Biti* is not much about Shaykh Zakariyyah at all. Metcalf maintains that Shaykh Zakariyyah's own life "gains significance not by individuality but by devotion to a particular pattern exemplified in specific anecdotal evidence about model figures both living and dead."[80] The text reinforces the teaching nature of such a genre. Maulānā Nadwī, who wrote an "official biography" of Shaykh Zakariyyah remarks that the *Aap Biti* contained "the episodes of his (Shaykh Zakariyyah's) life that offered instruction (*sabaq amuz hālāt*); the perfections (*kamālāt*) and conduct of life (*tarz-i-ẓindagī*) of his teachers and mentors (*shaykhs*); and finally episodes of sincerity and sacrifice (*ikhlās awr isār*)."[81] These comments by Maulānā Nadwī reveals his admiration for Shaykh Zakariyyah as the biography of the latter suggests. Yet Maulānā Nadwī in his presentation of Shaykh Zakariyyah was largely chronological in his approach in which he tried to analyse the subject's personality over his life course. This approach was in marked contrast with the

78. Barbara D. Metcalf, *Islamic Contestations,* 67.

79. Muḥammad Zakariyyah Khadhalwi, *Aap Biti,* vols. 1-7, *Yād-i-Ayyām,* Karachi: Mahd-ul-Khalil al-Islami, n.d.

80. Barbara Metcalf, *Islamic Contestations,* 72.

81. Nadwī, *Hadhrat Shaykh-ul-Ḥadīth Maulānā Muḥammad Zakariyyah,* Karachi: Majlis Nashriyāt-i-Islam, 1982, 106. Nadwī's *Kārwān-i-Ẓindagī* elaborates on his close affinity with Zakariyyah, a relationship that was based on "pastoral care and affection", vol. I, 442.

Indo-Persianite tradition which followed hagiographical trends and provided embellished accounts of personalities and events.[82] This new trend is evident in his own multi-volume autobiography, *Kārwān-i-Ẓindagī.* The parameters of Islamic authenticity are clearly defined. Shaykh Zakariyyah as representative of "traditional" Islam, had a profound influence on Maulānā Nadwī's formulation of *tajdīd* — a link with reformist thought developed over the last three centuries in the Indian subcontinent.

NAQSH-I-ḤAYĀT — MAULĀNĀ SAYYID ḤUSAYN AḤMAD MADANI (D. 1957)

Ḥusayn Aḥmad Maulānā Madani[83] occupies an important position as a scholar and a political activist. His autobiography *Naqsh-i-Ḥayāt* (Impressions of Life) is in marked contrast from his contemporary, Shaykh Zakariyyah who wrote *Aap Biti.* Maulānā Madani's autobiography "is two-thirds purely socio-political rather than religious discourse."[84] This statement does not imply that Maulānā Madani's fame as an illustrious scholar remains obscured; rather the *Naqsh-i-Ḥayāt* contains personal reminiscences that deal with Maulānā Madani's formative period. Three strands are conspicuous in his autobiography:

- Sense of gratitude to Allah for reviving his family's lost spiritual tradition after the 1857 uprising against British rule. "Spiritual knowledge and mysticism yielded place to ignorance and self-service. The events

82. Barbara Metcalf, *Islamic Contestations*, 79.

83. For a biographical detail on Maulānā Madani, see Mian Sayyid Mohammad, *Asirān-e-Malta*, English translation: Mohammad Anwer Hussain, *The Prisoners of Malta*, New Delhi: Manak Publications, 2005 and D.R. Goyal, *Maulānā Husain Aḥmad Maulānā Madani: A Biographical Study*, Kolkata: Anamika Publishers, 2004.

84. SHA Madani, *Naqsh-i-Hayāt*, Maktaba Diniya, 1999.

of 1857[85] destroyed even that and all the amassed wealth was plundered."

- Life in Madinah: challenges and trials as a *ḥadīth* teacher.[86] In addition it provided him an opportunity to study political developments in the world through his interaction with his students from different parts of the world.[87]
- Devotion to his mentor, Maulānā Maḥmud-al-Ḥasan[88] (Shaykh-ul-Hind), in their struggle for India's independence.

The episodes in the *Naqsh-i-Ḥayāt* are not recounted in a systematic manner and readers are expected to tie up the scattered incidents to form a coherent picture of Maulānā Madani's eminent personality. Maulānā Nadwī's assessment of Maulānā Madani's political struggle and moral standing is reproduced hereunder.

> Maulana Madani strove to the best of his ability, during the fateful years, to make the Muslims realise the folly of the Pakistan demand. He undertook extensive tours of the country, preaching the gospel of unity from town to town and village to village. Morally and religiously, his conduct remained absolutely stainless and above suspicion throughout that period of trial and crisis, and friend and foe are unanimous in their praise of his integrity and sincerity. After the Independence, too, when unlimited opportunities had opened up for personal gain, he sought no favours for himself, so much so that he politely declined to accept the title of Padma Vibhushan, which was conferred upon him by the President of India in 1954, saying that it was against

85. Goyal, *Maulānā Husain Aḥmad Madani*, 11.
86. Ibid., 16.
87. Quoted in Goyal, *Maulānā Husain Aḥmad Madani*, 16.
88. Sayyid Mohammad Mian, *The Prisoners of Malta*, 88-100.

the traditions of his precursors to receive honours from the government.[89]

Maulānā Nadwī shared a kindred spirit with Maulānā Madani on the future of Indian Muslims in a changed political scenario after Partition. His own *Payām-i-Insāniyat*[90] (Message for Humanity) movement reflected this change and through it he strove to promote the message of Maulānā Madani. Maulānā Nadwī maintained that Muslim corporate identity was safeguarded in the Indian Constitution which advocated democracy and secularism. This aspect is examined in Chapter 5. Two outstanding qualities which endeared Maulānā Nadwī to Maulānā Madani were the latter's unimpeachable sincerity and selflessness (*ikhlās wa be-gharẓī*)[91] which he internalised in his own life. Maulānā Madani's mission highlighted on a broader level the challenges Indian *'ulamā* faced in mapping out their future career and also offering alternatives to the realities — social, religious and political — caused by the Partition of India in 1947. Maulānā Nadwī was not immune to these changing circumstances and his contribution in this regard is analysed in Chapter 5. Maulānā Nadwī's ability to interact with *'ulamā* with varied understanding by the *tajdīd* tradition within a specific ideological orientation (Deobandi, for example) suggests his pragmation in reformulating his presentation of Islamic resurgence.

Autobiography: Non-Traditional Scholars

The study also examines the autobiographies of three scholars who though not trained in traditional Islamic institutions have

89. SAHA Nadwī, *Muslims in India,* Lucknow: Academy of Islamic Research and Publications, 1976, 121-22.

90. On the establishment of the *Payām-i-Insāniyat,* see SAHA Nadwī, *Kārwān-i-Ẓindagī,* vol. 2, 109-27.

91. SAHA Nadwī, *Purān-i-Chirāgh,* vol. 1, 110.

had a profound impact on contemporary Islamic thought. They have served as a nexus between traditionalist and Islamist interpretation as discussed in Chapter 1. As contemporaries of Maulānā Nadwī, their impact on his intellectual life cannot be ignored.

TADHKIRAH: MAULĀNĀ ABUL KALĀM ĀZĀD (D. 1958)

Maulānā Abul Kalām Āzād was a traditional Urdu journalist and religious scholar who symbolised the Muslim option for composite Indian nationalism. The *tadhkirah*[92] of Āzād[93] was intended to be his autobiography; however there appeared sketchy details of his own life. The editor Fazluddin Aḥmad's annotated comments[94] must be relied on to interpret the text. Āzād refers to the life and times of his ancestor Jamāluddīn and then branches out to other pre-eminent heroes of Islam with the reformist zeal. The matrix of his memoirs is on Aḥmad bin Ḥanbal[95] and Ibn Taymiyyah[96] who are considered to be ideologues of the *salafi* movement[97] which traces its sources to the classical interpretation of Islam. It is Ibn Taymiyyah who was to be his source of authority[98] to interpret

92. Abul Kalām Āzād, *Tadhkirah*, New Delhi: Sahitya Academy, 1985.

93. For a biographical account on Āzād, see Ian Henderson Douglas, *Abul Kalām Āzād: An Intellectual and Religious Biography*, Delhi: Oxford University Press, 1993; Humayun Kabir, *Maulānā Abul Kalām Āzād: A Memorial Volume*, Bombay: Asia Press, 1959.

94. Abul Kalām Āzād, *Tadhkirah*.

95. Muḥammad Abu Zahra, *The Four Imams: Their Lives, Works and their Schools of Thought*, tr. by Aisha Bewley, London: Dar-al-Taqwa, 2001, 436-500.

96. H. Laoust, "Ibn Taymiyyah", in *Encyclopaedia of Islam*, vol. 3, 951-5; Abdul Hakim Al-Matroudi, *The Hanbali School of Law and Ibn Taymiyyah*, Oxford: Routledge, 2005.

97. On the growth and development of the *salafi* movement see Emad Eldin Shahin, "Salafiyya" in John Esposito (ed.), *The Oxford Encyclopaedia of the Modern Islamic World*, vol. 3, 463-69.

98. Āzād, *Tadhkirah*, 212-26.

Islam in a changed Indian political landscape where Muslims were marginalised and disempowered of their former glory and political status. These two leading figures mentioned in the *tadhkirah* are also dealt with by Maulānā Nadwī in his *Saviours of Islamic Spirit*.[99] Āzād's *salafi* leanings are combined with his modernist interpretation of Islam. This approach is evident from his active participation in politics and like Maulānā Madani, his contemporary, he too expressed his opposition to the creation of Pakistan.[100]

A recent study by Sayyida Hameed[101] on the *tadhkirah* provides interesting insights on the reason for such writing:

> The autobiographical account, *tadhkirah* was obviously intended as an instrument of instruction. The author not only acknowledges his intention but considers it part of his mission. It also speaks about Āzād himself. He considers himself responsible for carrying forward the torch of *ṣidq-o-wafā* (truth and faith) lit by his ancestors. He aspires to become the *Momin-e-Kaamil* (perfect believer) as he believes he will become the *Fāteh-e-Waqt* (the conqueror of time).[102]

Āzād's political ambitions[103] have been analysed based on his personal mission as outlined above. Another memoir of Āzād,

99. Nadwī, *Saviours of Islamic Spirit*, vol. 1/2.

100. R. Subromani Iyer, *The Role of Maulānā Abul Kalām Āzād in Indian Politics*, Hyderabad: Abul Kalam Oriental Research Institute Publications, n.d.; Abul Kalām Āzād, *India Wins Freedom: An Autobiographical Narrative*, Calcutta: Orient Longman, 1964.

101. Sayyida Saiyidain Hameed, *Islamic Seal on India's Independence: Abul Kalām Āzād : A Fresh Look*, Karachi: Oxford University Press, 1998.

102. Ibid., 90.

103. Subromani Iyer, *The Role of Abul Kalām in Indian Politics*, Hyderabad, n.d. For a critrique on Āzād's nationalism and secularism views, see Maryam Jameelah, *Islam and Modernism*, Lahore: Mohammad Yusuf Khan, 1975, 77-87.

India Wins Freedom[104] was intended to be a supplement to his *tadhkirah*. It focuses on his political career and by and large is his personal narrative on the events leading to the Partition of India (in 1947). Here again Maulānā Nadwī's impressions on *India Wins Freedom* are interesting. The political profiles of *'ulamā* in the struggle for India's Independence of which Āzād is included reveal his admiration for Āzād's concern for Muslim as minorities in a changed political landscape. Āzād's versatility which mirrored Maulānā Nadwī's multi-faceted personality was acknowledged by the latter in the following words:

> It was Indian Muslims' misfortune or perhaps Āzād's restless soul and genius that saw the changing times in his career. From his debut as a journalist publishing his *Hilāl* magazine which had a revolutionary content for Indian Muslims to his *Ḥizb-Allah* (army of God) party advocating Islamic resurgence, Āzād could not achieve his goals. His last phase was evident in his involvement with the Indian National Congress through which he strove to serve both Muslim and Non-Muslim interests selfelessly. . . .[105]

Maulānā Nadwī's personal assessment of Āzād's contribution to composite nationalism illustrates the former's support of this concept which served as a precursor to his *Payām-i-Insāniyat*. Āzād's intellectual legacy beginning from his pan-Islamic vision to his nationalist standpoint in a way reflected the ambivalence of reformers in the Indian subcontinent striving to maintain a corporate Muslim identity in a rooted Indian context. Maulānā Nadwī was faced with similar challenges to which he responded pragmatically with the *iṣlāḥi-tajdīd* paradigm in a changed socio-political setting.

---

104. Abul Kalām Āzād, *India Wins Freedom*, Calcutta: Orient Longmans, 1964.

105. Nadwī, *Purān-i-Chirāgh*, vol. 2, 57-58.

KHUD NIWISHT: SAYYID ABUL 'AL'A MAUDŪDĪ (D. 1979)[106]

Maulānā Maudūdī's autobiography originally appeared in Pakistan after its publication in Hyderabad (India) in 1930 in Lahore's literary journal *Nuqūsh: Aap Biti Number* (June 1964). A synoptic overview of his autobiography is based on the English translation by Omar Khalidi.[107] The *Khud Niwisht* (Self-Reflections) succinctly describes Maulānā Maudūdī's early life and the formative period leading to his brilliant academic career. His precocious childhood and educational achievements are recounted to appreciate his self-study approach in his later life. Like Āzād, his upbringing followed a rigid pattern of compliance to social mores dictated by his father. Ironically, Maudūdī's later life as an ideologue of Islamic fundamentalism[108] was in sharp contrast to his early upbringing. Nasr's assessment of his secluded early years which influenced his intellectual career is extracted from his *Khud Niwisht:*

> Since I had originally been kept secluded, in this there existed benefits as well as drawbacks for me, such as when I became involved in society I was conscious and aware. My father in his talks and education had taught me how to distinguish between good and evil. My early education at his hand had left an

---

106. For biographical details on Maudūdī see Seyyed Vali Reza Nasr, *Maudūdī and the Making of Islamic Revivalism*, New York: Oxford University Press, 1996; Masudul Ḥasan, *Sayyid Abul A'la Maudūdī and His Thought*, vol. 1-2, Lahore: Islamic Publications (Pvt) Ltd., 1984 and Sarwar Sawlat, *Maudūdī*, Karachi: International Islamic Publications, 1984.

107. An earlier translation was produced by SVR Nasr, *Maulānā Maudūdī's Autobiography in the Muslim World*, LXXXV, no. 1-2, Jan-April, 1995, 49-62.

108. For an elaboration on his role in Islamic revivalism, see SVR Nasr, "Maudūdī and the Jamā'at-i-Islami: The Origins, Theory and Practice of Islamic Revivalism", in Ali Rahnema, *Pioneers of Islamic Revival*, London: Zed Books Ltd., 1994, 99-124.

> indelible mark upon me such that I would not easily fall under the sway of various influences.[109]

Maulānā Maudūdī's analytical approach nurtured in his early childhood rose in prominence when he developed his theory of *tajdīd* that set him apart from the traditional views on this concept. In fact, his self-study of the Islamic primary sources from which he drew his own understanding of *dīn* elicited harsh criticisms from the *'ulamā*. This aspect is discussed in subsequent chapters.

Maulānā Nadwī's critique on Maulānā Maudūdī which is examined in Chapter 4 deserves brief mention here. In his *Purān-i-Chirāgh* (Old Lamps)[110] which is a collection of obituaries, Maulānā Nadwī includes Maulānā Maudūdī, his contemporary, with scholars, *'ulamā*, political figures, etc. Maulānā Nadwī was primarily impressed by Maulānā Maudūdī's critique on Western civilisation, its genesis and decline.[111] Their shared worldview on the West was their common interest. The acknowledgement of sources for his major work, *Islam and the World*, however does not imply a total agreement on concepts[112] uniquely associated to Maulānā Maudūdī. This aspect is examined in Chapter 4.

THE ROAD TO MECCA: MUḤAMMAD ASAD

Before we attempt to discuss Maulānā Nadwī's impressions of Muḥammad Asad's writings it would be worthwhile for our study to examine Maulānā Nadwī's language proficiency

---

109. SVR Nasr, *Maudūdī and the Making of Islamic Revivalism*, 13.

110. SAHA Nadwī, *Purān-i-Chirāgh*, vol. 2, Karachi: Majlis Nashriyat-i-Islam, 1981, 300-20.

111. Ibid., 313.

112. For example, *The Theory of Jāhiliyyah* has strong political overtones. This concept is analysed in Chapter 4. See SAHA Nadwī, *Appreciation and Interpretation of Religion in Modern Age*, Lucknow: Academy of Islamic Research and Publications, 1982.

in English which is mentioned in his autobiography. Maulānā Nadwī described English studies as synonymous with progress and he too developed a "high fever" for it.[113] His mother Khayr-un-Nisā (d. 1968), a prolific writer in Urdu[114] discouraged him from pursuing post-graduate studies in English. However, Maulānā Nadwī remarked that his learning of English equipped him sufficiently to undertake extensive research in Islamic studies for his future writings.[115] Likewise it opened new vistas for his theorisation of Islamic resurgence.

Maulānā Nadwī was influenced by scholars beyond the Indian subcontinent periphery; Muḥammad Asad (Leipold Weiss) of Jewish origin was one notable example. Asad accepted Islam in 1926. His insightful books *Islam at the Crossroads* (1934) and *The Message of the Qur'ān* (1980) have earned him immortal fame in the Muslim world.

Asad's autobiography, *The Road to Mecca* (1954)[116] reveals the literary gems of his brilliance. The autobiography "gives us a rounded portrait of a restless man in search of adventure and truth. It is part autobiography, part summary of the author's intuitive insights into Islam, part an impressive travelogue."[117]

113. SAHA Nadwī, *Kārwān-i-Ẓindagī*, vol. I, 121.

114. Khayr-un-Nisa's influence on Nadwī's moral upbringing was profound. See Nadwī, Wadih, Rashid, Sayyid Abul Ḥasan Ali Nadwī, "Walida Sāhiba ke tarbiyati khutut aur duā ki roshni main", in *Ta'meer-i-Hayāt, Mufakkir Islam, Number*, 2000, 282-5.

115. SAHA Nadwī, *Kārwān-i-Ẓindagī*, vol. 1, 120-23.

116. Two important books on Asad's life and thought have been recently published: Ikram Chughtai, *Muḥammad Asad: Europe's Gift to Islam*, Lahore: The Truth Society, 2006; Abroo Andrabi, *Muḥammad Asad: His Contribution to Islamic Learning*, New Delhi: Goodword Books, 2007.

117. Muḥammad Asad, *The Road to Mecca*, London: Max Reinhardt, 1954.

The book is structured around the theme of the author's various journeys across Arabia and the Middle East. In the course of the narrative, Asad touches on his reflections of Islam. In his quest for Islamic authenticity a number of issues based on his accumulated experience of the West are re-examined.[118] This is best illustrated in his celebrated work *Islam at the Crossroads*. Maulānā Nadwī's appreciation of this work was based on Asad's competence to show the significance of the *shari'ah* in the light of contemporary problems Muslims faced across the world.[119] Years after its publication this book became the foundation of Maryam Jameelah's literary career[120] and one of the main influences for her accepting Islam.

It must be noted that *The Road to Mecca* and *Islam at the Crossroads* were written during the formative years of Asad's literary career. *Islam at the Crossroads* had a considerable impact on Maulānā Nadwī's critique of Western civilisation. This can be gleaned from two of his influential writings, *Islam and the World*[121] and *Western Civilisation, Islam and Muslims*.[122] His admiration for Asad's *The Road to Mecca* was undeniable; an Urdu version of the autobiography was published by Maulānā Nadwī.[123] Asad's indictment of the West did not imply that

---

118. Cited in Chughtai, *Muḥammad Asad: Europe's Gift to Islam*, 285-86.

119. Nadwī, *Kārwān-i-Ẓindagī*, vol. I, 23.

120. In one of her letters, Jameelah confesses that: "I can never forget that splendid chapter in his (Asad's) book *Islam at the Crossroads* about the necessity for Muslims to strictly follow the Sunnah as well as the Qur'ān if Islam is to survive and flourish." Maryam Jameelah, *Correspondence between Maudoodi . . .*, 18.

121. Nadwī, *Islam and the World*, 113-57.

122. Nadwī, *Western Civilisation . . .*, 10-32.

123. Cf. Nadwī, *Purān-i-Chirāgh*, vol. 2, 378-79. This book was translated in Urdu by Sayyid Muḥammad Nadwī, *Tūfān se Sāhil tak*, Lucknow: Academy of Islamic Research and Publications, 1970.

he was a fundamentalist. On the contrary his celebrated work, *The Message of the Qur'ān*[124] was resolutely modernist and Asad expressed his profound debt to the modernist commentator Muḥammad 'Abduh of Egypt.[125] Even Maulānā Nadwī stated that Asad's commentary like 'Abduh's did not meet the approval of the Muslims as it tended to promote liberal views against the established doctrines presented by the earlier commentators and the *ṣalf-al-ṣāliḥ*.[126] Nevertheless, Maulānā Nadwī's assessment of Asad's *tafsīr* set him apart from other scholars[127] in appreciating the latter's contribution to contemporary Islamic thought.

Islamic Authenticity: Kārwān-i-Ẓindagī[128]

Kārwān-i-Ẓindagī covering almost 2500 pages is a major work in the autobiography genre. Unlike the conventional form that characterises Urdu autobiography, *Kārwān-i-Ẓindagī* explores a world of events to which Maulānā Nadwī belonged. A salient feature is the narrator's presentation of the social milieu against a backdrop of "life-enriching experiences."[129]

---

124. Muḥammad Asad, *The Message of the Qur'ān*, Gibraltar: Dar-al-Andalus, 1980.

125. Ibid., v. A. Abroo, *Muḥammad Asad: His Contribution to Islamic Learning*, 57-116. Andrabi has attempted a comparative study of Asad's *tafsīr* with contemporary commentators of the Qur'ān.

126. Cited in Abdul Majid Daryabadi, *Tafsīr-ul-Qur'ān*, vol. I, xii.

127. Mention may be made of Maudūdī, an erstwhile admirer of Asad who was critical of *The Message of the Qur'ān*. His correspondence with Maryam Jameelah reveals his negative opinions on Asad's progressive outlook. See Jameelah, *Correspondence between . . .*, 14-15, cf. Ta'meer-i-Hayāt, 1993.

128. SAHA Nadwī, *Kārwān-i-Ẓindagī*, vols. 1-7, Lucknow: Maktaba-Islam, 1998.

129. For a detailed review on the *Kārwān-i-Ẓindagī*, see Tabish Mahdi, *Kārwān-i-Ẓindagī ek Mutāla'* in Muḥsin Uthmān Ma Nadwī, *Mutāla' Tasnifat Sayyid Abul Ḥasan Ali Nadwī*, Delhi: Arshi Publications, 2002, 352-61.

Maulānā Nadwī's early childhood to the last phase of his life is succinctly described in this work.

According to 'Ali Ṭanṭāwi (d. 1999), a noted Arabic littérateur, *Kārwān-i-Ẓindagī* is not merely biographical genre; it is a literary, political, social and religious document of his period.[130] It is in this context that *Kārwān-i-Ẓindagī* must be examined. The theme of Islamic authenticity is given much emphasis in this work. The Indian environment in which Maulānā Nadwī was raised and in which developed his formulation of Islamic resurgence is highlighted in the autobiography.[131] The thrust of Maulānā Nadwī's *da'wah* in the Arab world was to raise an awareness of Indian Muslims' contribution to the *tajdīdī* tradition. What sets Maulānā Nadwī apart from his contemporaries' autobiographical works is the absence of hagiographical literature.[132] A demerit of [the latter] is that the narrator's real contribution is obscured with exaggerated accounts. His personality is consecrated with infallible attributes and it is a daunting task to sift truth from myth. For our study purpose the following themes are elucidated by Maulānā Nadwī in his autobiography:

- The growth and development of Islamic resurgence in the Arab world and the Indian subcontinent.

130. Muḥammad Rāshid Nadwī, "Fi sirat-al-Hayāt main Sayyid Abul Ḥasan Ali Nadwī ki shakhsiyat" in *Kārwān-i-Adab*, Lucknow, 1997, 175-85.

131. *Kārwān-i-Ẓindagī*, vols. I, 115-19, 167-9, 241-6.

132. The hagiographical literature is not confined to writings belonging to Indo-Persian genre. A representative example is the Naqshabandi Sūfī order which has exerted a strong influence not only in the subcontinent but in West Asia as well. For this hagiographical trend see Muhammd Hisham Kabbani, *The Naqshabandi Sufi Way*, Chicago: Kazi Publications, 1995. Cf. Nadwī's, *Saviours of Islamic Spirit*, vol. 3 on the growth and development of the Naqshbandi order. For a comprehensive study on Islamic historiography, see Chase Robinson, *Islamic Historiography*, Cambridge: Cambridge University Press, 2003.

Biographical details of his ancestors who contributed to the *tajdīdī* traditions are given and their impact on contemporary Islamic thought are analysed by him. In a similar vein, Maulānā Nadwī provides a personal account of the resurgent movement in Egypt, Ikhwān, its ideologues like Ḥasan al-Bannā and Sayyid Quṭb. The imprint of a "mutual exchange of ideas" suggests their respective influence in shaping the current resurgence.[133]

- The emphasis of Islamic authenticity is derived from Maulānā Nadwī's claim that Muslims in the sub-continent have made a major contribution to Islamic culture. This theme resonates in another of Maulānā Nadwī's writings, *Muslims in India.*[134] Islamic authenticity advocated by Maulānā Nadwī as Zaman notes in his article "Muslim Identity in the Twentieth Century" is a call for the revival of an Islamic zeal among the Arabs who were the first bearers of Islam.[135]
- A stable Muslim society[136] in secular India, Maulānā Nadwī stressed, could progress only in a climate of peace, free from inter-communal violence. This implied that Muslims should build relations with others rather than alienating them. This view negated the position advocated by extremist Islamic groups against the Hindu majority.

Another important work may be considered as a "supplement" to *Kārwān-i-Ẓindagī. Mīr-i-Kārwān* (1999)[137] written

133. Nadwī, *Kārwān-i-Ẓindagī,* vol. I, 363-94, vol. 2, 64-81, 109-27.
134. Nadwī, *Muslims in India*, Lucknow, 1976.
135. Zaman, *Muslim Identity in Twentieth Century,* 292.
136. *Kārwān-i-Ẓindagī,* vol. 3, 111-60, vol. 6, 149-58.
137. 'Abdullāh 'Abbās Nadwī, *Mīr-i-Kārwān,* New Delhi: Majlis Ilmi, 1999.

in Urdu by Maulānā 'Abdullāh 'Abbās Nadwī explores aspects relating to Maulānā Nadwī's personality that have not been included in *Kārwān-i-Ẓindagī*. According to 'Abbās Nadwī, *Mīr-i-Kārwān* takes the reader on a personal journey to understand the multi-dimensional personality of Maulānā Nadwī.[138] The themes of Islamic resurgence, *da'wah* Arab nationalism and *tajdīd*[139] are examined in greater depth in this work.

Da'wah Series: An Overview

Maulānā Nadwī's *tajdīdī* writings focus on *da'wah* studies which are thematically linked to his presentation of Islamic authenticity. Muslim's commitment to the *shari'ah* and assimilation of Islamic values in promoting the universal message are issues discussed in the *da'wah* series.

ISMA'Ī WRITINGS: MOTIVATION

We now turn to another genre employed by Maulānā Nadwī in his *iṣlāḥi* efforts. His target audience is the Arab world and his writings entitled *isma'ī* address socio-political issues with an *iṣlāḥi* ethos. The word *isma'ī* used in its imperative form is a rhetorical device employed by Maulānā Nadwī to address the Arab world on assets relating to their commitment to Islam and their leadership role in the world of Islam. The motivation for employing this literary form is mentioned in his autobiography:

> Several days after my arrival in Cairo there was an urgent need to address the Egyptians so that they could be reminded of their status and mission. [Egypt] held the reigns of leadership in the Muslim world . . . the Suez Canal could serve metaphorically as a nexus between the East and the West. The

138. 'Abdullāh 'Abbās Nadwī, *Mīr-i-Kārwān*, New Delhi: Majlis Ilmi, 12-13.

139. Ibid., 326-66.

> cultural exchange could be an opportunity for the East (i.e. Egypt) to present its sublime message of Islam to the West while at the same time appreciating science and technology in which the latter has made great advances.[140]

Context is important to appreciate the impact of the *isma'ī* series. Arab nationalism and Western culture were embedded in the Egyptian soil; the intellectual climate nurtured by modernists such as Ṭāha Ḥusayn[141] posed a threat to the Islamic culture and tradition built over the centuries. Maulānā Nadwī laments at the Egyptians' failure to reconstruct the Egyptian society anchored on the lofty principles of Islam and the scientific outlook of the West.[142] If, however, Islamic values which gave Egypt its unparalleled position in the Muslim world were not maintained then the country was destined to a bleak future.[143]

Two points deserve mention here: the emphasis of an Islamic identity and a critique of Western civilisation.[144] It is in this context that his writings must be examined. The *isma'ī* genre has an emotive connotation: an impassioned appeal to Muslim societies (especially the Arab world) to adopt the Islamic civilisation wholeheartedly. The appreciative comments by Quṭb on *isma'ī* series[145] highlight their shared vision on Islamic resurgence[146] with special reference to the Arab world.

---

140. Nadwī, *Kārwān-i-Ẓindagī,* vol. I, 374.

141. On the life and thought of Ṭahā Ḥusayn, see Hourani, *Arabic Thought,* 324-40, Cf. Nadwī, *Western Civilisation,* 106-8.

142. Ibid., 97.

143. Nadwī, *Kārwān-i-Ẓindagī,* 374.

144. For an elaboration on this theme, see Nadwī, *Islam and the World,* 113-78.

145. The *isma'ī* series is included in Nadwī's Arabic work, *Al-Arab wa-l Islam* (Beirut, n.d.)

146. Nadwī, *Kārwān-i-Ẓindagī,* 375.

TUḤFAH WRITINGS: MOTIVATION

Like his *isma'ī* lectures, the *tuḥfah*[147] writings by Maulānā Nadwī address the Muslim societies in the Indian subcontinent. The *iṣlāḥi* content is evident in the *tuḥfa* which Maulānā Nadwī presented as a "gift" to the Muslim communities he addressed. Maulānā Nadwī believed that the reconstruction of Muslim society[148] cuts across barriers of ethnicity and linguistic prejudice. These two issues are critically examined in Maulānā Nadwī's *Calamity of Linguistic and Cultural Chauvinism.*[149] Implicit in his critique are Muslim countries like Pakistan and Bangladesh, which fought a civil war in 1971.[150] Maulānā Nadwī is unsparing in his criticism of linguistic chauvinism. He observes:

> But when languages are extolled and magnified, they are consecrated and raised to the pedestal of divinity, they become a curse rather than a blessing, a vehicle of destruction instead of a means of goodwill and amity.. . .[151]

---

147. The word *tuḥfah* has been interchangeably used for *ḥadīth* which conveys a similar meaning. Cf. M. Nadwī, *Hadith-i-Pakistan*, 1978.

148. This theme is elaborated in Nadwī's *Reconstruction of Indian Society: What Muslims can do,* Lucknow: Academy of Islamic Research and Publications, n.d.

149. Nadwī, *Calamity and Linguistic and Cultural Chauvinism*, Lucknow: Academy of Islamic Research and Publications, 1972.

150. The following comment by Fazlur Rahman on the great divide between Pakistan and East Pakistan (Bangladesh) is revealing:

 ". . . it might become difficult for East Pakistan and West Pakistan to stay together, for apart from their attachment to Islam, linguistically and culturally the two wings had little in common." Fazlur Rahman, *Some Issues in the Ayub Khan Era*, University of Chicago, Muslim Studies Sub-Committee Occasional Paper Series. The causes of the secession of East Pakistan have been analysed by Maudūdī in Masudul Ḥasan, *Sayyid Abul A'la Maudūdī and His Thought*, vol. 2, Lahore: Islamic Publications, 1986; 410-13.

151. Nadwī, *Calamity of Linguistics,* 15.

These traits, Maulānā Nadwī contends, are associated with a new Jāhiliyyah (which is discussed in Chapter 4).

The following passage of *Tuḥfah-i-Pakistan* summarises Maulānā Nadwī's message to the Pakistan nation:

> The most urgent need is a sustained effort to reform its society. It must be saved from the rivalry and obsession of amassing wealth. There can be no greater calamity for Pakistan than anarchy.. . . For Pakistan to maintain its distinctive identity and to be protected against anarchy, the reconstruction of society is crucial. Pakistan must be saved from two dangerous elements: religious and political anarchy.[152]

A close scrutiny of this passage shows Maulānā Nadwī's concern for the Islamic state of Pakistan. It is the Pakistani society that receives attention rather than the political dynamics that have shaped the destiny of the country. The rhetoric of anarchy does in no way imply Maulānā Nadwī's indifference to the socio-economic conditions prevailing in Pakistan; rather it is a diagnosis of the malaise affecting its society.

In contrast, Maulānā Nadwī touches on pertinent issues for the Indian Muslims. The *Tuḥfah-i-Insāniyat*[153] explores themes of Muslim self-esteem, co-existence with the Hindu majority and the message for humanity. Maulānā Nadwī observes:

> I do not reject things. . . . If universities are established, they are a source of pride and joy. I do not belittle such developments. I

152. SAHA Nadwī, *Tuḥfah-i-Pakistan*, Karachi: Majlis Nashriyāt-i-Islam, 1984, 38-40. The translation has been adapted. Cf. Nadwī, *Da'wat-i-Fikr wa Amal*, Lucknow, 1999 which covers a broader range of issues affecting Pakistani Muslims. The extract encapsulates the thrust of Nadwī's *iṣlāḥi* lectures in Pakistan.

153. SAHA Nadwī, *Tuḥfah-i-Insāniyat*, Lucknow: Majlis Tahqiqat wa Nashriyāt-i-Islam, 1992. Cf. Mawlānā Nadwī, *Tuhfa Din wa Dānish*, Lucknow, 1987 which emphasises Muslims' attachment to *shari'ah* and the promotion of a healthy stable society.

> only wish to see an addition — that respect for humanity is maintained. . . . It is my desire that our hearts reflect an exemplary character and be committed to humanity. We possess noble objectives and can reciprocate goodwill to others. We have the resources to provide benefit to humanity, and remove their pain and affliction. We can spread love in the world, reconcile hearts, avert corruption and prevent humanity's ship from sinking — this is my message![154]

The message for humanity (*Payām-i-Insāniyat*)[155] is a recurrent theme in his *iṣlāḥi* writings for the Indian Muslims. In their interaction with the significant "other"[156] — the Hindu majority — Muslims are exhorted to maintain an exemplary conduct and spread the universal values of love, compassion, etc. that Islam promotes. The conciliatory tone adopted by Maulānā Nadwī finds fuller expression in his *Payām-i-Insāniyat*.

Clearly Maulānā Nadwī's tone and tenor of *iṣlāḥi* writings vary from one Muslim society to another. To the Arab world represented by Egypt he shows how pervasive Western influence is. Likewise Pakistan, according to Maulānā Nadwī, needs to empower its people with moral values while the Indian Muslim's corporate identity rests on the spirit of goodwill and communal harmony. This approach provides useful insights to Maulānā Nadwī's broader understanding of *iṣlāḥ* and *tajdīd*.

---

154. Nadwī, *Tuḥfah Insāniyat*, 115-16.

155. A synopsis of the *Payām-i-Insāniyat* is provided in a monograph: Nadwī, *Payām-i-Insāniyat*, Lucknow, 2004. These lectures complement the *tuḥfah* series both in their content and outreach programme.

156. Nadwī's engagement with the Hindu community is extensively discussed in his multi-volume autobiography, *Kārwān-i-Ẓindagī*. The interfaith dialogue is analysed by several scholars. See Yoginder Sikand, *Muslims in India since 1947*, London: Routledge Curzon, 2004, 34-39.

Conclusion

In our study of autobiographical, biographical and *da'wah* writings with special reference to Maulānā Nadwī and his contemporaries, the *iṣlāḥ* and *tajdīd* are shared features for revivalist movements. Therefore Maulānā Nadwī's formal training as an *'ālim* did not inhibit his interaction with scholars and reformers of divergent Islamic backgrounds. This interaction does not suggest that Maulānā Nadwī compromised on his traditional Islamic background; rather it provided him with a broader base to develop his understanding of an Islamic order which is examined in subsequent chapters.

Maulānā Nadwī's choice of individuals in delineating their contributions to *iṣlāḥ* and *tajdīd* is illustrative of the multiple influences that shaped his understanding of Islamic resurgence. His critique of autobiographical and biographical writings from the Arab world endorses his important contribution in Arabic on the *tajdīdī* theme. Likewise his biographical writings on reformers and scholars with different ideological orientations underpin his ability to expand his notions of Islamic resurgence. The literary writings by no means express a uniformity of ideas; rather they highlight the emergent trends that defined the nature and scope of Islamic authenticity.

A defining feature of Islamic resurgence as it is clearly evident in Maulānā Nadwī's profile, is its *overlapping* characteristic. This does not however suggest a uniform and coherent trend; rather it points out to its adaptable forms in meeting the demands and challenges of the times. The next chapter will show how translocal scholarship, for example, contributed to these contrasting landscapes of Islamic resurgence.

3

The Development of Islamic Reformist Thought

A Comparative Analysis Between Maulānā Nadwī and His Contemporaries

ISLAMIC resurgence operates in specific historical settings. The time frame is linked to circumstances and personalities who define the parameters of Islamic resurgence. As discussed in previous chapters, the intellectual responses have influenced an interpretive reading of contemporary Islamic thought. However, ideological and theological viewpoints have also played a significant role in the formation of Islamic resurgence. These two approaches have a direct bearing on Maulānā Nadwī's interpretation of *tajdīd*. This chapter seeks to identify personalities and movements who are embedded in *tajdīdī* traditions and have had a formative influence on Maulānā Nadwī's conceptualisation of Islamic resurgence. His *tajdīdī* contributions are examined in the light of contrasting responses to Islamic resurgence. Furthermore, a comparative analysis will be made between Maulānā Nadwī and his contemporaries to understand how the dynamics of an Islamic ideal may vary in different historical circumstances. Maulānā Nadwī himself is no exception to this historical trend.

Three important trends that have contributed to the development of Islamic reformist thoughts are analysed in the chapter. Firstly, translocal scholarship or mobility among scholars for transmitting and acquiring knowledge with special reference to the Indian subcontinent especially during the nineteenth and twentieth centuries which brought in its wake several interpretations of Islamic thought that were inspired by the writings of the *ṣalf-al-ṣāliḥ* chief among which were the works of Ibn Taymiyyah. The growth of the Ahl-i-ḥadīth movement with its advocacy of *ḥadīth* against *taqlīd* upheld by the Deoband movement illustrates the influence of translocal scholarship in the Indian soil.

In the second place, the Salafiyyah movement originating in the Arab world had a direct impact on scholars like Maulānā Maudūdī who are associated with an Islamist understanding of Islamic resurgence. Although Quṭb does not belong to the category of intellectuals in the Indian subcontinent his conceptualisation of *tajdīd* is inextricably linked with his contemporaries, Maulānā Nadwī and Maulānā Maudūdī. These three scholars provide an insightful understanding on the dynamics of *tajdīd* in the twentieth century.

Thirdly, an interesting development in Islamic resurgence is the emergence of the *da'wah* movement, the Tabligh Jamā'at, which over the last few decades has grown into an international *iṣlāḥ*-based organisation. The Tabligh Jamā'at's presence is found in major parts of the world and has drawn adherents from all walks of life. It has a global presence and can be termed a transnational movement. Thus translocal scholarship, the Islamist profiles and transnational movements focus on an Islamic authenticity embedded in an ideal past. These trends fall within the ambit of cultural memory, a concept that is examined in the next section in relation to the *tajdīdī* tradition.

Cultural Memory in the Tajdīdī Framework

Cultural memory is a concept introduced to the archaeological disciplines by Jan Assmann. Assmann defines cultural memory as the outer dimension of human memory that embraces memory culture and reference to the past.[1] Memory culture is the way society ensures cultural continuity by preserving its cultural knowledge from one generation to the next so that they can reconstruct their own cultural identity. Likewise, references to the past reassure the members of a society of their collective identity and provide them with a historical consciousness by creating a shared past.[2]

A salient feature of cultural memory is that freedom exists to adapt to the past or life history to become part of a future collective memory. It is experience which is embedded in cultural memory that gives expression to authenticity, a longing to make reference to the past which validates this form of real feeling. Thus cultural memory also has a direct bearing on the Islamic past or life histories and Maulānā Nadwī's articulation of the Islamic past, be it individuals or organisations, is an expression of a cultural memory. In fact, Islamic authenticity (*turāth*) is one such example of cultural memory which not only links past events to present realities but provides new ideas drawn from these sources. The following section delineates these aspects of cultural memory.

Islamic Authenticity: Formative Influences on Maulānā Nadwī's Formulation

"Anatomy, psychology, ethics and sociology are all agreed that every man has certain inherited traits in his blood which have a role in shaping his character, aptitude, competence, inclinations and frame of mind. These traits are reflected in the following forms: the beliefs and values held strictly, cherished and revered by a family get inbuilt in the minds of

1. J. Assmann, *Das Kulturelle Gedächtnis: Schrift Erinnerung und Politische Identität in frühen Hochkulturen*, Munich: Verslag CH Beck, 1992, 19-20.
2. Ibid., 30-34.

the people belonging to it . . . they determine the inclinations and disposition and give a measure of judgement for these moral values."[3]

These traits were embodied in the distinguished family of Maulānā Nadwī. They had served as a "beacon of light" in the Indian subcontinent; their *iṣlāḥi* efforts combined with their exemplary piety and virtuous character changed the religious landscape of Muslim India.[4] In his writings Maulānā Nadwī has given detailed biographical accounts of his ancestors' contributions to the reform of the Muslim society. In his estimation, the *tajdīd* and *iṣlāḥ* traditions[5] were articulated in their reformatory endeavours. They formed a golden chain (*silsilat-al-dhahab*) of scholars and reformers to accentuate an Islamic authenticity which was linked to the global *ummah*.[6] The authenticity is best expressed in Maulānā Nadwī's anthology of Arabic prose, *Mukhtārāt*.[7] The choices of individuals are mostly classical and medieval religious scholars and saints within an *iṣlāḥi* framework. Zaman notes that Maulānā Nadwī's choice of individuals exhibits rather his self-conscious concern with creating an Islamic identity, and reveals his perception of who the "authentic" representatives of this identity are.[8] *Mukhtārāt* is a synopsis of Maulānā Nadwī's theme of authenticity elaborated in his multi-volume *Saviours of Islamic Spirit*.

---

3. SAHA Nadwī, *The Life of Caliph Ali*, Lucknow: Academy of Islamic Research and Publications, 1991, 11.
4. SAHA Nadwī, *Kārwān-i-Ẓindagī*, vol. 1, 20-3.
5. *The Sīrat-i-Sayyid Aḥmad Shahīd* by Nadwī reinforces this theme.
6. Nadwī, *Kārwān-i-Ẓindagī*, vol. 1, 26-7.
7. SAHA Nadwī, *Mukhtārāt min adab al-'Arab*, Beirut: Dār-al-Fikr, 1965.
8. Muḥammad Qasim Zaman, "Muslim Identity in Twentieth Century India" in *The Muslim World*, 283.

ISLAMIC AUTHENTICITY: AN OVERVIEW

The Islamic authenticity or *turāth* has been much debated in the Arab world. The interpretation of the *turāth,* as Leonard Binder observes, has elicited conflicting interpretations both in content and scope. Ideological tendencies[9] are influenced by a variant reading of Islamic tradition; thus a modernist interpretation differs radically from its conventional definition. Citing the Egyptian modernist, Zaki Nagib Mahmud, as an example, Binder points out to his hermeneutics of *turāth*: tradition merging with modernity.[10] Mahmud lavishes praise on heterodox sects like the *Mu'tazilah*[11] for their rational tendencies against Sunni orthodoxy — a clear sign of his antipathy towards the *turāth* evolved over the centuries.[12] In contrast to the above view, Binder's comment on Islamic authenticity shares common ground with Maulānā Nadwī's interpretation which is discussed elsewhere in the chapter. Binder says that the past is obviously not to be re-enacted like some ritual and it is not to be adjusted to someone else's preferred values. Thus Islamic authenticity is not subjected to changes as a result of a decline or rupture in a historical process. It transcends these barriers and reaffirms itself as a life-pulsating force and is focused on the perennial sources of Islam.[13] This approach to Islamic authenticity is forcefully expressed by Maulānā

---

9. Leonard Binder, *Islamic Liberalism: A Critique of Development Ideologies,* Chicago: The University of Chicago Press, 1988, 295.

10. Ibid., 299.

11. Ibid., 308, Mahmud remarks: "Tradition is merely expressive; modernity is productive." The statement clearly outlines his approach to *turāth.*

12. For a historical survey of these heteredox movements see Mohammad Kamal. *Heterodoxy in Islam: A Philosophical Study,* Karachi: Royal Book Company, 1993.

13. Leonard Binder, *Islamic Liberalism,* 300.

Nadwī to show the continuity of *tajdīd* in far-flung countries like the Indian subcontinent.[14]

Islamic authenticity is a key element in Maulānā Nadwī's conceptual framework of Islamic resurgence. Its parameters are clearly defined and as such Islamic reformers with *tajdīdī* credentials are selected. It would be worthwhile firstly to examine in this context the contributions of Sayyid Aḥmad Shahīd (d. 1831)[15] the illustrious ancestor of Maulānā Nadwī to appreciate his interpretation of Islamic authenticity. The choice of Sayyid Aḥmad is largely because of his *tajdīdī* efforts which had a direct bearing on Maulānā Nadwī's theorisation of Islamic resurgence. Moreover, other Islamic institutions like the Deoband *madrasa* and the Ahl-i-Ḥadīth movement draw their inspiration from Sayyid Aḥmad in their formulation of *iṣlāḥ-tajdīd* traditions.

SAYYID AḤMAD SHAHĪD: INDIAN REFORMIST

The selection of Sayyid Aḥmad Shahīd represents Maulānā Nadwī's ideal of Islamic authenticity and a potential realisation of an Islamic order. Sayyid Aḥmad's personality and core *tajdīdī* elements are articulated by Maulānā Nadwī. His two-volume *Sayyid Aḥmad Shahīd* (1987) is a detailed discussion on Sayyid Aḥmad's *tajdīdī* contributions. Maulānā Nadwī says:

> In its comprehensiveness and mass appeal and the methodology closely following the prophetic pattern, no contemporary

---

14. See Nadwī, *Muslims in India,* 7-21.

15. For a biographical account on Sayyid Aḥmad Shahīd, see SAHA Nadwī, *Sirat-i-Sayyid Aḥmad Shahīd,* vols. 1-2, Majlis Nashriyāt-i-Islam, 1987; Muḥammad Hedayatullah, *Sayyid Aḥmad,* Lahore: Sh. Muḥammad Ashraf, 1970; Mahmood Aḥmad Ghazi, *Islamic Renaissance in South Asia: 1707-1867,* Islamabad: Islamic Research Institute, 2002; Ishtiaq Husain Qureshi, *Ulema in Politics,* Karachi: Ma'aref Ltd., 1974, 140-56.

> revivalist movement comparable to the powerful movement of Islamic revival headed by Sayyid Aḥmad Shahīd is to be found in the nineteenth century.[16]

A scion of the Ḥasani family in Rae Bareli, the Sayyid established a reformist movement (*ṭariqa-i-Muḥammadī*) which emphasised the centrality of the *shari'ah* against the syncretic practices accumulated by Muslims from the Hindu rituals and deviant beliefs of some Sūfīs. The Sayyid wanted to reinstate the *shari'ah* in the Indian Muslim society with "the whole of practical and conceptual structure of Islam."[17] His *jihād* movement[18] which envisioned an Islamic state based on the pattern of the *Khulafā' Rāshidūn* (The Righteous Caliphs) was a powerful call for a reform of Muslim society. The *Taqwiyat-ul-Imān*[19] written by his close associate, Shāh Ismā'il Shahīd (d. 1831),[20] reformulated Islam in its pristine purity. This work attempted to reformulate Islamic authenticity against the established syncretic practices of Hinduism which

---

16. SAHA Nadwī, *A Misunderstood Reformer,* Lucknow: Academy of Islamic Research and Publications, 1978, 9.
17. Ibid., 12.
18. For a historical survey of the jihād movement, see SAHA Nadwī, *Sīrat-i-Sayyid Aḥmad Shahīd,* 318-464; Mohiuddin Aḥmad, *Sayyid Aḥmad Shahīd,* Lucknow: Academy of Islamic Research and Publications, 1975, 153-286. Cf. Abul A'ala Maudūdī, *A Short History of the Revivalist Movement in Islām,* Lahore: Islamic Publications Ltd., 1972, 99-116 for a critical review of the *jihād* movement.
19. Muḥammad Ismā'il Shahīd, *Taqwiyāt-ul-Imān,* Lucknow: Al-Maktaba al-Maulānā Nadwīyyah, 1991. The explanatory notes by Nadwī reveal their shared enthusiasm for an *iṣlāh* of the Indian Muslim society.
20. For a biographical sketch on Shah Ismā'il Shahīd, see Ansari Bazmee, "Ismā'il Shahīd" in *Encyclopaedia of Islam,* vol. 3, 196-97; SAHA Nadwī, *Kārwān-i-Imān wa Azimat,* Karachi: Majlis Nashriyāt-i-Islam, n.d., 17-39.

had a major impact on the Muslim society. The polemical tone of *Taqwiyat* provoked a wave of controversy among sections of the Muslim community for its anti-*bid'ah* position. Although the reformist mission of Shāh Ismā'il had a considerable appeal to *'ulamā* with Deobandi leanings, it highlighted the cleavage among ideological constellations in the subcontinent.

Sayyid Aḥmad's call for a return to the ideal past carried with it purificationist tendencies and an interpretation of physical *jihād*. The appellation "political-positivists"[21] to Sayyid Aḥmad's *jihād* movement by Habibul Haq Nadvi is to show its close parallel to the period of the righteous caliphs and indirectly give it a religious legitimacy. Maulānā Nadwī too showers praise on Sayyid Aḥmad in the following words:

> It was through the Sayyid's magnetic personality that the founders of the Deoband school, on the one hand, and a body of selfless workers by the great organisers of Sādiqpur, on the other, were initiated in the Mujaddidiyyah-Naqshbandi Sūfī orders. This first group exerted itself to establish educational institutions for religious reform while the second group worked against foreign influences alien to the spirit and teachings of Islam. [This] constituted a marvellous achievement of the Sayyid's movement which was not only unparalleled in the history of mysticism (Sūfīsm) and religious reforms but also protected the great Muslim community of this subcontinent against ever reverting back to unsound beliefs and polytheistic practices. . . . [These] achievements assign an honoured place to the Sayyid among the galaxy of *mujaddid*s whom we find giving a call to the faithful at every turning point of our history.[22]

The echoes of "political-positivism" are reflected in the above passage. Moreover the defining role of an Islamic order is

21. Habibul Haq Nadvi, *Islamic Resurgent Movements*, 53.

22. SAHA Nadvi, *Saviours of Islamic Spirit*, vol. 4, 333-34.

expressed both in terms of its goal and its diametric opposition to the entrenched influence of Hinduism on Muslim society in the subcontinent. The term political-positivist specifically refers to Sūfī-inspired reformers actively engaged in *jihād* either to establish an Islamic order or to rid Muslims on a political front of colonial rule during the nineteenth and twentieth centuries in the Muslim world. Habibul Haq Nadvi makes reference to several reformers who are considered freedom fighters in the Arab world. Shaykh 'Abdul Qādir of Algeria (d. 1883) is one example also considered to be a political-positivist by Maulānā Nadwī for his efforts to free Algeria from French colonial rule.[23]

Maulānā Maudūdī referred to the Sayyid's movement as "a rare phenomenon in our recent history."[24] This evocative description by Maulānā Maudūdī reflects his guarded admiration for the Sayyid's *jihād* movement. Maulānā Maudūdī observed:

> When they got a chance to establish their rule in a limited territory, they established it on the basis of "Caliphate after the pattern of Prophethood." It was characteristic of the same pious and God-fearing control, the same kind of equality and advisory body . . . they demonstrated and revived once again the type of rule established and guided by Abubakr Siddiq and 'Umar Faruq. . . .[25]

However, Maulānā Maudūdī points out that the *jihād* movement could not achieve the success it envisioned largely because it could not disassociate itself from *taṣawwuf* to which he (Maulānā Maudūdī) was averse and its failure to recognise

23. SAHA Nadvi, *The Life of Caliph 'Ali*, Lucknow: Academy of Islamic Research and Publications, 1991, 253-54.
24. A.A. Maudūdī, *Short History of the Revivalist Movement in Islām*, 33.
25. Ibid., 102.

the ascendancy of the West (European nations) both at political and military levels. Maulānā Maudūdī concluded:

> [The Islamic movement] demands the full support and backing of a comprehensive universal ideological movement which may bring a strong influence to bear upon all sciences and trends of thought . . . and master all possible strength and means to the service of Islam.[26]

The divergence of views between Maulānā Nadwī and Maulānā Maudūdī reinforces their different approaches to *tajdīd*. Maulānā Maudūdī critically examines the contributions of *mujaddids* to fit in with his own interpretation of reform. According to Maulānā Maudūdī, ideology is rooted in a political framework, a concept borrowed from Western models, which translates into Ḥākimiyyah (Sovereignty of God). In contrast Maulānā Nadwī does not depart from a traditional interpretation of *tajdīd*; rather he links the role of *mujaddids* to his understanding of Islamic authenticity where *shari'ah* co-exists with *taṣawwuf*.

The *jihād* movement of Sayyid Aḥmad also earned the appellation of "Wahhābi"[27] on account of its puritanical outlook to Islamic beliefs and practices. Ironically Maulānā

---

26. A.A. Maudūdī, *Short History of the Revivalist Movement in Islām*, 114.

27. On the Wahhābi movement see Aḥmad Abdol Ghafour Attar, *Muḥammad ibn Abdel Wahhab*, tr. Rashed al Barrawi, Makkah: Makkah Printing and Publishing Company, n.d. On the Nadwa's defence of the Wahhābi founder, see Masud Alam Nadwī, *Muḥammad ibn 'Abd-al-Wahhāb: Muslih, Mazlum and Muftara 'Alaih*, Zamzam Press, 1977. For a historical evaluation of the Wahhābi movement, see Syed Habibul Haq Nadvi, *Islamic Resurgent Movements in the Indo-Pak Subcontinent*, 245-63, Cf. SAHA Nadwī, *A Misunderstood Reformer*, 34-50.

    Recent studies attempt to highlight the anomaly between 'Abd-ul-Wahhāb's original teachings which were tolerant and broadminded to the official creed of Saudi Arabia which claims →

Nadwī was branded as a Wahhābi largely because of his close association with the Saudi *'ulamā* and its intellectuals.[28] This description ignores the Sayyid's Sūfī orientations which in the words of his biographer, Mohiuddin Aḥmad, "[was] a call for inner reclamation and redemption of the soul (*nafs*) and a struggle against external threats instead of meekly submitting to the powers of his time."[29]

The influence of *taṣawwuf* on *tajdīdī* tradition is examined in the following section particularly in respect of Maulānā Nadwī's formulation of Islamic resurgence.

Islamic Mysticism (Taṣawwuf): An Assessment

The Islamic mysticism (*taṣawwuf*) as envisaged by Maulānā Nadwī is best represented in his *Rabbāniyyah lā Rahbāniyyah* (1979)[30] which was largely written for an Arab audience. Implicit in this work is Maulānā Nadwī's discussion on the key concepts of *taṣawwuf*. The technical terms, Maulānā Nadwī argues, have obscured the essence of *taṣawwuf* and created a gulf between its admirers and critics. The result, Maulānā Nadwī laments, is self evident: ". . . [the] bitter experiments and grave errors of the flag-bearers of these

→ to follow Wahhābi doctrines in its interpretation of Islamic ideology. Cf. Natana J. De-Long Bas, *Wahhābi Islam*, London: I.B. Tauris, 2007, Bilal Aḥmad Kutty, "Muḥammad Ibn 'Abd-al-Wahhāb and his Reform Movement", in *Hamdard Islamicus*, vol. XX: 2, 43-9.

28. The Saudi connection has generated much debate among Arab intellectuals and dissidents. Their critique on scholars like Qardāwi and Nadwī is based on their so-called complicity with the Saudi state in terms of its *salafi* interpretation of Islam. See Aḥmad Ghorab, *Subverting Islam: The Role of Orientalist Centres*, Kuala Lumpur: The Open Press, 1995.

29. Reinhard Schulze, *A Modern History of the Islamic World*, London: I.B. Tauris Publishers, 2000, 173-74.

30. SAHA Nadwī, *Rahbāniyyah lā Rabbāniyyah*, Lucknow: Al-Majma' al-Islami-al-'Ilmī, 1979.

technical terms gave rise to such grievous misunderstandings that a great number of true and upright people have learnt to dread and dislike these aims and realities."[31] According to Maulānā Nadwī if the Qur'ānic term *tazkiyah*[32] (inner purification) and the *ḥadīth* description *iḥsān*[33] (virtuous actions) were employed, much misconceptions would be eliminated. The *taṣawwuf* Maulānā Nadwī pleads for is based on the *shari'ah*[34] and the lives of the illustrious Sūfīs which were "weighed and moulded according to the *shari'ah*."[35] Uthmāni observed that Maulānā Nadwī considered *taṣawwuf* a Divinely-inspired system (*ilhāmi nizām*)[36] that interiorised the whole body of Islam. The expansion of Islam was largely due to eminent personalities of pure acumen and whose lives reflected the training of the inner self.[37] Maulānā Nadwī thus strongly identifies these personalities as ideal representatives

---

31. Muḥammad Iqbal, *The Achievement of Love: The Spiritual Dimensions of Islam,* tr. Aftab Aḥmad, Vermont: Amana Books, 1987, 5. The English translation is taken from the *Introduction of Rabbāniyyah* which is included in this work.

32. Qur'ān: 62:2; cf. Vali-ud-din, Mir, *The Qur'ānic Sūfīsm*, Lahore: Sh. Muḥammad Ashraf, 1991, 17-43; Seyyed Hossein Nasr, *Islamic Spirituality Foundations,* New York: The Crossroad Publishing Company, 1985, 3-11.

33. *Sahih Muslim*: vol. 1:9. In his explanatory notes on *iḥsān* Siddiqi says that is to create a sense of inner piety in man and to train his sensibilities in a way that all his thoughts and actions flow from the fountainhead of the love of God. *Sahih Muslim,* tr. 'Abdul Hamīd Siddiqi, vol. IA, Lahore: Sh. Muḥammad Ashraf, 1990, 11.

34. For a detailed study, see Muḥammad Abdul Haq Ansari, *Sufism and Shari'ah: A Study of Shaykh Aḥmad Sirhindi's Effort to Reform Sufism,* Leicester: The Islamic Foundation, 1986, 61-100.

35. Muḥammad Iqbal, *The Achievement of Love,* 9.

36. Mụhsin Uthmāni, "Tazkiya wa Ihsān ya Taṣawwuf wa suluk: ek mutalā in Nadwī", *Mutāla' Tasnif āt Mawlana Sayyid Abul Hasan 'Ali Nadwī,* Delhi: Arshi Publications India, 2002, 332-33.

37. SAHA Nadwī, *Appreciation and Interpretation of Religion in the Modern Age,* 91.

of Islamic resurgence emphasising the inner aspects of the movement.

Of particular relevance to us is the role of Ibn Taymiyyah in Maulānā Nadwī's formulation of *tajdīd.* It is interesting to note how Ibn Taymiyyah is given much prominence in *Rabbāniyyah lā Rahbāniyyah.*[38] This work must be read together with *Saviours of Islamic Spirit*[39] to understand Maulānā Nadwī's portrayal of Ibn Taymiyyah as a Sūfī. The polemical response to the above works by *salafi* critics has been covered by 'Abbās Nadwī in his *Mīr-i-Kārwān.*[40] There exists no definitive study on Ibn Taymiyyah as a Sūfī. Ideological bias sets to portray him either as a *salafi* or a Sūfī-oriented intellectual. As such there are alternative views by Maulānā Nadwī's contemporaries which highlight the conflicting portraits of Ibn Taymiyyah as a *mujaddid.*

The impact of Ibn Taymiyyah as a *salafi* ideologue emerged during the nineteenth century. The term *ṣalf-al-ṣāliḥ* was accentuated in Egypt in response to a colonial encounter by Afghānī and his successor 'Abduh. As discussed in previous chapters the intellectual ferment in Egypt and India during this period saw the rise of Salafiyyah albeit in different forms to re-state and re-define Islamic thought couched in a

38. SAHA Nadwī, *Rabbāniyyah lā Rahbāniyyah,* 55-70.

39. SAHA Nadwī, *Saviours of Islamic Spirit,* vol. 2, 3-146. Two books written by Nadwī based on the *taṣawwuf* genre deserve mention:

- *Sawānih Hadhrat Maulānā Qadir Raipuri* (1977)
- *Suhbat-i-bā ihl-i-dil* (1982)

40. 'Abdullāh 'Abbās Nadwī, *Mīr-i-Kārwān,* New Delhi: Majlis 'Ilmi, 1999, 423-24. The diatribe against specific Islamic institutions in India notably Dār-ul-'ulūm Deoband, the Tabligh Jamā'at by a segment of *salafi* scholars gained momentum in the 1990s. Nadwī wrote a monograph to leading *'ulamā* and intellectuals in Saudi Arabia and the Gulf States to correct the misrepresentations in *salafi* writings. See SAHA Nadwī, *Aḍwā,* Lucknow: Majlis Tahqiqāt wa Nashriyāt-i-Islam, n.d.

language of *ijtihād* and *iṣlāḥ*. Thus the Islamic resurgent movements expanded gradually and made meaningful strides not only in the Arab world but in the Indian subcontinent as well. However, parallel to the resurgent influence was the already established translocal scholarship which gave fresh impetus to *iṣlāḥ* and *tajdīd* in institutionalised forms. This aspect had far-reaching implications for Maulānā Nadwī and his contemporaries. As we will note elsewhere in the chapter the transformative influence of *tajdīd* opened up new forms of contestations based largely on doctrinal differences and diverse methodological approaches.

Translocal Scholarship

To speak of Muslim scholarship in relation to a specific region is somehow misleading as it seems to suggest the existence of regionally-defined scholarly traditions. According to Hartung, the mobility among scholars is a connector for transmitting and acquiring knowledge.[41] The *riḥlah* (travel)[42] factor to a large extent developed the translocal character of scholarship over the centuries. Another circumstance which consolidated the translocality was the affiliation of scholars

41. Jan-Peter Hartung, *'Ulamā of Contemporary South Asia: Globalising the Local by Localising the Global.* The term "translocality" has been analytically covered in L.E. Guarnizo, "The Locations of Transnationalism" in L.E. Guarniz, Smith and P. Michael (eds.), *Transnationalism from Below*, London: Transaction Publishers, 1998, 15-20.

42. On the *riḥlah* genre see the following:

    I.R. Netton, "Rihla" in *Encyclopedia of Islam. New Edition,* Leiden: Brill, 1960, vol. 8, 528; S.I. Gellens, "The Search for Knowledge in Medieval Muslim Societies: A Comparative Approach" in Dan Eickelman and J. Piscatori (eds.), *Muslim Travellers, Pilgrimage, Migration and the Religious Inauguration*, Berkeley: UCP, 1990, 50-65; Siddiqi Muḥammad Zubayr, *Ḥadīth Literature: Its Origins, Development and Special Features,* Cambridge: The Islamic Texts Society, 1993, 40-42.

with Sūfī orders.[43] An important development that saw translocal scholarship gain momentum was the Muslim encounter with European colonialism.[44] More specifically it was the cultural encounter led to the introduction and adoption of new technology and "helped to develop expanded notions of space which had been much more confined to smaller units before. Once such space was communication which facilitated the introduction of bookprint."[45] Muslims could now study with relative ease religious texts outside the framework of *madrasa* institutions and the authoritative interpretation of the *'ulamā*. Moreover this "new freedom of access led to freedom of interpretation (of text) represented by the modernist and Islamist strands as well as a host of sectarian positions."[46] This remark is important to understand the contesting nature of *tajdīd* in the Indian subcontinent.

The following sections discuss aspects of translocal scholarship that have had a formative influence on Maulānā Nadwī's presentation of *tajdīd*.

43. South Asian Sūfī groups may be considered an exception to the mobility factor. For example, the Chistiyyah in South Asia was localised and adopted Sūfī paraphernalia peculiar to its *silsilah*. See S.A.A. Rizvi, "The Chistiyyah" in Seyyed Hossein Nasr (ed.), *Islamic Spirituality: Manifestations*, vol. 2, New York: Crossroad Publishing Company, 1991, 127-43.

44. Marshall G.S. Hodgson, *Venture of Islam: Conscience and History in a World Civilisation*, vol. 3, Chicago, 1974; Lewis Bernard, *The Muslim Discovery of Europe*, London: Phoenix, 1994. Lewis' account aims to portray the Muslim encounter with Europe by subtly reinforcing the expansionist power of Europe.

45. Robinson's *Islam and the Impact of Print in South Asia* is a useful introduction to the *'ulamā*'s response to print in the subcontinent. The historical survey provides a rationale for the diffusion of Islamic knowledge through the publications of important Islamic writings. F. Robinson, *Islam and Muslim History in South Asia*, 66-104.

46. Francis Robinson, *Islam: South Asia and the West*, 54.

NADWAT-UL-'ULAMĀ AS A REFORMIST INSTITUTION

Of much relevance to our study is the development and impact of Islamic institutions that are run without governmental or financial support since its inception. The Nadwat-ul-'ulamā has a transnational significance and has maintained its status as a premier institution of Islamic learning.

The Nadwat-ul-'ulamā (hereafter Nadwah) was established in 1893 at Lucknow, India. Its chequered history both in scope and content is examined in order to evaluate its contribution to a "reformed" curriculum and adopting a progressive mission statement.[47] The Nadwah's primary focus was anchored on a synthesis between a classical interpretation of Islam (*qadīm-al-ṣāliḥ*) and beneficial contemporary knowledge (*jadīd al-nāfi'*).[48] The reformers of Nadwah according to Habib-ul Haq Nadvi "stimulated contemporary Islamic resurgence and emerged triumphant in the reconstruction of Islamic education through restructuring the curriculum from time to time."[49] The curriculum reform implied the *Dars-i-Nizāmi*[50] system which is attributed to the influence of Mullah Nizām-al-din Muḥammad (d. 1748). The *Dars-i-Nizāmi* was composed of texts

47. B.D. Metcalf, *Islamic Revival in British India, Deoband, 1860-1900,* Karachi: Royal Book Company, 1982, 315-47. Cf. Dietrich Reetz, *Islam in the Public Sphere: Religious Groups in India 1900-1947,* New Delhi: Oxford University Press, 2006; Jamal Malik, *Islamische Gelehrtenkultur in Nordindien: Entwicklungsgeschichte und Tendezen am Beispiel von Lucknow,* Leiden: Brill, 1997, Muhammad Ishāq Jalīs Nadwī and Shams Tabrez Khan, *Tārikh Nadwat-ul-'Ulamā,* vols. 1-2, Lucknow: Daftar Nizamat Nadwat-ul-'ulamā, 1984.

48. For an elaboration on this mission statement, see Syed Habibul Haq Nadvi, *Islamic Resurgent Movements in the Indo-Pak Subcontinent,* 72-76.

49. Ibid., 72.

50. For a detailed discussion on the *Dars-i-Nizāmi*, see Francis Robinson, *The 'Ulamā of Farang-i-Mahal,* Delhi: Permanent Black, 2001.

largely of Central Asian, Iranian and Indian origin. It acquired the status of a "curriculum" in the latter half of the nineteenth century. The *madāris*, Zaman notes, "have continued, however, to differ in their versions of this curriculum, which has scarcely been impervious to change after its standardisation in the late nineteenth century."[51] The Dār-ul-'ulūm Deoband resisted any attempts for a curriculum reform and was critical of institutions like Nadwah which made efforts to foster new interpretations of Islamic thought.

The Nadwah sought to re-define Islam in the contemporary idiom; however its religious character as a *madrasa*[52] did not undergo any radical changes. While affirming traditional Islamic education, several reformers from Nadwah wanted to incorporate Western knowledge or science into Islam or "to interpret their achievements in an Islamic idiom."[53] It was Shibli Nu'māni (d. 1914)[54] an illustrious scholar of Nadwah who argued

51. Muḥammad Qasim Zaman, *The 'Ulamā in Contemporary Islam*, 68.

52. The *madrasas* grew out of the nineteenth-century movements in India. After the Partition of India in 1947 Muslims in India who now formed a minority were under "an atmosphere of suspicion" — their loyalty to India for ever in question. In these volatile circumstances, *madrasas* have come to be identified, not with the struggle to create an Islamic state, but with the cultural reproduction of an imperiled identity. The corporate Muslim identity or consciousness and Islamic authenticity by Nadwī which are discussed (in the Chapter 5) mirror the Islamic order the study seeks to examine.

53. Barbara Metcalf, "Madrasas and Minorities in Secular India" in Hefner Robert & Muḥammad Qasim Zaman (eds.), *Schooling Islam: The Culture and Politics of Modern Islamic Education*, 87-106.

54. Shibli Nu'māni (1857-1914) was an illustrious scholar whose intellectualism bore traces of Muslim glory and its impact on world civilisation combined with the rational spirit which saw the flowering of an Islamic tradition that borrowed liberally from Greek, Indian and Hellenic sources. He was also a proponent of a new *kalām* (scholastic theology) that confronted contemporary challenges. →

in favour of reforming traditional Islamic education according to the needs of the present day. His contributions to Islamic historiography[55] which is marked by scientific methods and scholarly arguments carved out a niche for Nadwah as a progressive Islamic institution. This observation is also echoed by Maulānā Nadwī that the scholars of Nadwah made an invaluable contribution to Islamic historiography and the presentation of Islamic teachings in modern literary style.[56] Maulānā Nadwī's *Islam and the World* and *Saviours of Islamic Spirit* were written in the *tajdīdī* mould to justify the view that Nadwah had a resurgent vision. However Maulānā Nadwī expresses his candour at these efforts:

> The profound changes envisaged in the Nadwah did not materialise mainly on account of the wide gulf which separated

---

→ Shibli despite his major contribution to Islamic thought and culture remains a controversial figure. Murad's analysis that it was his complex personality and enigmatic traits which led people to view him differently. Mehr Afroz Murad, *Intellectual Modernism of Shibli Nu'mani*, Lahore: Institute of Islamic Culture, 1976. In contrast Sayyid Sabahuddin 'Abdur Rahmān echoes the sentiments of his teacher Sayyid Sulāyman Nadwī that Shibli represented a merger of the classical Islamic tradition and modern sciences. This view is gleaned from Shibli's prolific writings. Abdur S.S. Rahman, *Maulānā Shibli Nu'māni par ek nazar*, Azamgarh, 1942. The view is embodied in Sulāyman Nadwī's *Hayāt-i-Shibli*. Cf. SAHA Nadwī, *Western Civilisation: Islam and Muslims*, 64-5.

55. Written in seven volumes, the *Sīrat un-Nabi* is considered to be one of the most authoritative works on the *sīrah* genre. To date, several volumes have been translated in English and Arabic. Shibli's student, Sayyid Sulāyman Nadwī (d. 1953) played a pioneering role in the compilation of the *Sīrat-al-Nabi*. For a biographical account on Sayyid Sulāyman Nadwī, see Muḥammad Na'im Siddiqui Nadwī, *'Allāmah Sayyid Sulāyman Nadwī: Shakhsiyat wa Adab Khidmāt*, Lucknow: Maktaba Firdaus, 1985.

56. SAHA Nadwī, *Western Civilisation: Islam and Muslims*, 66.

> the orthodox from the modern sections of Muslim society, it could not receive from either of the two the support it merited.[57]

In its reformist zeal, Nadwah focused on Arabic for its cultural authencity with the Arab world. The cultural authenticity is interchangeably used for Islamic authenticity by Maulānā Nadwī to present his interpretation of Islamic resurgence.

ARABIC AS A REFORMIST VEHICLE

Maulānā Nadwī's exposure to the Arabic language and Arabic Islamic culture began early in life. Though his father, Sayyid 'Abdul Ḥayy al-Ḥasani (d. 1923), was a prolific scholar of Arabic,[58] Maulānā Nadwī's brother, Dr Sayyid 'Abdul 'Ali al-Ḥasani (d. 1961), the Rector of Nadwah, continued to supervise his education in Arabic.[59]

If Maulānā Nadwī was predisposed towards Arabic education, so too was the Nadwah's focus on Arabic as a living, contemporary language. To them the promotion of Arabic was to enable active intellectual and cultural exchange between scholars of India and of the Arab and Islamic world.[60]

---

57. SAHA Nadwī, *Western Civilisation: Islam and Muslims*, 65.

58. For a biographical account, see SAHA Nadwī, *Hayāt-i-'Abdul Ḥayy*, Karachi: Majlis Nashriyāt-i-Islam, 1985. His biographical dictionary, *Nuzhatut-ul-Khawātir* written in eight volumes covers 4500 scholars and men of genius born in India during the past 1,300 years of Islamic era. Cf. Nadwī's introduction in S. Abdul Hayy, *India During Muslim Rule*, Lucknow: Academy of Islamic Research and Publications, 1977, 1-22.

59. Dr 'Abdul 'Ali's pastoral care is poignantly recounted in Nadwī's *Kārwān-i-Ẓindagī:*

    "A father to his brother and an obedient son to his mother; with his unbounded affection for me, he extended his patronage to all of us, reflecting a role model as was now before us," vol. 1, 78.

60. Muḥammad Qasim Zaman, *Muslim Identity in Twentieth-Century India*, 279. Cf. Abdus Salam Kidwai Nadwī, *85 Years of Nadwatul 'Ulamā*, Lucknow, 1975, 10-12.

The institution's emphasis on Arabic was a powerful statement of its cultural orientation and a mark of its distinction from other *madāris* in the Indian subcontinent. This language proficiency, Zaman noted, became the basis of a sustained intellectual engagement with the contemporary Arab and Muslim world.[61] Arabic was considered a marker for Islamic authenticity which fitted in the Islamic resurgence paradigm envisaged by Maulānā Nadwī.

We now turn to two important leading figures whose contributions to Arabic at Nadwah had a significant influence on Maulānā Nadwī's academic career. However, it would be worthwhile to discuss the phenomenon of translocal scholarship, albeit briefly, in context of its influence on Maulānā Nadwī. The *tajdīdī* and *salafi* influences were embedded in this cultural encounter and had a direct bearing on Nadwah's Islamic orientation. It is this historical context that saw Maulānā Nadwī as a beneficiary of translocal scholarship.

THE AHL-I-ḤADĪTH AS SALAFI REPRESENTATIVES IN THE INDIAN SUBCONTINENT

The translocal character of Islamic scholarship became institutionalised in the post-colonial era. The pioneering role was played by Sayyid Siddīq Ḥasan Khan (d. 1890)[62] in reformulating the reformist trends in the subcontinent. Tracing his intellectual lineage to the Yemeni reformist,

61. Muḥammad Qasim Zaman, "The Scope and Limits of Islamic Cosmopolitanism and the Discursive Language of the 'Ulamā" in Miriam Cooke & Bruce Lawrence (eds.), *Muslim Networks from Hajj to Hip Hop*, Chapel Hill: The University of North Carolina Press, 2005, 95.

62. For biographical details, see Al-Ḥasani, 'Abdul Ḥayy, *Nuzhat-al-khawātir*, Rae Bareli: Da'rat al-Shah 'Alam-Allah, 1991, vol. 8.

Muhammad al-Shawkāni (d. 1834),[63] Sayyid Siddīq enlisted several scholars from Yemen to Bhopal, an Indian princely state which was ruled by Begums.[64] His marriage to Shāh Jahān Begum (d. 1901) raised his rank as a Nawāb, a royal title. His reforms were twofold: to disseminate his religious ideas through print and enlist scholars of *salafi* orientation to teach in the princely state. Sayyid Siddīq and Sayyid Nadhīr Husayn Dehlawi (d. 1902)[65] are credited for the establishment of the Ahl-i-Ḥadīth movement.[66] Metcalf observed that the Ahl-i-Ḥadīth was "one of the most visible of the Muslim intellectual movements of the late nineteenth century both because of its avowedly sectarian character and because of its membership from among the educated and well-born."[67] In Muslim countries no *ḥadīth*-based movement emerged with doctrinal tendencies that emphasised sectarian differences. The movement shared similar characteristics with the Salafiyyah in respect of its rejection of *taqlīd* and publishing

---

63. The global impact of Shaukāni is expressed in the following words: "Shaukāni is a towering figure in both Yemeni Islam and modern Islamic reformist thought. His encyclopaedia oeuvre is studied and referred to throughout the Sunni world today, from Nadwatal-'ulamā in north India to the *madrasas* of Kano in Nigeria. . . . It is his formulations of the problems facing the community of Muslims (*ummah*) and the solutions he proferred for solving these — his intellectual project — as well as his attempt to put these into practice in his own lifetime that account for his enduring appeal." Bernard Haykel, *Revival and Reform in Islam: The Legacy of Muḥammad al-Shaukāni*, Cambridge: Cambridge University Press, 2003.

64. Claudia Preckel, *Begums of Bhopal*, New Delhi: Roli Books, 2000, 105-72.

65. Cf. Sayyid Abdul Hayy al-Ḥasani, *Islam*, vol. 8, 523-27.

66. On the Aḥl-i-Ḥadīth movement, see B.D. Metcalf, *Islamic Revival in British India*, 268-96.

67. Ibid., 268.

the works of Ibn Taymiyyah in the Arab world and Indian subcontinent. Daniel Brown has made a pertinent comparison between the Ahl-i-Ḥadīth and the *salafis* in his *Rethinking Tradition in Modern Islamic Thought*. He observes:

> The Salafiyyah are akin to the Ahl-i-Ḥadīth in their rejection of classical authority and their claim to be capable of reviving the pure, unadulterated sunnah of the Prophet. . . . Moreover, by their emphasis on a return to the Qur'ān and the *sunnah* both movements offer a radical critique of the whole classical tradition.[68]

Sharply different were the Deobandis who too followed a reformist outlook within the framework of *taqlīd*.[69] The duality between these movements was to have serious implications in the contesting discourse of what was considered to be "authentic" Islam.

Maulānā Nadwī's response to the Deobandi institution may be viewed from two angles. Firstly, he defended Dār-ul-'ulūm Deoband when it was subjected to a spate of polemical literature by the emergent *salafi* group in the Indian sub-continent. In his response he wrote an Arabic monograph, *Aḍwā*[70] for an Arab audience to highlight the contributions of the Deobandis to *iṣlāḥ* and *tajdīd*. The monograph is a brief survey of Islamic movements and personalities who have contributed to the growth and development of a corporate

---

68. Daniel Brown, *Rethinking Tradition in Modern Islamic Thought*, Cambridge: Cambridge University Press, 1966, 32.
69. The *taqlīd* was a principal factor that distinguished the Ahl-i-Ḥadīth and Deobandi movements. See Dietrich Reetz, *Islam in the Public Sphere*. For an analysis on *taqlīd*, see Bernarch Weiss, "Taqlīd" in J. Esposito (ed.), *The Oxford Encyclopedia of the Modern Islamic World*, vol. 4, 187-89.
70. SAHA Nadwī, *Aḍwā*, Lucknow, Majlis al-Ilmi, 1995, 21. Cf. Nadwī, *Kārwān-i-Ẓindagī*, vol. 6, 155-56.

Islamic identity (*tashakhkhus*) in the subcontinent. This approach falls within Maulānā Nadwī's framework of *tajdīd* and his vision of an Islamic order. Secondly, Maulānā Nadwī's critique of Deoband is based on its religious conservatism. Maulānā Nadwī makes a critical assessment of this aspect in his *Western Civilisation, Islam and Muslims*:

> But as far as meeting the challenge of the times is concerned, Deoband has failed to make any noteworthy contribution. It has not been able to provide suitable answers to the questions thrown up by modern civilisation. Its graduates have done little to bridge the gulf between the old and new generations. Much as the Deoband people are advanced in their political views, in their educational outlook and in the appreciation of the law of social change they have tended, more or less, to be conservative and tradition-bound.[71]

Their sectarian outlook and rigidity of views which assumed forms of theological disputations with other Islamic movements pursuing a reformist mission have been critically examined by Maulānā Nadwī in several of his important writings.

A similar picture emerges in Maulānā Nadwī's relationship with the Ahl-i-Ḥadīth movement. An important question is raised: Was Maulānā Nadwī and his family receptive to the Ahl-i-Ḥadīth? Several *ḥadīth* scholars were of *salafi* leanings under whom Maulānā Nadwī studied. Mention may be made of the eminent *ḥadīth* scholar, Shaykh 'Abdur Rahmān Mubārakpuri (d. AH 1353).[72] Another scholar, Ḥusayn bin Muḥsin al-Yemeni[73] taught *Ḥadīth* to Maulānā Nadwī's father, Sayyid 'Abdul Ḥayy al-Hasani. These intellectual

71. Nadwī, *Western Civilisation: Islam and Muslims*, 63.

72. On 'Abdur Rahmān Mubarakpuri, a pupil of Nadhir Husayn Dehlawi, cf. al-Ḥasani, *al-'Islam*, op. cit., vol. 8, 259F; Nadwī, Abu Suhban Ruh al-Quds, *Maulānā 'Ali Mia aur Ilm-i-ḥadīth*, Lucknow: Majlis Tahqiqāt wa Nashriyāt-i-Islam, 2000, 37.

73. Ibid., 121-25.

figureheads belonged to the Ahl-i-Ḥadīth movement. Maulānā Nadwī did not accentuate this influence; rather the versatility in his academic career prepared him for his multi-faceted role to accommodate divergent views in contemporary Islamic thought.

The above responses illustrate the developmental stages in Maulānā Nadwī's formulation of *tajdīd.* Maulānā Nadwī faced the daunting task of reconciling ideas with influences drawn from contrasting religious situations. It was largely his pragmatic approach that set him apart from his contemporaries in their respective understanding of Islamic resurgence.

Arab Scholars

SHAYKH KHALĪL BIN MUḤAMMAD AL-YEMENI

The presence of Arab scholars in the Indian subcontinent was largely due to the efforts of Sayyid Siddīq of Bhopal. Arabic and *ḥadīth* studies were their areas of specialisation. Although their *salafi* leanings were not pronounced, they wielded considerable influence in providing alternative views to *taqlīd* and emphasising the primacy of Qur'ān and *sunnah* on contemporary Islamic thought. It would be difficult to assume that Maulānā Nadwī remained immune from such influences. One such example was Shaykh Khalīl al-Yemeni.

The famous Yemeni scholar, Shaykh Khalīl (d. 1966)[74] taught Arabic language and literature at the Nadwah. His influence on Maulānā Nadwī's proficiency in the Arabic language was profound; his (Maulānā Nadwī's) meteoric rise among the Arab literati was largely due to Shaykh Khalīl's efforts. Maulānā Nadwī stated:

---

74. Shaykh Khalīl's influence on Nadwī was profound. His personal impression of his teacher are profiled in *Purān-i-Chirāgh*, vol. 1, 207-28.

> His (Shaykh Khalīl's) eloquence and mastery left indelible imprints in our appreciation of the language. He was without a peer and gave us the opportunity to share in its literary excellence and spoke Arabic with a powerful zeal and elegance. It would be no exaggeration to say that his consummate skills of the language was a divine gift.[75]

Two other traits of Shaykh Khalīl were embedded in Maulānā Nadwī's personality: the promotion of *tawḥīd* (oneness of Allah) and *da'wah* (propagation).[76] This twin concept was an anchor for Maulānā Nadwī's *Payām-i-Insāniyat.* It implied on a broader level the possibilities of engaging in an interfaith dialogue with the Hindus[77] without Muslims compromising their basic credo-*tawḥīd.* Simply put, the moral regeneration of values was emphasised; however it would not compromise on doctrinal issues. Maulānā Nadwī received the ire of fundamentalist movements[78] which perceived his *Payām* as a breach of "unalloyed" *tawḥīd.* This criticism was directed at Maulānā Nadwī for attempting to diminish the core beliefs of the *salafi*s on which their vision of Islam rested. Their rigidity underlined their inability to recognise a Muslim minority co-existing with a Hindu majority. Notwithstanding these criticisms Maulānā Nadwī saw the pragmatism of interacting with other faiths for *da'wah* purposes.

75. SAHA Nadwī, *Kārwān-i-Ẓindagī,* vol. 1, 91.

76. For an elaboration of these themes, see SAHA Nadwī, *Inviting to the Way of Allah,* London: Ta-Ha Publishers, 1996, 8-14; *Islam and Civilisation,* Lucknow: Academy of Islamic Research and Publications, 1986, 7-18. Cf. Nadwī's enormous debt to Shaykh Khalīl for his endearing mentorship in *Be Mithāl Ustādh aur Be Mithāl Shāgird* in 'Abdul Qayyum Haqqāni, *Al-Qāsim,* 466-76.

77. According to Sikand, Nadwī's call for an interfaith dialogue meant a form of joint effort to build a more harmonious and just society. Yoginder Sikand, *Muslims in India Since 1947: Islamic Perspectives on Interfaith Relations,* London: Routledge Curzon, 2004, 43. Cf. SAHA Nadwī, *Muslims in India,* 76.

78. 'Abdullāh 'Abbās Nadwī, *Mīr-i-Kārwān,* 443.

A noteworthy feature of Maulānā Nadwī's pragmatism is the discourse of the "other" which is articulated in an Indian context. The marginalised Muslim community (*millat*), Maulānā Nadwī argued, "can come to the aid of India in the reconstruction of a healthy, honest and egalitarian society."[79] This overriding concern idealised as a theme in Maulānā Nadwī's writings shaped his perception of an Islamic order in India. A careful reading of Maulānā Nadwī's *Muslims in India* for example is intended to reach out to a Hindu audience to show that the Muslims have made major contributions in the evolution of Indo-Islamic culture. Maulānā Nadwī lamented that "one of the curious contradictions of Indian national existence is that one important part of the population is totally in the dark about the ancient heritage and background of the other important part. . . . There is a campaign to present the history of our land in a manner as if the Muslim era in India was an era of foreign imperialistic domination."[80] The rhetoric of Muslim contribution to India's progress is also expressed in Maulānā Nadwī's *Payām-i-Insāniyat.*

'ALLĀMAH TAQĪ-AD-DĪN AL-HILĀLI

The chequered history of the Moroccan scholar, 'Allāmah Taqī-ad-dīn al-Hilāli (d. 1987)[81] has been discussed by Maulānā Nadwī. An embodiment of the translocal *salafi* scholarship, 'Allāmah al-Hilāli played a leading role with the Egyptian *salafi* reformist Muḥammad Rashīd Rīḍā (d.

79. SAHA Nadwī, *Reconstruction of Indian Society: What Muslims Can Do*, Lucknow: Academy of Islamic Research and Publications, n.d., 34.

80. Nadwī, *Muslims in India,* 2-3.

81. SAHA Nadwī, *Kārwān-i-Ẓindagī*, vol. 1, 115-20. Cf. Muḥammad Majahub, *'Ulamā wa Mufakkirun 'Araftahum*, Cairo: Dar-ul-I'tisām, vol. 1, 200-202 Cf. Muḥammad Manzoor Alam, *100 Great Leaders of the 20th Century*, New Delhi: Institute of Objective Studies, 2005, 323-26.

1935)[82] in promoting "a conscious return to the ethical ideals of the early Islamic period without ignoring the general conditions of the prevailing time."[83]

Maulānā Nadwī became acquainted with 'Allāmah al-Hilāli in 1930 when the latter was employed for a short period of three years to teach Arabic language and literature at Nadwah.[84] During this period, 'Allāmah al-Hilāli served as an important link to consolidate the network of translocal scholarship[85] between Nadwah and the Arab world. The cultural exchange of publications and journals[86] was a corollary to an intensive exchange of ideas between reformist scholars of the Arabic-speaking world and South Asia.

The expansion of these translocal relations had a personal impact on Maulānā Nadwī. 'Allāmah al-Hilāli was responsible for the publication of an Arabic monograph *Tarjamat-ul-Imām*

---

82. On the pan-Islamic movements represented by Jamal-ud-din Afghani, Muḥammad 'Abduh and Rashid Riḍā, see A. Hourani, *Arabic Thought in the Liberal Age: 1798-1939*, Cambridge: Cambridge University Press, 1970.

83. R. Schulze, *A Modern History of the Islamic World*, 18-20. The *salafi* representation in the quotation may be read in conjunction with Nadwī's elaboration of Islamic authenticity. This term has been critically examined in Zaman Muḥammad Qasim, *The 'Ulamā in Contemporary Islam*, 165-67.

84. SAHA Nadwī, *Kārwān-i-Ẓindagī*, vol. 1, 116-17.

85. The production of Arabic texts and exchange of Arabic journals and periodicals between Nadwah (facilitated by 'Allāmah al-Hilāli) and Arab institutions was a turning point for Nadwī's intellectual profile. For Nadwī, 'Allāmah al-Hilāli prepared him for a significant role. "During my first visit to Egypt in 1951, I was not overwhelmed by any personality nor was there any unfolding of new realities." *Kārwān*, vol. 1, 48-49.

86. For example, the Arabic journal, *al-Ḍiyā*, published by Nadwa received critical acclaim in the Arab world.

Sayyid Aḥmad bin 'Irfān Shaḥid[87] by Maulānā Nadwī in Rashid Rīḍā's journal, *al-Manār.* This work marked the beginning of Maulānā Nadwī's publishing activities and was a forerunner to his promotion of Islamic resurgence in the Arab world. The influence of 'Allāmah al-Hilāli was significant.

> An international scholar who was peerless in Arabic, 'Allāmah Hilāli drew capable students from across the country and developed their skills — his *sanad* (certificate) was a testimony of his students' proficiency in Arabic.[88] In the company of Hilāli, two realities unfolded before us for the first time: the difference between language and literature. Language is the foundation of *adab* (literature) which is the gallery of the former and adorns its words with portraits. *Adab* represents the highest form of literary expressions through which progressive thoughts are a vehicle.[89]

The use of Arabic was an appropriate vehicle for Maulānā Nadwī to promote his *tajdīdī* activities and also spread his ideas of Islamic authenticity, a key concept in his *tajdīdī* paradigm.

Al-Hilāli's *salafi* orientations in India had far-reaching implications. He was successful in preparing a team of scholars for publishing Arabic works[90] that had a niche market

---

87. Nadwī's monograph on his ancestor, Sayyid Aḥmad Shahīd, was a first serious attempt to portray the reformer in a positive light. See Nadwī's voluminous account, *Sirāt-i-Sayyid Aḥmad Shahīd,* vol. 1, 47-55 for a detailed account of his first literary work.

88. SAHA Nadwī, *Kārwān-i-Ẓindagī,* vol. 1, 115.

89. SAHA Nadwī, *Meri 'ilmi wa mutāli'āti ẓindagī,* Rae Bareli: Sayyid Ahmad Shahid Academy, n.d., 16.

90. Mention may be made of Maulānā Mas'ud 'Ālam (d. 1954) a contemporary of Nadwī. Al-Hilāli's influence on his literary output was profound. In fact, he was the Arabic translator for several of Maulānā Maudūdī's major works written originally in Urdu. Again Nadwī's worldview encompassed scholars from a diversity of thoughts. See SAHA Nadwī, *Purān-i-Chirāgh,* vol. 1, 317-57.

in the Arab world. Several decades later, 'Allāmah al-Hilāli was involved in a collaborative initiative: the translation of the Qur'ān into English.[91] The *salafi* influence stands out clearly in the translation with Saudi patronage making this work easily available worldwide. The proliferation of such works created contestations for Islamic authenticity and at the same time gave rise to polemical literature dealing with the nature and scope of Islamic resurgence.[92]

The antecedents for Maulānā Nadwī's fame in the Arabic-speaking world rested to a large extent on scholars like 'Allāmah al-Hilāli. Translocal scholarship saw a matrix of Islamic authenticity develop into a discourse for both *'ulamā* and Islamists. The contributions of the Islamists with specific reference to Maulānā Nadwī's contemporaries are discussed in the following sections to examine their input on the Islamic resurgent movements.

ISLAMIST PROFILES

Maulānā Nadwī's contemporaries included *'ulamā* and Islamists. Although they promoted different visions of Islamic resurgence largely because of their ideological backgrounds, they played a pivotal role in the formulation of *tajdīd*. The tradition of translocal scholarship has followed a somewhat predictable pattern in terms of its influence on Maulānā Nadwī's which is consistent with the growth and development of translocal scholarship in the Indian soil. In this context the role of the Islamists tend to project a set of opposing views. As discussed in Chapter 1, the Islamist profile merges with *salafi* orientations making it problematic to

91. Muḥammad Muhsin Khan and Muḥammad Taqi-ud-din 'Allāmah al-Hilāli, *Interpretation of the Meanings of the Noble Qur'ān in the English Language*, Riyadh: Dar-us-Salam Publishers, 1995.

92. For an elaboration on *salafi* orientations and refutations, see Aḥmad Ghorab, *Subverting Islam*, 32-63.

separate the two groups. Of course, Salafiyyah emerged much earlier; however Islamists have embraced the *salafi* vision of Islamic resurgence albeit in a strict ideological sense with traces of Western influence which characterise the former's strategies of Islamic resurgence. This approach is evident in two of Maulānā Nadwī's contemporaries, Maulānā Maudūdī and Quṭb. In the spectrum of intellectual exchange their specific writings have had an impact on Maulānā Nadwī on Islamic resurgence. An attempt is made to present their respective contributions to contemporary Islamic thought.

SAYYID ABUL A'LĀ MAUDŪDĪ[93]

Abul A'lā Maudūdī (d. 1979) is regarded as one of the most influential and prolific of contemporary Muslim thinkers[94] whose interpretation of Islam has contributed greatly to the articulation of Islamic revivalist thought and has influenced Muslim thinkers and activists from Morocco to Indonesia.[95]

93. For a thorough discussion of Maulānā Maudūdī's biography, see Seyyed Vali Reza Nasr, *Maudūdī and the Making of Islamic Revivalism*, New York: Oxford University Press, 1996; Khurshid Ahmed and Zafar Ishaq Ansari, Maulānā Sayyid Abul A'la Maudūdī, "An Introduction to His Vision of Islam and Islamic Revival", in *Islamic Perspectives: Studies in Honour of Maulānā Sayyid Abul A'la Maudūdī*, Leicester: The Islamic Foundation, 1979, 360; Masudul Hasan, *Sayyid Abul A'ala Maudūdī and His Thought*, vols. 1-2, Lahore: Islamic Publications Pvt. Ltd., 1984.

    On Maulānā Maudūdī's impact on expression of Islamic revivalism, see John L. Esposito, *The Islamic Threat: Myth or Reality*, New York: Oxford University Press, 1992, 154-55; Zainab Anwar, *Islamic Fundamentalism in Malaysia*, Kuala Lumpur, 1989; Hamid Enayat, *Modern Islamic Political Thought*, Austin, 1982; Ishtiaq Husain Qureshi, *Ulema in Politics*, Karachi: Ma'aref Ltd., 1974, 339-54.

94. Charles J. Adam, "Maudūdī and the Islamic State", in John L. Esposito, *Voices of Resurgent Islam*, New York: Oxford Univerity Press, 1983, 99.

95. Seyyed Vali Reza Nasr, "Sayyid Abul al-A'la Maudūdī", in John L. Esposito (ed.), *The Oxford Encyclopedia of the Modern Islamic World*, Oxford: Oxford University Press, 1995, 71.

According to Wilfred Cantwell Smith, "perhaps the most significant constituent of Maulānā Maudūdī's position has been the gradual and continual elaboration of an impressive system of ideas. Maulānā Maudūdī would appear to be the most systematic thinker of modern Islam."[96]

A study of Maulānā Maudūdī's formative years is important to analyse his presentation of Islam in contemporary Islamic thought. Maulānā Maudūdī was born in Aurangabad (India) in December in 1903 in a respectable family known for its religious piety. His education was rather short and somewhat unsystematic.[97] After completing his "Maulvi" examination (equivalent to a secondary school certificate) in 1914, he was admitted to Dār-ul-'ulūm College, Hyderabad for higher education. This was disrupted, however, due to his father's illness. During this period, Maulānā Maudūdī developed proficiency in both Arabic and Urdu and mastered difficult texts, which exceeded the expectations of his teachers.[98]

Two important developments took place during his stay in Delhi. In 1925 he was appointed by the Jami'at-ul-'ulamā Hind (JUH)[99] to edit their paper, *Al-Jami'at.* Once more, Maulānā Maudūdī resumed his studies of the *Dars-i-Nizāmi* and completed the course under reputable Deobandi *'ulamā.* His *ijāzah*[100] (certificate to teach religious sciences) was discovered after his death and began to appear in the Jamā'at-

96. Wilfred Cantwell Smith, *Islam in Modern History*, Princeton, 1957, 236.

97. Seyyed Vali Reza Nasr, *Maudūdī and the Making of Islamic Revivalism*, 11-12.

98. Ibid., 13.

99. On the Jami'at-ul-'Ulamā Hind (JUH), see Dietrich Reetz, *Islam in the Public Sphere*, 34-44.

100. Sayyid Abu'l A'la Maudūdī, *Wathā'iq-i-Maudūdī*, Lahore, 1986.

i-Islami literature to refute claims that he was not a traditional *'ālim* by training.

Maulānā Maudūdī by common standards was a Deobandi *'ālim* and absorbed many of their ideas and concerns. Like the Deobandis, Maulānā Maudūdī sought to emulate the practice of an authentic text of an idealised historical period.[101] He also strove to create a normative order in which Muslims could lead their lives according to the teachings of Islam. Maulānā Maudūdī's vision was essentially that of carrying out a total reconstruction of human life and establishing a new social order and *state* (emphasis added) and thereby using it in a new era in human history.[102] In other words, Maulānā Maudūdī envisioned a radical change in Muslim societies which did not reflect, in his view, Ḥākimiyyah (sovereignty of God). This was only possible if Muslims had a firm conviction and "an uncompromising resolve to do the will of God."[103] This theoretical generalisation is clearly spelt out in Maulānā Maudūdī's *The Islamic Movement* (1984):

> Islam desires, above all, that people should commit themselves to God's truth and they should serve and worship God. . . . The aims cannot be realised so long as power and leadership in society are in the hands of ruling disbelievers gone astray, and the followers of Islam confine themselves to worship rites. . . . It is therefore the primary duty of all those who aspire to please God to launch an organised struggle for this purpose.[104]

---

101. Seyyed Vali Reza Nasr, *Maudūdī and the Making of Islamic Revivalism*, 18.

102. Khurshid Aḥmad and Zafar Ansari, *Islamic Perspectives in Honour of Sayyid Abul A'la Maudūdī*, Leicester: The Islamic Foundation, 1979, 369.

103. Ibid., 371.

104. S.A.A. Maudūdī, *The Islamic Movement: Dynamics of Value, Power and Change*, Leicester: The Islamic Foundation, 1984, 79.

The rhetoric of an Islamic movement faithfully translating Maulānā Maudūdī's vision of an Islamic state is evident. The key concepts of Jāhiliyyah and Ḥākimiyyah are Maulānā Maudūdī's salient features of Islamic resurgence. According to Nasr, Maulānā Maudūdī's political ambitions prevented him from identifying with the *'ulamā* fraternity as the title of an *'ālim* was more a liability than an asset.[105] The synthesis between the new and old educational systems in Maulānā Maudūdī's view was the ideal. He observed:

> I do not have the prerogative to be in the class of the *'ulamā*. I am a man of middle cadre, who has imbibed something from both the systems of education, the new and the old; and have gathered my knowledge by traversing both paths by virtue of my inner light. I conclude that neither the old school nor the new is to be in the right.[106]

Maulānā Maudūdī's "inner light," a euphemism for independent thinking (*ijtihād*) was severely condemned by the *'ulamā*. Moreover Maulānā Maudūdī castigated the *'ulamā* for their obsession with the past and their inability to interpret the principles and laws of Islam in the light of the changing conditions. The article "Sick Nations of the World" includes among other issues a critique on the *'ulamā* fraternity.[107] Maulānā Maudūdī's observation focused on the Muslims in the Indian subcontinent before the Partition in 1947. Thereafter much of Maulānā Maudūdī's writings were an elucidation on the nature and functions of an Islamic state in the newly-established Pakistan.

The echoes of the "old" (*qadīm*) and new (*jadīd*) dichotomy

105. S.A.A. Maudūdī, *The Islamic Movement: Dynamics of Value, Power and Change*, Leicester: The Islamic Foundation, 1984, 79.

106. Cited in Abu'l Afaq, *Sayyid Abu'l A'la Maudūdī: Sawānih wa afkār, Tahrik*, Lahore, 1971, 73.

107. Cited in Masudul Hasan, *Sayyid Abul A'ala Maudūdī and His Thought*, vol. 1, Lahore: Islamic Publications, 1984, 109-10.

are also evident in Maulānā Nadwī's interpretation of knowledge. In a keynote address at the Kashmir University in 1981, Maulānā Nadwī noted:

> I regard knowledge a truth which is a gift of Allah and does not and should not belong to a particular race or community. I see unity even in its diversity. The unity is truth, the search for truth, the aptitude for it, and the joy of its realisation.[108]

The universal message of humanity's claim to knowledge is articulated by Maulānā Nadwī. Unlike Maulānā Maudūdī, Maulānā Nadwī's construct of knowledge is based on its utilitarian value, i.e. the purpose of knowledge is to impart a new life and a new soul to the country and to the nation.[109] This pragmatic approach is evident in Maulānā Nadwī's interpretation of an Islamic order which is discussed in Chapter 5. These preliminary remarks are important to contextualise the conflictual relationship between Maulānā Maudūdī and Maulānā Nadwī.

MAULĀNĀ MAUDŪDĪ AND THE QUEST FOR A HOLY COMMUNITY: AN ASSESSMENT

Maulānā Nadwī's interest in Maulānā Maudūdī stemmed from the latter's critique of the West. The revivalist programme Maulānā Maudūdī set out before him was partly inspired by Maulānā Nadwī's biography of the revivalist leader, Sayyid

108. SAHA Nadwī, *The Place of Knowledge and Responsibilities of Those Who Acquire It*, Lucknow: Academy of Islamic Research and Publications, n.d., 8. Cf. SAHA Nadwī, *Islam and Knowledge*, Oxford: OCIS, 1988. His pertinent remarks reinforce his view on knowledge in its holistic dimension:

 "[the] contribution of Islam in integrating different disciplines of learning and guiding them to play a positive, constructive role for the service of humanity, was even more significant than extending the frontiers of knowledge and creating a zest for its cultivation," p. 5.

109. SAHA Nadwī, *The Place of Knowledge . . .*, 14.

Aḥmad Shahīd.[110] The revivalist theme attracted several *'ulamā* including Manzur Nu'māni (d. 1997)[111] who after the establishment of the Jamā'at-i-Islami was to become Maulānā Maudūdī's staunchest opposition on doctrinal differences.[112]

A cursory view of the *tajdīdī* movement promoted by Maulānā Maudūdī highlights some interesting observations: "Maulānā Maudūdī advocated an interpretive reading of Islam, one which aims to mobilise piety and faith for the purpose of political action. He placed emphasis on religious works, discouraged traditional religious practices and rationalised the Islamic faith. . . . Maulānā Maudūdī viewed Islam as a holistic ideology similar to Western ideologies. His notion of Islamic ideology, one of the most prolific and systematic articulations of its kind, has been most influential in giving shape to Islamic revivalism as a distinct reading of Islam, its history, and its purpose across the Muslim world."[113] Maulānā Maudūdī's revivalist programme had two distinct messages: traditional Islam was an obstacle to Muslim progress in the comity of nations; ideology which is synonymous with *dīn* (way of life) had a far more encompassing influence than rites of

---

110. Seyyed Vali Reza Nasr, *The Vanguard of the Islamic Revolution: The Jama'at-i-Islam of Pakistan*, Berkeley: University of California Press, 1994, 22.

111. On Nu'māni, see SAHA Nadwī, "Rafiq-i-Muhtaram", in Atiqur-Rahman Sambhali (ed.), *Hadhrat Maulānā Muḥammad Manzur Nu'māni*, Lucknow, 1997 is a useful introduction to his academic and *tablīgh* career.

112. For a detailed account of Nu'māni's critique of Maudūdī, see Muhamad Manzur Nu'māni, *Maulānā Maudūdī mere sath rifaqat ki sarguzash aur ab mera mu'qaf*, Lahore, 1980. Cf. Seyyed Vali Reza Nasr, *Maudūdī and the Making of Islamic Revivalism*, 28, on Nu'māni's censure of Maudūdī for not complying with the Islamic moral of conduct.

113. Seyyed Vali Reza Nasr, *Maudūdī and the Jama'at-i-Islami*, 104-05.

worship.[114] The ideological implication was an attempt to break the shackles of Muslim conservatism and usher in a new world order: Maulānā Maudūdī says:

> This call of mine is not to sustain and develop the so-called Muslim society, which has in itself gone adrift of the Islamic way. In fact this call means: . . . *to* raise *de novo* (a new and perfect) world on the Qur'ānic plane. . . .

Thus Maulānā Maudūdī's concept of ideology was a blueprint for the future of an Islamic state.

Maulānā Maudūdī's ideology was also elaborated as social action.[115] This system was enunciated as *dīn*.[116] It was applied to every aspect of Islamic thought and practice and produced a comprehensive interpretation of Islam[117] which had a major impact across the Muslim world and was used as a standard manual for Islamic resurgence.[118] It is interesting to note Maulānā Maudūdī's early writings were translated into

---

114. S.A.A. Maudūdī, *Towards Understanding Islam*, I.I.F.S.O., n.d., 131-40.

115. Cf. Tāriḳ Jān, "Maulānā Maudūdī's Critique of the Secular Mind" in *The Muslim World*, vol. 93, nos. 3 & 4, 503-20 for Maulānā Maudūdī's critical appraisal of a secular mind *vis-à-vis* the Islamic ideology.

116. For a variant interpretation of *dīn* see Charles J. Adams, "The Ideology of Maudūdī" in Donald E. Smith (ed.), *South Asian Politics and Religion*, Princeton, 1966; Abul A'lā Maudūdī, *Towards Understanding of Islam*, Kuwait, IIFSO; Khurshid Aḥmad, *The Religion of Islam*, Lahore: Islamic Publications, 1976.

117. Originally written in Urdu, *Risāla-i-Dīniyāt* in 1930 for the government of the Nizām in Hyderabad, the book was met with critical acclaim in the Muslim world. It has been translated into major languages of the world. S.A.A. Maudūdī, *Towards Understanding Islam*, tr. Khurshid Aḥmad, Leicester: Islamic Foundation, 1990.

118. According to Fathi Osman, Maudūdī's impact on Islamic thinking has been tremendous. His concepts and the terms he →

Arabic[119] largely through the efforts of Maulānā Nadwī. This period was in the 1940s when Maulānā Nadwī's own formulation of *tajdīd* was not clearly articulated and his admiration for Maulānā Maudūdī's presentation of Islam was during the initial years of his association with the Jamā'at-i-Islami.

Maulānā Maudūdī's formulation of an Islamic ideology incorporated modern ideas and values and was, as Nasr argued, "a hybrid ideological perspective."[120] There is no doubt to assume that Maulānā Nadwī's association with the Jamā'at-i-Islam of which he was the founding member presented him with ideological challenges. Apart from Maulānā Maudūdī's theory of Ḥākimiyyah (sovereignty) Maulānā Nadwī's critique of the Jamā'at-i-Islami was based on the following reasons:

Firstly, the "persona" of Maulānā Maudūdī[121] was considered above criticism by members of the Jamā'at. His writings were widely regarded as definitive for an authentic interpretation of Islam. Hence, the reformatory endeavours

→ coined have become widely used in contemporary Islamic literature. He has been followed, studied, quoted and criticised. For example, the impact of Maulānā Maudūdī's thought can be seen in the works of Sayyid Quṭb and his brother Muhammad. Fathi Osman, "Maudūdī's Contribution to the Development of Modern Islamic Thinking in the Arabic-speaking world", in *The Muslim World,* vol. 93, 480.

119. The contribution of Maulānā Mas'ud 'Ālam to promoting Maulānā Maudūdī's writings in the Arab world may be mentioned. See SAHA Nadwī, *Purān-i-Chirāgh,* vol. 1, 345.

120. Seyyed Vali Reza Nasr, *The Vanguard of the Islamic Revolution,* 8.

121. In a similar vein, Nadwī lamented the fact that the party (Jamā'at-i-Islami) "[should] exhibit, on the part of its members and supporters such hyper-sensitiveness against criticism or objections of others to their creating a halo of sanctity round the founder of the party." SAHA Nadwī, *Appreciation and Interpretation of Religion in the Modern Age,* 28.

of scholars and *'ulamā* were considered inconsequential.[122] Secondly, an alarming sign of Maulānā Maudūdī's "liberal outlook" was the trenchant and often hostile critique of *'ulamā* and Islamic institutions[123] drawn from epoch-making periods of Islamic history. Lastly, the absence of spirituality was glaring in Maulānā Maudūdī's writings. Sūfī-oriented Islam[124] was an anathema for Maulānā Maudūdī — a view in sharp contrast to Maulānā Nadwī's articulation in his multi-volume *Saviours of Islamic Spirit*.[125] However, Maulānā Nadwī's disassociation with Jamā'at-i-Islami did not stop him from maintaining a cordial relationship[126] with Maulānā Maudūdī. His "shift of allegiance" although not publicly announced was in marked contrast to other erstwhile members of the Jamā'at[127] who were scathing in their criticism of Maulānā Maudūdī.

---

122. SAHA Nadwī, *Kārwān-I-Ẓindagī*, vol. 1, 244.

123. Ibid.

124. Cf. S.A.A. Maudūdī, *A Short History of the Revivalist Movement in Islam*, 105-6. Maulānā Maudūdī's trenchant criticism of *taṣawwuf* was toned down after his retirement from the Jama'āt-i-Islami, According to Nasr, Maudūdī endorsed the Sūfī concept of *tazkiyah-i-nafs* (purification of the soul) and initiated several members into Sūfīsm by the authenticity of his Chistī lineage. See Seyyed Vali Reza Nasr, *Maudūdī and the Making of Islamic Revivalism.*

125. Faruqi's comment of the *Saviours of Islamic Spirit* reflects Nadwī's role of the *'ulamā* in the *tajdīd* process. He says:

    "[*Saviours*] provides an alternative view of looking at Islamic history as a history of *'ulamā* and intellectuals instead of as a chronicle of sultans and regimes, some noble and some horrible. Depending on their respective circumstances some of the *'ulamā* even took part in or even led *jihād*, others concentrated on winning the hearts and some of people," M.H. Faruqui, "Abul Hasan Ali Nadwī" in *The Fragrance of East*, January-June 2000, 130.

126. Cf. SAHA Nadwī, *Purān-i-Chirāgh*, vol. 2, 312-18.

127. Manzur Nu'māni stood out as a staunch critic of Maudūdī and his tirade against the former was based on his breach of the *shari'ah*. See Reza Seyyed Vali Nasr, *The Vanguard of the Islamic Revolution*, 25-26.

The opposing views between Maulānā Maudūdī and Maulānā Nadwī expressed their respective orientations to *tajdīd*. Maulānā Maudūdī formulated his Islamic resurgence theorisation in the light of his wide reading of Western writings on philosophy, science, etc. Maulānā Nadwī on the other hand drew his understanding on Islamic resurgence from traditional sources of Islam and selectively augmented them with contemporaneous writings (which included Maulānā Maudūdī) to articulate his *tajdīdī* paradigm. If Maulānā Maudūdī expressed an anti-*'ulamā* position, Maulānā Nadwī in contrast advocated the importance of traditional scholarship.[128] This conflictual relationship was unavoidable in view of their different ideological backgrounds.

VIEWS ON MAULĀNĀ MAUDŪDĪ'S CONTRIBUTION TO THE ISLAMIC RESURGENCE

Of much relevance to a critique of Maulānā Maudūdī's writings are the works of Maryam Jameelah (b. 1934).[129] An ardent admirer of Maulānā Maudūdī[130] who played a major role in her conversion to Islam, Jameelah presents a traditionalist interpretation of Islam and a polemical response to the West.[131] Even Maulānā Nadwī admired her critique of

128. Nadwī was an ardent admirer of *'ulamā* with a traditional background. His biography on his spiritual guide, Maulānā 'Abdul Qādir Raipūri reinforces this view. See SAHA Nadwī, *Sawānih Hadhrat Maulānā Abdul Qadir Raipuri,* Lahore: Maktaba Rashidiya, 1977.

129. On Maryam Jameelah, see J.L. Esposito, vol. 1, JO, *Makers of Contemporary Islam,* 54-67.

130. The following books reveal Maulānā Maudūdī's profound influence on Jameelah's literary career:

 - *Who is Maudūdī,* Lahore, 1970.
 - Correspondence between Maulana Maudūdī and Maryam Jameelah, Lahore, 1973.
 - *Islam in Theory and Practice,* Lahore, 1976, 260-385.

131. Esposito, *Makers of Contemporary Islam,* 58.

the West in particular her *Islam versus Ahl-al Kitab: Past and Present.*[132] Jameelah's *Islam and Modernism*[133] is a critique of many intellectuals, including *'ulamā* associated with Muslim modernism. According to Jameelah, the pioneers of Westernisation in the Muslim world "were merely the end-product of their circumstances and more specifically, the result of an overwhelming sense of inferiority which engulfed the East after its humiliating capitulation under the feet of the imperialist West."[134]

The rhetoric associated with Jameelah's polemics against the West is also evident in several of her other writings.[135] Jameelah has been among the staunchest defenders of the *'ulamā* and is not prepared to concede the right to re-interpret Islam to modernists. However her critics argue that in her defence of the *'ulamā* she focuses on idealism rather than pragmatism.[136]

Esposito for example has remarked that Jameelah supports her indictment of the West and its concomitant decadence by "employing Islamic sources as well as Western sources very selectively, restricting herself to Western critics of the process of modernisation and its impact on religion and society."[137] The stereotypical representation of the West is prominent in Muḥammad Asad's *Islam at the Crossroads* which was written in 1930s and was widely consulted by Maulānā

---

132. Maryam Jameelah, *Islam versus Ahl-al-Kitab, Past and Present*, Lucknow: Academy of Islamic Research and Publications, 1983; cf. SAHA Nadwī, *Kārwān-i-Ẓindagī*, vol. 2, 269.

133. Maryam Jameelah, *Islam and Modernism*, Lahore, 1971.

134. Ibid., 153.

135. A notable example is *Islam and Western Society*, New Delhi: Adam Publishers, 1982.

136. Muḥammad Manzoor Alam, *100 Great Muslim Leaders of the 20th Century*, New Delhi: Institute of Objective Studies, 2005, 277-78.

137. Esposito, *Makers of Contemporary Islam*, 63.

Maudūdī, Maulānā Nadwī and Jameelah for their respective critiques of Western civilisation.

Jameelah's ardent admiration for Maulānā Maudūdī as a *mujaddid* of the present day[138] is in marked contrast to her later criticism of his modernisation tendencies. In her article, "Modern Ideas and Concepts in the Works of Maulānā Sayyid Abul A'la Maulānā Maudūdī", Jameelah criticises Maulānā Maudūdī for condemning Muslim conservatism and promoting modernisation as a vehicle to change the trends of world events.[139] According to Jameelah, Maulānā Maudūdī "expresses his faith in evolutionism and progressivism and contempt for tradition."[140]

The element of "ambiguity and ambivalence," to coin a phrase, recurs in Maulānā Maudūdī and Jameelah's writings. A critique of the West, as it appears in their writings, does not reflect a consistent standpoint. Their vagueness in presenting a systematic and coherent response to the West is much evident.

Likewise, Maulānā Nadwī's ambivalence towards the West is clearly shown in two important writings, *Muslims in the West*[141] and *Islam and the West*.[142] Maulānā Nadwī refers to the synthesis of science and technology rooted in spirituality which would have promoted "co-operative endeavour between different nations instead of generating the spirit of contest, collision

138. Maryam Jameelah, *Who is Maudoodi*: Lahore, Yusuf Khan Publishers, n.d.

139. Maryam Jameelah, "Modern Ideas and Concepts in the Works of Maulana Sayyid Abul A'la Maudūdī", in *Islamic Studies*, vol. 42, no. 2, 348-49.

140. Ibid., 350.

141. SAHA Nadwī, *Muslims in the West: The Message and Mission*, Leicester: The Islamic Foundation, 1983.

142. SAHA Nadwī, *Islam and the West*, Lucknow: Academy of Islamic Research and Publications, 1983.

and conflict." The pragmatism is also expressed by Maulānā Nadwī in his interaction with the significant "other" — the Hindu majority in India in his formulation of an Islamic order.[143]

Opposition to Maulānā Maudūdī's writings and the Jamā'at-i-Islami was largely by Deobandi *'ulamā*. The appellation Maudūdīyat was a diatribe against his interpretation of Islamic beliefs and teachings. Also the sectarian bias of Deoband *'ulamā* can be gleaned from their scathing criticism of Maulānā Maudūdī. For example, *Maudūdī, Akābir-i-ummat ki nazar me*[144] is a compilation of opinions and critique on Maulānā Maudūdī's "deviant" beliefs. The book also attempts to expose the baseless claims of Jamā'at-i-Islami which is considered a modern version of the earliest sects[145] in Islam. Compare the incisive analysis by Israr Aḥmad in *Tahrik-i-Jamā'at Islami*[146] which offers a balanced historical account of Maulānā Maudūdī and the Islamic movement. While praising the Islamic credentials of the movement in its initial stages, he laments the politicised agenda[147] followed by Maulānā Maudūdī and the Jamā'at-i-Islami in promoting Islam as a *dīn* (way of life).

Against this background, Maulānā Nadwī's balanced approach to Maulānā Maudūdī's contribution to contemporary Islamic thought is expressed in the following words:

> Maulānā Maudoodi (Maulānā Maudūdī) has not followed the apologetic and defensive style of Sir Syed Aḥmad Khan

143. SAHA Nadwī, *Islam and the West*, Lucknow: Academy of Islamic Research and Publications, 1983, 12.

144. Hakim Muḥammad Akhtar, *Maudūdī, Akābir-i-ummat ki nazar me*, Lahore: Maktaba al-Qāsim, n.d.

145. Ibid.

146. Isrār Aḥmad, *Tahrik Jamā'at-i-Islami: Ek Tahqiqi Mutāla*, Lahore: Markazi Maktaba Tanzim-i-Islami, 1983.

147. Ibid., 150-77.

> . . . but boldly attacked the very foundations of the Western cultural and intellectual edifice in the manner of Muḥammad Asad and the other writers of the same group, and presented the teachings of Islam with greater confidence and in a positive and convincing style.[148]

This statement does not reflect Maulānā Nadwī's total agreement with other views; however it does indicate that Maulānā Maudūdī had considerable influence on Maulānā Nadwī's earlier years particularly during the latter's theorisation of *tajdīd.* Maulānā Nadwī's interaction with scholars from the Arab world advanced his understanding of *tajdīd* in significant ways. His association with the Ikhwān introduced him to the writings of its ideologue, Sayyid Quṭb.

SAYYID QUṬB

This section explores important aspects of Sayyid Quṭb's formative period[149] of his intellectual career and discusses the ideas and responses that were developed into his later writings and which had a major impact on Muslim movements across the world.

Quṭb (d. 1966) was born in the village of Musha in the province of Asyut, Egypt. His early education was completed at a *kuttāb* (traditional school)[150] and thereafter he pursued modern education at the Dār-ul-'ulūm, Cairo. He was there from 1925 until 1929. This period provided him with a sound

---

148. SAHA Nadwī, *Western Civilisation, Islam and Muslim,* 90-91.

149. The principal sources used for information on the life of Sayyid Quṭb are: Muhammad Tawfiq Barakat, *Sayyid Quṭb,* Beirut: Dār-al Da'wah, n.d.; A.A. Musallam, *The Formative Stages of Sayid Quṭb's Intellectual career and his Emergence as an Islamic Dā'i,* 1906-52, Ph.D Thesis on University of Michigan, 1983; Sayed Khatab, *The Political Thought of Sayyid Quṭb: The Theory of Jahiliyyah,* London: Routledge, 2006.

150. Sayed Khatab, *The Political Thought of Sayyid Quṭb,* 44-45.

education in applied science, humanities as well as Arabic and Islamic studies. His interest in modern science remained with him throughout his life. In his important writings, Quṭb provided an incisive analysis of modern science and its impact on modern civilisation. However, he did not reject modern science as such but identified the critical problem of civilisation detached from God and a loss of spirituality.[151] This theme is largely drawn from the distinguished scientist Dr Alexis Carrel's voluminous book *Man, The Unknown.*[152]

Quṭb's literary output[153] during this period (1930s) was a true reflection of his state of mind and search for spiritual fulfilment. Later, his literary works showed an intellectual maturity and spiritual inclination with special reference to his studies of the Qur'ān. Quṭb developed an aesthetic theory of the Qur'ān (*taṣawwur*).[154] The book, *al-Taswir al-fanni fi-al-Qur'ān*[155] (*Artistic Representation in the Qur'ān*) completed in 1944 resonates with the theme of the Islamic conception of life (*al-taṣawwur-al-Islami li-l-hayāh*). According to Quṭb, the whole of the Qur'ān is "marvellously integrated by a remarkable

151. Sayed Khatab, *The Political Thought of Sayyid Quṭb,* 44-45.

152. Details are found in Quṭb's *Islam, the Religion of the Future,* IIFSO, n.d., 79-88.

153. Adnan A. Musallam, "Prelude to Islamic Commitment: Sayyid Quṭb's Literary and Spiritual Orientaiton, 1932-1938" in *The Muslim World,* 1982, 132-46. Cf. SAHA Nadwī, *Mudhākarāt sa'ih fi al Sharq al-'Arabi,* Beirut: Mu'assasat al-Risalah, 1975, 69-96.

154. For an analysis on the Qur'ānic (aesthetics) developed by Quṭb, see Leonard Binder, *Islamic Liberalism,* 188-94. In summing up his perspectives, Quṭb writes: "Taṣwīr is the instrument of preference for the Qur'ānic method. Taṣwīr expresses intellectual meanings and mental states by means of sensuous and imaginative depiction; and, by the same token the Qur'ān expresses the experiences of events, and the perception of spectacles," p. 193.

155. Sayyid Quṭb, *Al-taṣwir al-fanni fi-al-Qur'ān,* Cairo, Dar-al Shuruq, 1995.

singleness of purpose and method."[156] This conception of life is associated with the term *dīn* which played a pivotal role in his theorisation of Jāhiliyyah.

According to Quṭb, the Qur'ān's relationship to literature (*adab*) is unambiguous: the Qur'ānic text "offers life with its motion, not description of life."[157] Quṭb emphasised that the Qur'ān came to establish a comprehensive creed — *tawḥīd.*[158] The *taṣawwur* (aesthetics) are repeated in the Qur'ān to reinforce the portrayal of *tawḥīd.* Islamic literature draws its inspiration from *tawḥīd* and its fundamental objective should be the strengthening of this *tawḥīd-consciousness.*[159]

Quṭb and Maulānā Nadwī's shared view on *tawḥīd* provides two interesting perspectives on this doctrine. According to Quṭb *tawḥīd* is the anathema to all systems — political and social, that are *jāhilī* in content. This approach was a prelude to the confrontational politics that would characterise his call for an Islamic state in Egypt. For Maulānā Nadwī, *tawḥīd* represented a distinct Muslim community in the Indian subcontinent striving towards a corporate Islamic identity against the background of a Hindu majority embracing polytheistic practices.

In an insightful article, "Towards an Islamic Theory of Literature"[160] Shukri has succinctly discussed the relationship between Islamic literary tradition and the revival of Islamic thought. In his view, Quṭb and Maulānā Nadwī may be

---

156. Cited in Leonard Binder, *Islamic Liberalism,* 191.

157. Sayyid Quṭb, *Al-taswir,* 36.

158. Sayed Khatab, *The Political Thought of Sayyid Quṭb,* 84.

159. Seyyed Ali Ashraf, "Literary Education and Religious Value: The Islamic Approach" in *Muslim Educational Quarterly,* vol. I, no. 4, 54-56.

160. M.A.M. Shukri, "Towards an Islamic Theory of Literature in Islamic Studies" in *Islamic Studies,* 31:4, 411-21.

considered pioneers[161] in the field of Islamic Literary Theory. Both these scholars have formulated the parameters of literature based on Islamic aesthetics[162] and their writings are anchored in the *iṣlāḥ* and *tajdīd* tradition. Of particular relevance are the works of Quṭb that deal with his theorisation of Islam as a *dīn* and its implications in the Islamic resurgence paradigm.

SOCIAL JUSTICE IN ISLAM

Before we attempt to discuss Maulānā Nadwī's relationship with Quṭb, it is important to refer to Quṭb's *Social Justice in Islam*[163] written in 1948. The context of this book is important to evaluate Quṭb's other writings which speak of an Islamic order. The text of *Social Justice in Islam* was also developed before Quṭb's departure to United States during the period 1948-50.

161. Quṭb oulined the general features of the Islamic literary theory in his *al-Tarikh Fikratun wa Minhajun* which Nadwī gave an exposition of his thought in the introduction of his book, *Mukhtārāt min adab al-'Arab.* Cf. Wādih Nadwī's, *Towards an Islamic Theory of Literature,* 413-14, See Muḥammad Wādih Rashid Nadwī, *Al-Mashat al Adabiyyah,* Lucknow: Rabita al adab al Islami al-Alamiyyah, 2004.

162. Cf. Sayed Khatab, *The Political Thought of Sayyid Quṭb,* 92-115; Muḥammad Rābey Nadwī, *Kārwān-i-adab,* 2001-2, vol. 8, 149-202.

163. Sayyid Quṭb, *Social Justice in Islam,* tr. John B. Hardie, New York: Islamic Publications, International, 2000. The Arabic version, *Al-'Adalah al-ijtima'iyyah fi'l-Islam.* The translation has been revised and includes a useful introduction by Hamid Algar. *Social Justice* has seen seven editions in Arabic. William Shephard maintains the changes in this important work reflect the radical Islamist that Quṭb espoused and by the ideological influences of Maudūdī. Cited in *Social Justice in Islam,* 17. The work "allows us to follow the changes in Sayyid Quṭb's views over a period of sixteen years, comprising not only whole period of his Islamic activism but also a compact period for the incubation, of some of the most trends in the Islamic world today." William E. Shephard, , *Sayyid Quṭb and Islamic Activism: A Translation and Critical Analysis of Social Justice in Islam,* Leiden: EJ Brill, 1996.

Quṭb's stay in the United States[164] was aimed at studying the educational system for which he was sent by the Egyptian Ministry of Education. This was also a productive phase in Quṭb's intellectual career to formulate his critique on Western civilisation.[165] As early as the 1940s Quṭb was critical of Egypt's cultural surrender to the West. Abu Rabiʻ contends that Quṭb's notion of Islamic order was incorporated in *Social Justice in Islam* and derived a "new intellectual synthesis."[166] According to Khatab, Quṭb presented Islam as a "worldwide" and ideal system of life. "Islam has one universal theory that covers the universe, life and humanity."[167]

For Quṭb the Islamic socio-political system "can keep up with the times and conditions while preserving its spirit and general principles and assuring the achievements of a sound, virtuous, strong and growing life."[168]

A contemporary response to Quṭb's *Social Justice in Islam* is Aḥmad Moussalli's critique.[169] He also maintains that Quṭb's visit to the United States had a great impact on his formulation of an Islamic society. Islam provided the alternative as a "superior creed and ideology." He furthermore felt that Islamic revival was necessary and that the West entertained a deep hatred of Islam. Therefore

---

164. Abu Rabiʻ has ably stated that *Social Justice in Islam* "should be viewed as a critical commentary on the social, economic, cultural and educational conditions and policies of the Egyptian State in the interwar period." Ibrahim Abu-Rabiʻ, *Intellectual Origins of Islamic Resurgence in the Modern Arab World*, 108.

165. Sayed Khatab, *The Political Thought of Sayyid Quṭb*, 145.

166. Ibid., 114.

167. Cited in Sayed Khatab, *The Political Thought of Sayyid Quṭb*, 116.

168. Ibid.

169. Aḥmad Moussalli, *Moderate and Radical Islamic Fundamentalism*, Gainesville: University Press of Florida, 1999.

Western civilisation could not be used as a basis for a moral and political regeneration of Islam.[170]

Salwa Ismail expresses a similar view like Moussalli with regard to Islamists for whom Quṭb is considered to be the ideologue of the movement. According to Ismail the confrontation with the West is articulated in terms of opposing systems of values which are expressed within two notional indexes. The first index is comprehensive and unitary for Quṭb and it represents Islam. The second index is associated with change and progress and is represented by the West.[171] The second index negates the values of justice and equality as argued by Quṭb in his *Social Justice in Islam.* Thus the discourse of fundamentalism and modernity has provoked ideological tension between Islamists and their critics on important issues relating to Islamic resurgence.

MAULĀNĀ NADWĪ AND QUṬB: RECIPROCAL INFLUENCES

Sayyed Khatab has described Maulānā Nadwī's meeting with Quṭb in Hijaz (Saudi Arabia) as significant: it was as indicated by Maulānā Nadwī, a conference of "information exchange" about the condition of the Muslim *ummah.*[172]

It was during this meeting that Quṭb presented Maulānā Nadwī with *Social Justice in Islam.* Maulānā Nadwī says:

> It was a great honour for me, that is, to be gifted by his book, *Social Justice in Islam.* In this holy place I concentrated on reading this book in this peaceful and pleasant atmosphere. I have found in the book a new style of writing of research and exposition

170. Aḥmad Moussalli, *Moderate and Radical Islamic Fundamentalism,* Gainesville: University Press of Florida, 1999, 132-54.

171. Salwa Ismail, "Confronting the Other: Identity, Culture, Politics and Conservative Islamism in Egypt", in *International Journal of Middle Eastern Studies,* 30 (1998), 206.

172. Sayed Khatab, *The Political Thought of Sayyid Quṭb: The Theory of Jahiliyyah,* Abingdore: Routledge, 2006.

> that I have not found in the writings of the Islamist writers in general and the writings of the Arabs, in particular.[173]

Maulānā Nadwī's book *Islam and the World* published in early 1950 was read by Quṭb. As Maulānā Nadwī noted, "[it] was a meeting I would never forget. I felt that he (Quṭb) spoke to me openly as he had read my book which interested him and appeared to be closer to his soul and spirit and in harmony with his style and ideas."[174] However, this affinity does not suggest a total agreement of ideas in respect of the characteristics of Islamic resurgence. The differences of views are examined in Chapter 4.

The intellectual affinity between Quṭb and Maulānā Nadwī can be gleaned from their respective works. Maulānā Nadwī's admiration of Quṭb's call for Islam's comprehensiveness (*al-shumuliyyah*)[175] in his *Social Justice in Islam* also resonated in the Quṭb's Introduction[176] to his *Islam and the World.* The reciprocal and shared vision drew them closer in both spirit and ideas. Quṭb's role as the ideologue to the Ikhwān which he joined after return from the United States in 1950 was a turning point in the movement's *da'wah* programme and unequivocal demand for an Islamic order in Egypt.[177]

The influence of Maulānā Nadwī's writings was also evident in Quṭb's *magnum opus, Fī-Zilāl-al-Qur'ān*[178] (*Shades of the*

---

173. Sayed Khatab, *The Political Thought of Sayyid Quṭb: The Theory of Jahiliyyah*, Abingdore: Routledge, 2006.

174. Ibid.

175. Ibid., 153.

176. SAHA Nadwī, *Islam and the World*, Lucknow: Academy of Islamic Research and Publications, 1973, 1-7.

177. For preliminary remarks on Quṭb's vision of an Islamic order, see Sayed Khatab, *The Power of Sovereignty : The Political and Ideological Philosophy of Sayyid Quṭb*, Abingdon: Routledge, 2006, 39-40.

178. Quṭb cites Nadwī's assessment of idolatory and human dignity →

Qur'an). According to Oliver Carre, *Fī-Zilāl-al-Qur'ān* is an icon text not only for Islamists across the Arab world but its popularity in South Asia is attributed to the declared influences of two Indo-Pakistan thinkers, Maulānā Maudūdī and Maulānā Nadwī.[179] Manazir Ahsan observes that Quṭb's *tafsīr* is "an effort to reflect on the dynamic and revolutionary message of the Qur'an in its comprehensive sense and invite not only Muslims but of all of humanity to come and enjoy the shade and blessings of the Qur'ān."[180]

Fī-Zilāl-al-Qur'ān was written during Quṭb's prolonged term of imprisonment (1954-64). Maulānā Nadwī's admiration for Quṭb couched in literary elegance also reveals his antipathy towards the Nasserist regime[181] responsibe for Quṭb's execution in 1966. Maulānā Nadwī says:

> I am confident Sayyid Quṭb's imprints (*āthār*) will continue. In this regard people will focus their attention on his works which form his intellectual legacy. [These works] will be elaborated by those who seek to perpetuate his name and contributions. I believe the glad tidings of *ḥayāt* (living) conferred on a martyr (*shahīd*) by Allah is comprehensive. These are people who embrace death and Allah allots for them their span of life and eradicates all traces of their adversaries. Allah decides the extent

---

→ from the latter's *Islam and the World*, 29-31. See Sayyid Quṭb, *In the Shade of the Qur'ān*, vol. 2, Leicester: The Islamic Foundation, 2000.

179. Olivier Carre, *Mysticism and Politics: A Critical Recording of Fī-Zilāl-al-Qur'ān* by Sayyid Quṭb 1906-1966, Leiden: Brill, 2000, 13. For Nadwī's influence on Quṭb's *Fī-Zilāl* see Ali Rahmena, *Pioneers of Islamic Revival*, 161-63.

180. Quṭb, *In the Shade of the Qur'an*, vol. 1, viii. Cf. Badmas Yusuf, "A History of Fī-Zilāli al-Qur'ān", in *Hamdard Islamicus*, vol. XXV, no. 2, 17-27.

181. Nadwī's critique of Nasser who is considered the forerunner of Arab nationalism is elaborated in several of his writings. See SAHA Nadwī, *Western Civilisation, Islam and Muslims*, Lucknow: Academy of Islamic Research and Publications, 1974, 112-23.

of their respect and popularity and it is Allah who enforces such decisions.[182]

The 1950s was a crucial period in Maulānā Nadwī's intellectual career: his association with the Ikhwān coincided with his affiliation to the Tabligh Jamā'at as in the 1940s. Two resurgent movements nurtured in two different countries had a decisive influence on Maulānā Nadwī's. The following section explores the role of the Tabligh Jamā'at among the resurgent movements and Maulānā Nadwī's contribution to the movement.

Tabligh Jamā'at as a Resurgent Movement

The Tabligh Jamā'at[183] (hereafter TJ) as a transnational movement[184] is probably most widespread in the world today. Like any other social movement, the TJ has undergone a process of evolution over time. A recent study by Yoginder Sikand in *The Origins and Development of the Tablīghi Jamā'at (1920-2000)* has referred to the TJ as the single largest and one of the most influential Islamic movements of contemporary times.[185] The term transnationalism is used to describe the TJ operating in a nation-state framework. This implies that the TJ has adopted transnational travel and physical movement as a means of *da'wah*.[186] Travel in a *tablīghi* discourse refers to a *hijrah* (migration): "it is a migration from corruption to purity,

182. SAHA Nadwī, *Purān-i-Chirāgh*, vol. 3, 37-38.

183. The following works deal with the growth and development of the Tabligh Jamā'at and may be regarded as primary sources to understand the movement. Abul Hasan 'Ali Nadwī, *Hadhrat Maulānā 'Ilyās aur unki Dīni Da'wat*, Karachi: Majlis Nashriyāt-i-Islam, 1985; Muḥammad Manzur Nu'mani (ed.), *Da'wat Tablīgh*, Lahore: Maktaba Zakariyya, n.d.; M. Anwaral Haq, *The Faith Movement of Mawlana Muḥammad Ilyās*, London: George Allen, 1972.

184. Muhamad Khalid Masud, *Travellers in Faith*, Leiden: Brill, 2000, xv.

185. Yoginder Sikand, *The Origins and Development of the Tablīghi Jamā'at*, New Delhi: Orient Longman, 2002, 252.

186. Masud, *Travellers in Faith*, xvi.

withdrawing from worldly attachments to the Path of God."[187] The dichotomy of *dunyā* (worldly pursuits) and *dīn* (religious concerns) is a favourite theme of the TJ and it is the special characteristic that has attracted millions of adherents across the globe.

Transnationalism for the TJ has no political connotation.[188] This is evident from its apolitical agenda, although Sikand has argued that the TJ had envisaged an Islamic society in its initial stages.[189] This aspect may best be understood within the context of political developments in twentieth-century India. Its founder Maulānā Ilyās believed that religious leadership was not trained for politics. According to Maulānā Nadwī, "Maulānā (Ilyās), the founder of the TJ, had a fixed idea, rather the essence of Islamic history in his mind was that the *'ulamā* had lost the ability to deal with political matters since they had possessed no political power for centuries."[190] Khalid Masud argues that the TJ activities were political because it made "Muslims conscious of their separate identity and aware of their social obligations from a religious perspective [which] ultimately serves a political purpose."[191]

The TJ's focus on a separate Muslim identity bears similar resemblance to Maulānā Nadwī's advocacy of a corporate

187. Masud, *Travellers in Faith,* xvi.

188. Ibid., xv.

189. Sikand, *The Origin and Development*, 268-70. This assessment is further elaborated by Sikand: The different political roles thus the TJ has played have been determined essentially by the needs of survival and expansion of the movement and the importance to carry forward the movement's agenda for promoting Islamic teachings. Yoginder Sikand, "The Tablīghi Jama'at and Politics: A Critical Reappraisal" in *The Muslim World*, vol. 96, January 2006, 192.

190. Cited in Muḥammad Khalid Masud (ed.), *Travellers in Faith*, 97.

191. Ibid., 99.

Muslim identity (*tashakhkhus*). However the TJ's discourse on this concept differs significantly with Maulānā Nadwī's theorisation on the possibilities of engaging non-Muslims in changed socio-political situations. The latter concept was developed in response to post-Partition developments in the Indian subcontinent.

The *iṣlāḥi* tradition in the TJ is embedded in the broader perspective of social reformism.[192] Its programme of *da'wah* exclusively to the Muslims created a discourse peculiar to the TJ. The *tablīghi* literature highlighted the model character of the Prophet (SAW) and "sought to foster among their followers exact imitation of the Prophet (SAW) and his Companions."[193] This is evident in its emphasis on the detailed minutiae of Prophetic emulation which in a sense "accessorised" Islam. Such a discourse narrowed down any form of intellectual engagement in contemporary Islamic thought. Its pietistic and quietest character shows traces of *taṣawwuf* which had a direct influence on Islamic movements espousing a Deobandi reformist Islam.[194]

The TJ in its constant stress on Islamic communitarian spirit and brotherhood has opened up new channels of symbolic support and linking Muslims with the worldwide *ummah*.[195] In his evaluation of the TJ, Masud discusses the pivotal role of *iṣlāḥ* and *tajdīd* in its ideology. Like the Islamists, the TJ emphasises on this twin concept of *iṣlāḥ* and *tajdīd* albeit in a restrictive form. These terms have a specific semantic structure in a *tablīghi* discourse: a revival or restoration of the *sunnah*, i.e. the practice of the Prophet Muḥammad (SAW) and his

192. Reetz, *Islam in the Public Sphere*, 164.

193. Ibid., 127.

194. For an elaboration on the role of the Sūfīs within a Deobandi-reformist tradition see Metcalf, *Islamic Revival in British India*, 138-97.

195. Sikand, *The Origin and Development*, 268.

companions.[196] It is precisely this vision that has provided the TJ with transnational linkages[197] to gain a measure of legitimacy among a sizeable segment of Muslims across the globe.

MAULĀNĀ NADWĪ AND TJ : AN ASSESSMENT

Maulānā Nadwī's association with the TJ took place in 1942 after he terminated his membership with the Jamā'at-i-Islami. It was a turning point in his life "when God sent me to Maulānā Ilyās."[198] His disillusionment with the Jamā'at-i-Islami which insisted on an Islamic political order in a changed landscape in the subcontinent paradoxically drew him closer to the TJ. This movement eschewed political activity and refrained from communal controversy.[199] Maulānā Nadwī saw pragmatic strategies for Muslims in India. It was largely through Maulānā Nadwī's efforts that the TJ made forays in the Hijāz (Saudi Arabia).[200]

According to Sikand, Maulānā Nadwī saw the TJ with its vast network of activists all over the country and abroad playing a pivotal role in preserving Muslim identity and spreading Islamic consciousness among the masses. It was Nadwah under the guidance of Maulānā Nadwī that took the lead to promote the TJ.[201] The first comprehensive

---

196. Masud, *Travellers in Faith*, xix.

197. The transnational character of the TJ is in marked contrast with Muslims residing in Europe with challenges of multiple identities to preserve Islam. Cf. Ralph Grillo, "Islam and Transnationalism", in *Journal of Ethnic and Migration Studies*, vol. 30, no. 5, September, 2004, 861-78.

198. Cited in *The Fragrance of East*, 121.

199. Yoginder Sikand, *Muslims in India Since 1947 : Islamic Perspectives on Interfaith Relations I*, London: Routledge Curzon, 2004, 38.

200. Nadwī, *Kārwān-i-Ẓindagī*, vol. 1, 326-41.

201. Sikand, *Muslims in India Since 1947*, 39.

biography on its founder Maulānā Ilyās[202] was written by Maulānā Nadwī. Although Maulānā Nadwī remained associated with the TJ till the end, his pragmatism made him realise the need for interfaith dialogue with his largely dominated Hindu counterparts. The *Payām-i-Insāniyat* (Message for Humanity)[203] as he saw it pointed to the most appropriate way in which Muslims could join hands with others in building the country[204] for their lives were inextricably linked with the others. The shift of allegiance by Maulānā Nadwī reflected his pragmatism to changing realities that affected the Muslim community in the country. Maulānā Maudūdī's interpretation of Islamic resurgence with emphasis on an Islamic state was impractical to Maulānā Nadwī's espousal of an Islamic order for a Muslim minority rooted in an Indian soil. Likewise, his exposure to the Arab resurgent movements like the Ikhwān and an array of intellectuals and scholars sharpened his vision of *da'wah* beyond the confines of the TJ of which he was an active supporter. This new approach enabled him to establish his *Payām-i-Insāniyat* reaching out to a wider audience of Muslims and non-Muslims sharing common concerns on India's destiny. In fact, the *Payām*, enhanced Maulānā Nadwī's *da'wah* vision in sharp contrast to the TJ's restrictive *da'wah* programme.

The sense of pragmatism adopted by Maulānā Nadwī has subtle connotations. His dissociation with the Jamā'at-i-Islami came to light in 1978 when he wrote his *Appreciation and*

202. SAHA Nadwī, *Life and Mission of Mawlana Mohammad Ilyās*, Lucknow: Academy of Islamic Research and Publications, 1979.

203. For a detailed account on the *Payām-i-Insāniyat*, see Nadwī, *Kārwān-i-Ẓindagī*, vol. 2, 109-27. It is interesting to note that the *Payām* had not registered offices and revolved around the charisma of Nadwī. It had enjoyed limited success; however it has spawned other organisations sharing similar ideals.

204. This vision is elaborated by Nadwī in his monograph, *Reconstruction of Indian Society*, Lucknow, n.d.

Interpretation of Religion in the Modern Age.[205] Similarly, Maulānā Nadwī was provoked to declare at a large *tablīghi* gathering at Aurangabad in 1998 that it was regrettable that the TJ had restricted its sphere of activity to just the six principles propagated by the movement.[206] Maulānā Nadwī's re-appraisal of the TJ is echoed by two of his contemporaries, Maulānā Maudūdī and Maulānā Wahiduddin Khan. Maulānā Maudūdī, an erstwhile admirer of the TJ wrote an account[207] of his trip to a *tablīghi* meeting praising Ilyās' work and his efforts to revive Islam to create an Islamic society in India. Later he was to be the TJ's harshest critic as he saw the movement's "preoccupation with purely religious concerns."[208] Also active in the TJ for some years and appreciating its "Islamisation" of individual Muslims,[209] Khan gradually became disillusioned with it too and by 1975 had completely disassociated himself from it. Sikand noted that Khan saw the movement's hostility to *ijtihād* and aversion to critical thinking as a "betrayal of the Islamic imperative itself."[210]

---

205. The book provides a detailed critique on Maulānā Maudūdī's *Four Basic Qur'ānic Terms* which apart from its political overtones discusses on the sovereignty of God. This concept is discussed in detail in Chapter 2.

206. Sikand, *The Origins and Development,* 104.

207. Cited in *Tarjumān-al-Qur'ān*, Lahore, 1939.

208. Nasr, *The Vanguard of the Islamic Revolution,* 16, Cf. Sikand, *The Origins and Development,* 96-102. The rigid ritualistic observances and *dīn-duniyā* refrain are among some of the criticisms against the TJ.

209. Wahiduddin Khan, *Tablīgh Movement*, New Delhi: The Islamic Centre, 1986. Like Maulānā Maudūdī's account, the monograph contains personal reminiscences of the TJ. Generally there is no evidence to interrogate critically the textual sources or evaluate its ideological content. The tendency to provide narratives embellished with hagiography is evident in some of the sources on the TJ.

210. Sikand, *Muslims in India Since 1947,* 51.

Conclusion

Islamic authenticity draws a parallel with cultural memory in terms of the past having an unbroken link with the present. Maulānā Nadwī and his contemporaries are a case in point of the dynamics of change embedded in Islamic resurgence. It also shows the contested claims to "Islamicity"[211] among various Islamic groups and scholars about the monolithic character of Islam as a "fixed well-defined body of beliefs, principles and practices." This rigidity is in direct contrast to the idea that reformation and critical evaluation are salient features in Islamic thought. The *'ulamā*, *salafi*s, Islamists and Islamic movements like the TJ share a reformist vision invariably with conflicting approaches and methodologies. This perhaps explains the divergence of views in the Islamic resurgent movements which do not always articulate the vision of an Islamic state. Politics tend to dominate a religious discourse and this is clearly evident in Maulānā Maudūdī's theorisation of this concept. Likewise, idealisation may yield conflicting responses to the conceptualisation of a practicable Islamic society. Quṭb is representative of this trend. The TJ on the other hand pursues a pietistic Islam that strives to replicate the Prophetic model. Its reformist spirit is imbued with a literalist understanding of Islam. Yet its interpretation diverges with the *salafi*s who espouse a *ṣalf-al-ṣāliḥ* vision which is free from *taqlīd* and *taṣawwuf*, two key concepts that are interwoven in the TJ resurgent paradigm. Maulānā Nadwī's position perhaps reflects an equilibrium between two divergent positions striving for an Islamic ideal. As we have noted, there are traces of his contemporaries' and movements' influence on his theorisation of Islamic resurgence. The socio-political realities in the Indian

211. Sikand, *Origins and Development*, 89.

subcontinent had a major impact in Maulānā Nadwī's pragmatic approach that set him apart from other intellectuals pursuing the *tajdīdī* vision. This aspect is examined in subsequent chapters.

4

Towards an Islamic Order
An Evaluation of Jāhiliyyah and Ḥākimiyyah

THE development of Islamic resurgence as a political movement is closely associated with particular individuals and their intellectual contributions to it. Their ideas have reshaped public debate in the Muslim world on issues pertinent to the resurgent trends. In this regard, Maulānā Nadwī, Maulānā Maudūdī and Quṭb occupy a unique position in contemporary Muslim thought. All three scholars emerged as pre-eminent figures in the articulation of an Islamic order.[1] This term has been interchangeably used for an Islamic state or society in the study. The chapter seeks to examine two important concepts, Jāhiliyyah (ignorance)[2] and Ḥākimiyyah[3] (sovereignty) which have shaped the discourse of Islamic

1. The study does not elaborate on the various theories of an Islamic state/order. The following writings may however be consulted: Sayyed Vali Reza Nasr, *The Vanguards of the Islamic Revolution*, Berkeley: University of California Press, 1994; Leonard Binder, *Islamic Liberalism*, Chicago: The University of Chicago Press, 1988; Ishtiaq Husain Qureshi, *Ulema in Politics*, Karachi: Ma'aref Ltd., 1974.
2. Sayed Khatab, *The Political Thought of Sayyid Quṭb*, London: Routledge, 2006. This study provides useful insights into Quṭb's theory of Jāhiliyyah.
3. Sayed Khatab, *The Power of Sovereignty*, London: Routledge, 2006. The book is a coherent study of Quṭb's theory of Ḥākimiyyah and its impact on contemporary Muslim political systems.

political movements. Quṭb, Maulānā Maudūdī and Maulānā Nadwī have played pioneering roles in the propagation of these concepts. It is through the prism of these two concepts that Islamic political movements "divide the world into two camps of potential clash."[4] The statement is also examined to show how these concepts are fluid and overlapping in relation to Islamic resurgence. An important point that informs our understanding of these concepts is how individuals and Islamic movements articulate a vision of an Islamic order. The beginnings of an Islamic order have been discussed, albeit briefly in Chapter 3 to highlight its growth and development during the twentieth century.

The theories of Ḥākimiyyah and Jāhiliyyah have had major impact on movements claiming to be true representatives of the *tajdīd* tradition. The theory of Ḥākimiyyah refers to Divine rule possessing distinctive characteristics which govern the lives of Muslims. In contrast, Jāhiliyyah is associated with man's rule embodying qualities that negate the moral system envisaged by Islam. Against this background, Maulānā Nadwī's contribution to these concepts will be analysed. The impact of Jāhiliyyah is the focus of Maulānā Nadwī's major work, *Islam and the World*.[5] It is however on issues relating to Ḥākimiyyah that Maulānā Nadwī presents his view that are diametrically opposed to Quṭb and Maulānā Maudūdī's theories. In this context the divergence of views is investigated to understand Maulānā Nadwī's alternative presentation of an Islamic order. Moreover Maulānā Nadwī's theorisation of Jāhiliyyah is set against the backdrop of Indian Muslims having a minority status after the Partition of 1947. In this context, Maulānā Nadwī's formulation of *dīn* is examined in

---

4. Sayed Khatab, *The Power of Sovereignty*, London: Routledge, 2006, 2.

5. Nadwī, *Islam and the World*, Lucknow: Academy of Islamic Research and Publications, 1973.

relation to his conception of an Islamic order. These historical developments in post-Partition India have a direct bearing on the efforts of Maulānā Nadwī and his contemporaries in India to develop models of an Islamic society that operate in a political system at variance with Quṭb and Maulānā Maudūdī's Ḥākimiyyah theorisation. This aspect is investigated in the chapter in order to show the historical linkages to Maulānā Nadwī's Islamic order.

Sources of Study: Content and Context

The study on Jāhiliyyah and Ḥākimiyyah by Quṭb, Maulānā Maudūdī and Maulānā Nadwī is enunciated in several of their important writings. However the study attempts to locate primary sources of these respective authors to form a coherent understanding of their contributions to these concepts. This aspect is also discussed to evaluate Maulānā Nadwī's motivation for a different presentation of an Islamic order.

The primary sources for this chapter are Quṭb's *Milestones*[6] and his Qur'ānic commentary, *Fī-Zilāl-al-Qur'ān*.[7] The significance of these works is contextualised in the evolution of his intellectual thought and relating these two concepts to the environment within which he was functioning and to which he was responding. *Milestones* is Quṭb's last work which embodies his manifesto of an Islamic society. As a strategist of Islamic resurgence Quṭb wrote this important work to define his concept of what according to him constitutes a true Islamic society — the *ṣalf-al-ṣāliḥ* paradigm. The implications of his Islamic society are clear: the present

6. Originally written in Arabic, *Ma'alam fi-al-Tariq* was translated into English. Sayyid Quṭb, *Milestones*, IIFSO, 1977.

7. Sayyid Quṭb, *Fī-Zilāl al Qur'ān*, vols. 1-6, Cairo: Dār-al-Shuruq, 1992. Several volumes have been translated into English entitled *In the Shade of the Qur'ān* by Adil Salahi, Leicester: The Islamic Foundation, 1999.

Muslim countries have degenerated into Jāhiliyyah and do not represent the Ḥākimiyyah that is integral to the ideal Islamic society based on the Prophetic model. The militant tone of the book has been scrutinised by scholars since its publication and the opinions reflect their respective ideological orientations. It is outside the purview of our study to examine the impact *Milestones* has had on Islamic movements with a *jihādi* agenda against Muslim governments which do not espouse Islam as a comprehensive way of life (*dīn*).

Maulānā Maudūdī's *Four Basic Qur'ānic Terms*[8] and *A Short History of the Revivalist Movements in Islam*[9] are considered icon-texts on Jāhiliyyah and Ḥākimiyyah. Like Quṭb, Maulānā Maudūdī's *tafsīr, Towards Understanding the Qur'ān*[10] has been written in a distinct revivalist vein. The thrust of these books is Maulānā Maudūdī's theorisation of Islamic resurgent movements in a political setting. Maulānā Maudūdī's radical departure from a traditional understanding of the term *dīn* and his conceptual framework of an Islamic order are salient features in the above works.

Likewise, Maulānā Nadwī's *Islam and the World* has been an important book for Islamic resurgent movements. The book undertakes a study of the impact of Islam on history: the role Islam has played for mankind's progress and the loss humanity has suffered by its downfall. Implicit in the study is Maulānā Nadwī's assertion that Islam possesses the perennial sources, Qur'ān and *sunnah*, to provide impetus on the material and spiritual progress of humanity. Maulānā

8. S.A.A. Maudūdī, *Four Basic Qur'ānic Terms*, Delhi, 1980. The Urdu version is entitled, *Qur'ān ki char buniyādī istilāhen*, Delhi, 1978.

9. Maudūdī, *A Short History of the Revivalist Movements in Islam*, Lahore: Islamic Publications, 1972.

10. S.A.A. Maudūdī, *Towards Understanding the Qur'ān*, vols. 1-7, tr. Zafar Ishaq Ansari, Leicester: Islamic Foundation, 1988.

Nadwī's worldview on Islamic resurgence is succinctly discussed in the book. An important work, *Appreciation and Interpretation of Religion in the Modern Age*[11] by Maulānā Nadwī is a critique on Quṭb and Maulānā Maudūdī's theories. According to Maulānā Nadwī, the motivation for this book was the apprehension that Maulānā Maudūdī's *Four Basic Qur'ānic Terms* was "giving a new direction to the religious attitude and there was a great danger that a new meaning and interpretation of religion and new set of values and new standards were likely to evolve."[12] Maulānā Nadwī sets out to show how Maulānā Maudūdī's interpretation of specific Qur'ānic terms in relation to Ḥākimiyyah is likely to have a radical impact on the traditional understanding of these terms.

The above works serve as a reference point to understanding the variant expressions of Jāhiliyyah and Ḥākimiyyah. These twin concepts form the core of *tajdīdī* discourse and have influenced Islamist movements pursuing goals of an Islamic order. As we noted in the previous chapters, Islamic resurgent movements' visions tend to overlap with the above concepts and therefore require a detailed assessment.

The overlapping of ideas among these scholars does not in any way reflect a consensus of viewpoints as the study will show. This is largely based on their different scholarly backgrounds and intellectual orientations.

Jāhiliyyah and Islam

JĀHILIYYAH : AN OVERVIEW

Etymologically, the term Jāhiliyyah comes from the Arabic

11. SAHA Nadwī, *Appreciation and Interpretation of Religion in the Modern Age*, tr. Syed Athar Husain. Written originally in Urdu: *Asr-i-hādir me dīn ki tafhīm-o-tashrīh*, Lucknow: Dar-i-Arafat, 1978.

12. Ibid., 24.

root (*jhl*). This term Jāhiliyyah is an abstract noun derived from the substantive *jahl*.[13] For many a scholar Jāhiliyyah is antithetical to knowledge of *'ilm*. Turning to the Qur'ān the single and plural forms of *jahl* and *jāhil* are used as descriptive expressions Therefore adjectival expressions such as *jāhilī* people or *jāhilī* society are employed from a social or moral position.[14]

In this section we will be discussing the term Jāhiliyyah and its connotation in the Islamic tradition. In English the word Jāhiliyyah is conventionally translated as the "The Age of Ignorance." It is taken to refer to the pre-Islamic Arab society. The term is rooted in the Arabic language and expanded in several verses of the Qur'ān. Toshihiko Izutsu states in his *God and Man in the Qur'ān* that Jāhiliyyah refers to a tendency to go to the extremes.[15] Another explanation is that the word is antithetical to knowledge or *'ilm*.[16] In fact, the concept of Jāhiliyyah in pre-Islamic Arabic has several contradictory meanings due to linguistic variations.[17] In a specific context it refers to haughtiness, arrogance and insolence.[18] These definitions point out to the general characterisation of the people of Jāhiliyyah and emphasise their moral shortcomings. In Izutsu's view, these attributes of Jāhiliyyah were embedded in "the psychology of the pre-Islamic Arabs and it was but natural that the word should occur frequently in *jāhilī*-poetry."[19]

---

13. Ibn Manzur, *Lisān*, vol. 11, 130-31.
14. Ibid.
15. Toshihiko Izutsu, *God and Man in the Qur'ān: Semantics of the Qur'ānic Weltanschauung*, Kuala Lumpur: Islamic Book Trust, 2002, 220-21.
16. See Nadwī, *Islam and the World*, 29-44 for an elaboration on this concept.
17. Ibrahim Al-Samurrai, *Fi-al-lahajat al-'arabiyyah*, 112-13.
18. Izutsu, *God and Man in the Qur'ān*, 222.
19. Ibid., 223. For a detailed discussion on the *jāhili* poetry, see R.A. Nicholosn, *A Literary History of the Arabs*, Delhi: Adam Publishers, 1996.

Tribal prejudice, for example, dominated the Arab outlook in life. The tribal hierarchy was given much prominence in their interaction with others. The Quraysh, direct descendants of the prophet Ibrahim, considered themselves to be of noble stock and did not intermingle with other pilgrims during some of the *haj* rites as they were deemed inferior to them. Tribal prejudice combined with the Arabs' warlike temperament could provoke internecine wars with other tribes over trivial matters. Thus tribal conflicts served to perpetuate the culture of Jāhiliyyah in their lives.[20]

It was the Qur'ān that however standardised the concept of Jāhiliyyah. The term Jāhiliyyah appears four times in the Qur'ān with no specific reference to simple ignorance or lack of knowledge. We may refer to two examples that provide variant meanings to this concept. "Do not make a display of yourselves in the manner of the former Jāhiliyyah."[21] The social aspect of Jāhiliyyah is emphasised in this verse. The political connotation according to Quṭb is suggested in the following verse. "Do they desire to be ruled by the law of pagan ignorance (*ḥukm-al-jāhiliyyah*). But for those who are firm in their faith, who can be a better lawgiver than God?"[22] This verse is very important for Quṭb's interpretation of Jāhiliyyah. A few comments from *Fī-Zilāl al-Qur'ān* reveal Quṭb's interpretation of Jāhiliyyah and Ḥākimiyyah:

> The state of darkness (Jāhiliyyah) as used in an Islamic context does not refer to a particular period of history. Rather, it refers to a particular condition, which may be present in any period of time. . . . A judgement according to laws other than that revealed by God means evil, corruption and turning away from faith as the Qur'ān says.[23]

20. Nadwī, *Islam and the World,* 31-2.
21. Qur'ān, 33:33.
22. Qur'ān, 5:50.
23. Quṭb, *Fī-Zilāl al-Qur'ān*, vol. 4, 112-13. Cf. vol. 1, 369 where Quṭb →

Here Quṭb's formulation of Jāhiliyyah is categorical: It is a violation of Divinely sanctioned laws expounded in the Qur'ān. In this regard Maulānā Maudūdī's comment on Jāhiliyyah in this verse is also significant:

> Islam is the way of *'ilm* (true knowledge), since it is God Himself Who has shown this way, and His knowledge embraces everything. In contrast is the way that diverges from Islam — the path of Ignorance (Jāhiliyyah). . . . The appellation of Jāhiliyyah will apply to every aspect of life which is developed in disregard of the knowledge made available by God.[24]

The phrase "every aspect of life" is synonymous with *dīn* which Maulānā Maudūdī employs to advance his theory of Ḥākimiyyah.

Maulānā Nadwī's own understanding of *dīn* (as explained elsewhere in the chapter) is in marked contrast with Maulānā Maudūdī's presentation of this term.

The intellectual and more importantly the political overtones of Jāhiliyyah are clearly evident. This trend as re-examined in subsequent sections points to a reinterpretation of specific Qur'ānic verses by reformers to advance their understanding of this concept. Of course, the radicalisation of the concept by Quṭb and Maulānā Maudūdī, albeit in a less militant tone by the latter, has had a significant impact on contemporary trends influencing Islamic resurgence.

JĀHILIYYAH : IN THE WRITINGS OF THREE MAJOR SCHOLARS

The doctrine of Jāhiliyyah has distinct strands represented by Maulānā Maudūdī, Maulānā Nadwī and Quṭb. However

---

→ denounces the capitalist system as Jāhiliyyah for perpetrating economic deprivation and misery to societies and nations across the world.

24. Maudūdī, *Towards Understanding the Qur'ān*, vol. 2, 171.

Jāhiliyyah has far-reaching implications in Quṭb's writings[25] and continues to have its impact on resurgent movements across the Muslim world. William Shephard in his article, *Sayyid Quṭb's Doctrine of Jāhiliyyah*[26] states that both Maulānā Maudūdī and Maulānā Nadwī had a profound influence on Quṭb's Jāhiliyyah doctrine. This statement is analysed in the chapter to show that an oversimplification of this theory has led to this assumption. However Shephard opines that both these scholars have not applied the doctrine to the Islamic world in a radical way as Quṭb did.

JĀHILIYYAH IN MAULĀNĀ MAUDŪDĪ'S WRITINGS

Maulānā Maudūdī defines Jāhiliyyah as "every such conduct which goes against Islamic culture, morality and the Islamic way of thinking."[27] This definition is a sweeping assumption on the pervasive presence of Jāhiliyyah in Muslim societies. The negative connotations have a loaded semantic purpose by Maulānā Maudūdī: to show that the decline in the Muslim world was caused by a loss in political authority or sovereignty (Ḥākimiyyah). The phenomenon of Jāhiliyyah, Maulānā Maudūdī argues, has been present in the Muslim world after the period of the rightly-guided caliphs.

Maulānā Maudūdī diagnosed two forms of Jāhiliyyah which began "eating into the body of the community life like cancer:"

- Atheism which was associated with monarchy

25. For a comprehensive analysis of Quṭb's thought, see William Shephard, *Sayyid Quṭb and Islamic Activism: A Translation and Critical Analysis of Social Justice in Islam*, Leiden: EJ Brill, 1996; Ibrahim Abu Rabiʿ, *Intellectual Origins of Islamic Resurgence in the Modern Arab World*, Albany: Suny Press, 1996.
26. William Shephard, "Sayyid Quṭb's doctrine of Jāhiliyya" in *International Journal of Middle East Studies*, 2003: 35, 521-45.
27. Maudūdī, *The Meaning of the Qur'ān*, vol. 10, 106.

replaced the caliphate. It brought in its wake "the downpour of all admixtures of philosophy, literature and science from the Greek, Iranian and Indian skies on the Muslim soil.[28] Here the term atheism refers to *la madhabiyat*, the state of irreligiousness that Maulānā Maudūdī says swept across the Muslim countries ruled by the Abbasid caliphate. The periodisation of irreligiousness is selectively used by Maulānā Maudūdī to develop his formulation of Jāhiliyyah. The emergence of Muslim sects was patronised by these monarchies. This presupposition is elaborated in Maulānā Maudūdī's other controversial work, *Khilāfat wa Mulukiyat* (Caliphate and Monarchy) which makes harsh criticism on the monarchy established after Caliphate rule.[29] Maulānā Maudūdī's endorsement of the Caliphate as the only embodiment of the Prophetic model restricts the historical process which spawned a number of political systems which indirectly shaped the *tajdīdī* movements. Nasr has rightly remarked that "[Maulānā Maudūdī's] interpretive reading of Islam broke entirely with the traditional view to purge it of everything through which the Islamic revelation had manifested itself. Philosophy, literature, the arts, mysticism were all derided by Maulānā Maudūdī as a syncretic and impure adulteration of the Islamic faith."[30] This reaction rested largely with Maulānā Maudūdī's formulation of an Islamic resurgent movement where sovereignty of God determines human activity and conduct in Islam.

- Polytheism (*shirk*) made incursions in the lives of

28. Maudūdī, *A Short History*, 28.
29. See Nasr, *Maudūdī and the Making of Islamic Revivalism*, 116-19.
30. Ibid., 59.

ordinary people who began to perform un-Islamic rituals like saint-worship. These syncretic practices were implicitly endorsed by world-seeking *'ulamā* with the result that pristine Islam was hardly distinguishable from polytheistic practices.[31] Monasticism, in Maulānā Maudūdī's view, as an "anti-social creed" retarded the progress of Islamic arts and sciences "by narrowing down (the) outlook, and restricted the whole religious life to a few special rituals and ceremonies only."[32] These statements create the impression that Islam was engulfed by un-Islamic practices which offered bleak prospects of an Islamic revival.

For most of what we know as *taṣawwuf,* Maulānā Maudūdī's comments reflect a puritanical approach to this esoteric dimension of Islam. There is very little of the *fascinans* aspect of the divine nature[33] that emerged from his writings. Those verses which emphasise the nearness of Allah and His ubiquitous presence are taken by Maulānā Maudūdī to refer to the surveillance of the stern judge who sees all that we do and who will one day call to reckoning. For Maulānā Maudūdī, there is no mystical quest, a position dissimilar to Maulānā Nadwī whose *mujaddin* are drawn from the rank and file of *taṣawwuf.*

Maulānā Maudūdī's ambiguous position on *taṣawwuf* brought about his symbiotic relationship with *'ulamā.* According to him syncretism was antithetical to the aura of puritanism which the Prophet (SAW) advocated and the *'ulamā,* by and large, condoned practices which he (Maudūdī)

31. Nasr, *Maudūdī and the Making of Islamic Revivalism,* 29.

32. Ibid., 30.

33. See Charles Adams, "Abul A'la Maudūdī's Tafhim al-Qur'ān", in Rippin Andrew, *Approaches to the History of the Interpretation of the Qur'ān,* Oxford: Clarendon Press, 1988, 316-17.

deemed un-Islamic. Thus saint-worship, for example, was associated with Sūfī-laden rituals and in Maulānā Maudūdī's view repugnant to the spirit of Islam. In other words, Sūfīsm was responsible for the decline in the Muslim world over the centuries.[34]

Similarly, Maulānā Maudūdī's criticism of the *'ulamā* stemmed from his belief that they opposed all forms of *itjihād* and also the work of *tajdīd* espoused by him.[35] The number of *fatwās* by *'ulamā* denouncing his works relating to *tajdīd* were symptomatic of the conflict that existed between *'ulamā* and Islamists, pursuing similar goals to Maulānā Maudūdī's reconstruction of Islamic thought.

The mixture of Jāhiliyyah and Islam does not suggest that the latter succumbed to un-Islamic practices. On the contrary, Maulānā Maudūdī states that Muslim people all over the world have always been morally superior to non-Muslim communities.[36] This approach explains his critique on Western civilisation in order to develop his theories of Jāhiliyyah and Ḥākimiyyah.

WESTERN CIVILISATION AND JĀHILIYYAH

Maulānā Maudūdī considers Western civilisation to be the extension of modern Jāhiliyyah. He analyses the reasons behind Western domination and Muslim subordination and traces Muslim decline to religious, social and intellectual causes. In his pursuit to understand the reasons for Western domination he identifies extreme nationalism and secularism for its success. In spite of his criticism of the West, Maulānā Maudūdī encouraged his followers to understand some of its positive values in order to trace the causes of Muslim

34. For an elaboration on Maudūdī's views on Sūfism, see Maudūdī, *A Short History of the Revivalist Movement*, 129-35.

35. Ibid., 114-15.

36. Ibid., 5-27, 53, 78.

cultural deterioration.[37] A salient feature of Maulānā Maudūdī's Jāhiliyyah concept is Ḥākimiyyah (sovereignty), which he argues is notably absent in the modern Muslim world because Muslims have ignored God's sovereignty and guidance. The dichotomy between nationalism/secularism and God's sovereignty has been a challenge for Maulānā Maudūdī for the following reasons:

Firstly, his concept of Ḥākimiyyah although derived from his interpretation of specific Qur'ānic verses is based on his reading of Western political science. The theoretical and logical anomalies even Maulānā Maudūdī concedes in juxtaposing Ḥākimiyyah with tools of political science show a flawed understanding of this concept.[38] Secondly, to invest the Prophets with political authority so that Ḥākimiyyah could be established negates the actual role as Messengers of Allah. Maulānā Nadwī's *Islamic Concept of Prophethood* repudiates Maulānā Maudūdī's assertion in respect of the Prophets' assumed political role. Maulānā Nadwī writes: "[the] Prophets do not summon the people to accept only a creed and a law — Islam, but they also lay the foundation of a new way of life which carries the seed of a new culture; a new civilisation."[39]

Lastly, the Jamā'at-i-Islami, founded by Maulānā Maudūdī to give a tangible expression to his Ḥākimiyyah theory was

---

37. Maudūdī's bold critical appraisal of the revivalists' failure in establishing an Islamic state in the subcontinent during the nineteenth century is in line with his doctrine of Ḥākimiyyah. Maudūdī argues that there was no systematic study of the Western civilisation's domination in terms of its scientific and military success. Muslims' decline rests largely with their failure to appreciate the force of scientific progress. *Maudūdī: A Short History. . .*, 110-14.

38. For a detailed understanding of this concept, see Maudūdī, *The Islamic Law and Constitution*, 147-92.

39. Nadwī, *Islamic Concept of Prophethood*, 90.

influenced by democracy. Nasr's observation of the Jamā'at is instructive:

> The political fortunes of the party may yet improve; only time will tell. It is obvious now, however, that operating in the political process, especially in a *democracy* (emphasis added) will require the party associated with the rise of contemporary Islamic revivalism to embark upon changes that will inevitably diminish its commitment to its original ideology if it is to succeed.[40]

It can be argued that Ḥākimiyyah shared specific characteristics of Western democracy which Maulānā Maudūdī attempted to repudiate. The contradiction of isolating Jāhiliyyah and Ḥākimiyyah from the historical process particularly from the twentieth century becomes clearly evident. In fact Maulānā Maudūdī, Maulānā Nadwī and Quṭb's theorisations of Jāhiliyyah are connected with historical and political developments in the Muslim world.

The Islamists' hostitlity towards the West has been examined in Chapter 1. According to their thesis (Maulānā Maudūdī is a pioneer in this line of thinking), a complete epistemological break has to be effected with modern civilisation if Muslims are to be real Muslims. In order to arrive at this conclusion, modern civilisation has been divorced, in their analysis, from its intellectual sources, and a simplistic reading of its shortcomings and drawbacks is offered which is based on the readings of a few basically conservative and pessimistic critics of European civilisation. Furthermore the critique of modern civilisation is not presented as a thesis that may be discussed and debated but is used as a militant ideology to castigate the West. The binary opposites of Jāhiliyyah and Ḥākimiyyah are also elaborated in Quṭb's critique of Muslim societies.

---

40. Nasr, *The Vanguard of the Islamic Revolution*, 223.

Maulānā Maudūdī and the Islamists are also representatives of this line of thinking.

A NEW JĀHILIYYAH : MAULĀNĀ NADWĪ'S CRITIQUE

Maulānā Nadwī in his influential work, *Islam and the World* sees the Jāhiliyyah of ancient Greece and Rome resurrected in modern Europe and Muslims and Muslim societies have become its allies and camp followers. Maulānā Nadwī states that the real fundamentals of the Greek civilisation were the rationalistic and eclectic spirit that pervaded its life. It carved a niche for itself in the field of philosophy and politics, by producing intellectuals like Aristotle and Plato whose writings wielded a decisive influence on Islamic culture and civilisation. Nevertheless, Maulānā Nadwī asserts that the basic structure of the theological metaphysics of the Greeks left hardly any room for the development of the spirit of religious reverence and awe. This was evident in its repudiation of the Attributes of God and of His personal control of the universe, which he argues, could only lead to the "destruction of spirituality."[41] The disregard for transcendental truths and its exaggerated emphasis of material comfort, described in detail by Maulānā Nadwī, have negatively impacted on the character of this great civilisation.

The Roman civilisation, according to Maulānā Nadwī, had never been a source of moral enthusiasm. Being wholly paganish and superstitious, it was incapable of checking scepticism and the spirit of disbelief among its followers. Consequently, as the Romans advanced culturally, they grew openly contemptuous of their faith. Materialism combined with aggressive imperialism was the benchmark of Roman civilisation. A natural corollary of the materialism of the Romans was the exploitation of the weaker nations for selfish

---

41. Nadwī, *Islam and the World*, 113-19.

motives. Maulānā Nadwī observes that these characteristics have been inherited by modern Europe. He is also critical of Muslim societies that have absorbed the *jāhili* traits of Western civilisation which in turn was influenced by Greek and Roman civilisations. However he has resisted generalising the Muslim community as embracing Jāhiliyyah in totality, a position assumed by Quṭb. Maulānā Nadwī argues in his *Saviours of Islamic Spirit* that in Islam there has been a continuity of reformative (*tajdīdī*) movements and that there were no long intervals of inaction in Islamic history.[42]

Maulānā Nadwī illustrates a candid observation of Muslim ambivalence towards the West. Two conflicting trends are discernible: rejection and assimilation. According to Maulānā Nadwī both these trends have a negative impact on Islamic culture and identity. An alternative trend, in Maulānā Nadwī's view is the correct use of technology and science advocated by the West for the betterment of mankind. However Muslims should not surrender their cultural and spiritual identities.[43]

JĀHILIYYAH : MAULĀNĀ MAUDŪDĪ AND MAULĀNĀ NADWĪ COMPARED

The tone of Jāhiliyyah in the writings of Maulānā Maudūdī and Maulānā Nadwī deserves mention. Maulānā Maudūdī's outright rejection of the philosophical and cultural contributions by Greek, Iranian and Indian civilisations is an oversimplification of the historical process over the centuries to which Islam was not immune. The impact of these civilisations created a discourse on Islamic philosophical thought. A synopsis of these philosophical trend is expressed in Mujahid Sharif's two-volume *A History*

---

42. Nadwī, *Saviours of Islamic Spirit*, vol. I, 11-13.

43. For a discussion on Islam and the West, see Nadwī; *Islam and the World*, 158-68; Nadwī, *Western Civilisation, Islam and Muslims*, 165-90.

of Muslim Philosophy.[44] Maulānā Maudūdī's scathing criticism of the doctrine of Jāhiliyyah influenced his formulation of Ḥākimiyyah in political terms.[45] In contrast to this approach, Maulānā Nadwī argues that elements of spirituality absent in Greek and Roman civilisations brought about a materialistic culture in the West. Its pervasive influence is in Maulānā Nadwī's estimation the hallmark of the present Jāhiliyyah. The political implication of the doctrine does not feature in Maulānā Nadwī's theorisation; rather the *tajdīdī* elements which are in consonance with his worldview are given prominence. This view is reiterated in his important monograph, *The New Menace and its Answer.* Maulānā Nadwī says:

> The cure of the ills of the Muslim World lies in our capacity to produce a band of dedicated workers who may be above all personal considerations and have no worldly aspirations for themselves. Their entire endeavour should be directed towards loosening the intellectual and psychological knots of the ruling classes of the society through establishing personal contacts with them and bringing forth for them an effective religious literature, and reforming them through their own piety, sanctity of character, earnestness of purpose, sincerity and selflessness and Prophet-like moral conduct.

JĀHILIYYAH IN QUṬB'S WRITINGS

Sayed Khatab in his recent study, *The Political Thought of Sayyid Quṭb*[46] has traced the development of Jāhiliyyah theory by Quṭb. According to Khatab the Jāhiliyyah concept underwent gradual changes which represented the

44. M.M. Sharif, *A History of Muslim Philosophy*, Karachi: Royal Book Company, 1983.
45. Maudūdī, *Towards Understanding Islam*, IIFSO, 1979.
46. Sayed Khatab, *The Political Thought of Sayyid Quṭb*, London: Routledge, 1006.

intellectual development of Quṭb's career. It was however the period (1950-66) that brought a mature and coherent formulation of his theory.[47]

In 1951 Quṭb wrote the *Introduction* of the second edition of Maulānā Nadwī's *Islam and the World*. Quṭb brought his constructs to emphasise what he had discussed in his own work *Social Justice in Islam* which was read and appreciated by Maulānā Nadwī. The central theme in Maulānā Nadwī's influential work touches, *inter alia*, on two issues relevant to this study: Islam is a universal system that sought to liberate humanity from the *'ubudiyyah* (servitude) to anything other than Allah, and Jāhiliyyah was a condition, not a period in time or place.[48] Shephard's important remarks are also expressed by Quṭb to show his affinity with Maulānā Nadwī in respect of the Jāhiliyyah theory. Quṭb says:

> [After] describing this age of ignorance (Jāhiliyyah) and its salient features, the author has outlined the part played by Islam in the reconstruction of humanity. He has shown how, when it had the opportunity, Islam liberated the soul of man from superstitions and banalities, emancipated him from the evils of slavery and degradation, and lifted him out of the slough of filth and disease. The author had made it clear how, during its days, Islam saved human society from degradation, and civilisation from disintegration and ruin, and liberated man from the tyranny of kings and the dominance of priests.
>
> [A] praiseworthy feature of the book is that the author, whenever he speaks in it of the general depravity of mankind (the depravity that has come because the Muslim failed in his leadership), he calls it ignorance (Jāhiliyyah). This approach shows clearly what, according to the author and his way of thinking, is the difference between the spirit of Islam and the

47. Sayed Khatab, *The Political Thought of Sayyid Quṭb*, 147.

48. See Shephard, *Sayyid Quṭb and Islamic Activism*, 351-52.

> spirit of materialism which prevailed before the advent of Islam and which has been prevailing in the world ever since Islam lost its world leadership.[49]

Quṭb's assessment of Maulānā Nadwī's *Islam and the World* according to Khatab, especially the theory of Jāhiliyyah, illustrates the overlapping of views by these two reformers. However Khatab maintains that Quṭb did not borrow the theory of Jāhiliyyah from Maulānā Nadwī as his earlier writings confirmed his statements on it. Moreover, the period (1950-66) was crucial to Quṭb's definitive formulation of the theory for two reasons as discussed by Khatab: Firstly, Quṭb was moving in a consistent direction, and secondly "there was an intercontinental similarity of Muslim thought and ideological response to the conditions Muslims faced at the time."[50]

The intercontinental similarity of views appears in Quṭb's *Fī-Zilāl-al-Qur'ān.*[51] Quṭb's extensive quotations from *Islam and the World* express his appreciation of Maulānā Nadwī's ideas on Jāhiliyyah. However Quṭb expanded on this theory and developed his own interpretation based largely on his personal circumstances at the time.

Here we will consider the doctrine in its most radical form based on Quṭb's writings published in 1964 or later. Quṭb's association with the Ikhwān as an ideologue had enabled him to present his ideas and views more clearly. The banning of Ikhwān in 1954 and Quṭb together with other leading figures was based on an alleged assassination attempt on President Nasser of Egypt. In 1955 he was charged with subversive

---

49. Khatab, *The Political Thought of Sayyid Quṭb*, 150. Cf. Nadwī's appreciation of Quṭb's *Introduction in Kārwān*, vol. 1, 269-70.

50. Khatab, *The Political Thought of Sayyid Quṭb*, 150.

51. See for example, *Fī-Zilāl-al-Qur'ān*, vol. 2, 276-79.

activity and was sentenced to fifteen years hard labour.[52] It was during this period of confinement and hardship that Quṭb was to write his most important works dealing with Jāhiliyyah and Ḥākimiyyah. His major work *Fī-Zilāl al Qur'ān* was commenced in 1952; however the larger part of this work was written when the author was in jail in the period 1954-64.[53] According to Muhammad Quṭb, a distinguished contemporary writer on Islam and Quṭb's brother, *Fī-Zilāl al-Qur'ān* is a "campaign of struggle."[54] It is an attempt "to achieve the implementation of Islam in the shape of a community which practises Islam in its life and preaches the need for its realisation until it becomes the actual code of practice for the society as a whole."[55] In this work Jāhiliyyah is discussed in greater depth with supporting details from Maulānā Nadwī's writings.[56] These remarks provide a synopsis of the role of Quṭb's *tafsīr* in his elaboration of Islamic resurgence and the theories of Jāhiliyyah and Ḥākimiyyah.

In Quṭb's view, Islam and Jāhiliyyah are antithetical and a complete epistemological break was therefore needed.

> Either Islam or Jāhiliyyah there is no other state, half-Islam and half-Jāhiliyyah that Islam accepts. Islam clearly indicates that the truth is one, not multiple, that everything other than the truth is perdition and the two cannot be mixed. Either God's

52. For details on Quṭb's role in the Ikhwān and his subsequent imprisonment by the Nasserist regime, see Musallaa, *The Formative Stages of Sayyid Quṭb's Intellectual Career and His Emergence as an Islamic Da'iyan: 1906-1952,* Ann Arbor: University of Michigan, 1983; Ismail Abu-Rabi' *Intellectual Origins of Islamic Resurgence in the Modern Arab Word,* Suny Press, 1996.
53. Khatab, *The Political Thought,* 160.
54. Quṭb, *Fī-Zilāl-al-Qur'ān,* vol. I, xi.
55. Ibid.
56. See *Fī-Zilāl-al-Qur'ān,* vol. 2, 276-79.

> sovereignty or Jāhiliyyah government. Either divine law or human whim.[57]

The above passage illustrates a rigid demarcation of what Quṭb contends to be Ḥākimiyyah and Jāhiliyyah. There is no acknowledgement of the evolution of Islamic thought and a discursive tradition that accommodates diverse cultural and religious expressions rooted in a historical time frame. For his part, Quṭb insisted that his definition of *dīn* and Jāhiliyyah was not his but God's and his interpretation was drawn from the first community of believers. The dynamism that characterised the *ṣalf-al-ṣāliḥ* is notably absent in Quṭb's formulation of *dīn;* rather it is typecast as an immutable representation of an Islamic ideology envisaged by him. In the final analysis, Quṭb's idealistic presentation of Ḥākimiyyah sets him apart from both Maulānā Nadwī and Maulānā Maudūdī in terms of his uncompromising presentation of *dīn*. He contends:

> [The basic meaning of Islam] consists in believing that divinity (Ulūhiyyah) belongs to God, and no other; addressing the rites of worship to God, and no other; and surrendering one's fate, obedience and submission to God, and no other, in all the affairs of life [. . .]. Lack of compliance with any of those requirements, like lack of compliance with all of them, takes people out of Islam and into Jāhiliyyah and inevitably associates them to impiety [*kufr*] or idolatry [*shirk*].

The full implications of Jāhiliyyah and Ḥākimiyyah were developed in *Milestones* published in 1964. This was the book the Egyptian authorities used as the main item of evidence in the trial of Quṭb for conspiracy to overthrow the regime.[58]

---

57. Cited in Ana Belen Soage, "Hasan al-Banna and Sayyib Quṭb: Continuity or Rupture", in *The Muslim World,* vol. 99, 299.

58. Charles Tripp, "Sayyid Quṭb: The Political Vision", in Al Rahnema (ed.), *Pioneers of Islamic Revival,* London: Zed Books Ltd., 1994, 160. Cf. Khatab, *The Political Thought . . . ,* 162-63.

These doctrines have elicited varied responses particularly the importance of *Milestones* in defining Quṭb's vision of Islam as *dīn*. Badmas Yusuf is of the view that *Milestones* is a definitve elaboration of Quṭb's presentation of Jāhiliyyah.

He says:

> The doctrine is described as a revolution against all earthly authority that may lay claim to one of the main attributes of Allah, as it is also a revolt against all systems that are based on this false claim. It is also a call to disregard all authorities that govern with man-made laws not approved by Allah.[59]

However he makes a guarded remark that *Milestones* may be misunderstood as an open invitation for radicalism to establish an Islamic order. According to Adil Salahi, translator of *Fī-Zilāl al-Qur'ān* in English, Quṭb was an advocate of the Islamic cause which required commitment and sacrifice. The advocacy effort should present the believer with the "totality of Islam" envisaged by Quṭb as *dīn*. In a similar vein, Salahi refutes the view that Quṭb's view of Jāhiliyyah was a precursor to his radical thoughts on the Islamic order. He argues that a contextual reading of Jāhiliyyah as explained in the *Milestones* is articulated in the various *āyat* (verses) of the Qur'ān.[60] Quṭb's elaboration on this concept as expressed in the Qur'ān is as follows:

> . . . [They] apply to holding a wrong concept of God, rejecting His law and seeking alternative judgement, contravening the values of propriety and morality and allowing pride to bind oneself to truth and justice. This certainly covers a very wide area of life, for both individual and society.[61]

---

59. Badmas Lanre Yusuf, *Sayyid Quṭb, A Study of His Tafsir,* Kuala Lumpur: Islamic Book Trust, 2009, 92.

60. Salahi, *Fī-Zilāl al-Qur'ān,* vol. XVI, x-xxiv.

61. Ibid., xxii.

It is thus clear that Salahi's aim is to provide a coherent formulation of Quṭb's views and Jāhiliyyah and Ḥākimiyyah. However he too concedes that Quṭb "might have gone a little further in his last book *Milestones;*"[62] in other words, the militant tone of these concepts is unambiguously expressed. The ambivalence in Salahi's remarks illustrates the conflicting portrait of Quṭb's position in contemporary Islamic thought.

SALIENT FEATURES OF JĀHILIYYAH: MAULĀNĀ NADWĪ AND QUṬB COMPARED

First and foremost the defining characteristic of Jāhiliyyah is that it rejects divine authority for human authority. This is also echoed elsewhere by Quṭb when he says Jāhiliyyah is based on an attack against God's authority on earth and against the most distinctive characteristic of divinity (Ulūhiyyah) and sovereignty (Ḥākimiyyah), ascribing sovereignty to humans and making some people lords over others.[63] Although Quṭb[64] mainly emphasises the similarities among Jāhiliyyahs, there is one important difference: the present-day Jāhiliyyah is more sophisticated. It deceives people with its science which it borrowed from Islam and perverted it by removing it from its divine foundations. In a dramatic and well-known passage in *Milestones,* Quṭb insists that all existing societies are *jāhilī*.[65] Finally these societies that call themselves Muslim are *jāhilī* because they give political and social authority to others other than God.[66] Jāhiliyyah has wide political connotation for Quṭb: it includes secularism

62. Salahi, *Fī-Zilāl al-Qur'ān*, vol. XVI, xxiii.
63. Quṭb, *Milestones,* 15.
64. Cf. Quṭb, *This Religion,* 97.
65. Quṭb, *Milestones,* 148-55.
66. Ibid., 154. For a critical review on this doctrine, see Aref Ali Nayyed, *The Radical Qur'ānic Hermeneutics of Sayyid Quṭb in Islamic Studies,* 31:3, 355-64.

and nationalism. Implicit in his condemnation is Egypt and other Muslim countries that follow these *jāhilī* trends. Quṭb refers to a secular nationalism or an Arab nationalism that regards Islam as secondary to ethnic identity. Arab nationalism opposes the universality of Islam which includes Ulūhiyyah (divinity) and Ḥākimiyyah (sovereignty).[67] Maulānā Maudūdī's Jāhiliyyah negates the role of *taṣawwuf* in Islam and gives an ideological orientation to the concept of *dīn*. Unlike Maulānā Nadwī *tajdīd* is rigorously viewed in political terms and elements of spirituality are challenged and assumed to be expressions of Jāhiliyyah.

The polemics against Arab nationalism[68] is also expressed in the writings of Maulānā Nadwī. He laments the fact that factionalism which is synonymous with nationalism bore the imprints of linguistic and culutural chauvinism.[69] He observes that as a result of the Western assault on the Islamic world, factionalism is being held with fanatical enthusiasm of reverence. According to Maulānā Nadwī, it is the most powerful rival to religion judging by the extensiveness and intensity of its influence.[70] Maulānā Nadwī's critique of nationalism is based largely on Muslim countries' unconditional surrender to its influence.

However Maulānā Nadwī tacitly endorses nationalism in an Indian setting where there is no fear of investing it with a

67. Sayed Khatab, "Arabism and Islamism in Sayyid Quṭb's Thought on Nationalism" in *The Muslim World*, vol. 94, April 2004, 222-23.

68. Nadwī has been very forceful in his critique on Arab nationalism. His writings on this subject were widely acclaimed by *'ulamā* and Islamists in the Arab world. See Nadwī, *Al-Muslimun wa Qadiyat-al-Filistan*, Lucknow: Majlisal-Ilmi, 1972; Nadwī, *Western Civilisation and Muslims*, 106-24. Cf. Nadwī, *Kārwān*, vol. 2, 65-73 for Nadwī's critique on Nasser's regime.

69. Nadwī, *The New Menace and Its Answer*, Lucknow: Academy of Islamic Research and Publications, n.d., 8.

70. Ibid., 10.

religious content. This contradiction is discussed in the next chapter.

Maulānā Nadwī's admiration of Quṭb's contribution to Islamic resurgence did not imply that he accepted the latter's formulation of Jāhiliyyah and Ḥākimiyyah. The influence of Maulānā Maudūdī's *Four Basic Qur'ānic Terms* on Quṭb's views expressed in *Milestones* is analysed in Maulānā Nadwī's *Appreciation and Interpretation of Religion.*[71] Maulānā Nadwī disagrees with Quṭb's theory stating that it is exaggerated and exceeding the limits of *shari'ah* prescriptions.[72] The "militant" tone in *Milestones* spawned a number of Islamic movements advocating a violent overthrow of Muslim regimes displaying traces of Jāhiliyyah.[73] It is outside the scope of the study to evaluate its impact on these movements in the contemporary Muslim world.

ASSESSMENT: QUṬB AND MAULĀNĀ MAUDŪDĪ

In retrospect, one may point to some fundamental difference between Quṭb and Maulānā Maudūdī. For Quṭb Jāhiliyyah is specifically a transgression against God's sovereignty and authority by applying laws other than God's. Moreover Quṭb gave the concept a seemingly universal and physical character presenting it as a conflict between *jihād* and a revolution against tyrants (*tāghuts*). He also called on those committed to Islamic movement to mobilise against Jāhiliyyah by carrying out wholly any given divine injunction.[74] This

71. Nadwī, *Appreciation and Interpretation of Religion in the Modern Age,* 54-66.

72. Ibid., 61-62.

73. This phenomenon has been critically analysed by Khatab in several of his writings. For a detailed examination on the Islamic movements see Sayed Khatab, *The Power of Sovereignty: The Political and Ideological Philosophy of Sayyid Quṭb,* London: Routledge, 2006, 175-212.

74. Quṭb, *Milestones,* 148-53.

uncompromising view of God's sovereignty chalked out Quṭb's reading of an Islamic system. This is also different from Maulānā Maudūdī's thought; he believed that a comprehensive Islamic system would support and consolidate true faith in Ḥākimiyyah and not contradict it.

Ḥākimiyyah (Sovereignty)

The development of Islamic resurgence as a political movement is closely associated with political individuals and their intellectual contributions to formative ideas. In this respect both Maulānā Maudūdī and Quṭb emerged as pre-eminent figures in their articulation of the Ḥākimiyyah concept. Quṭb's concept of Ḥākimiyyah cannot be independent of his concept of Jāhiliyyah. It is through the prism of these two ideas that the Islamic political systems divide the world into "two camps of potential clash."[75] On the other hand, Maulānā Maudūdī's Ḥākimiyyah concept is less strident in comparison to Quṭb's formulation of ideas. Maulānā Maudūdī attempted to translate this concept in a specific socio-political setting: the creation of Pakistan in 1947. However his ideas continue to wield on Islamic movements seeking to establish Ḥākimiyyah. At variance with Quṭb and Maulānā Maudūdī's views is Maulānā Nadwī's critique on Ḥākimiyyah. Invariably, Maulānā Nadwī takes issues with Maulānā Maudūdī on the concept of *dīn* which is inextricably linked with Ḥākimiyyah. These aspects are examined in the following sections.

ḤĀKIMIYYAH IN MAULĀNĀ MAUDŪDĪ'S WRITINGS

Maulānā Maudūdī's *hukumat-e-ilāhiyah* or Islamic state was articulated after the establishment of the Jamā'at-i-Islami (hereafter JI) in 1941. Nasr has observed in his *The Vanguard of Islamic Revolution* that both Maulānā Maudūdī and JI faced a

75. Khatab, *The Power of Sovereignty,* 2.

number of challenges in their vision of an Islamic order.[76] His opposition stemmed largely from *'ulamā* of the Jami'at-ul-ulāma Hind (JUH) who believed in a secular composite India and did not regard "state" as essential to Islam. In his response, Maulānā Maudūdī developed his *hukumat-e-ilāhiyah* deriving his sources from the Qur'ān and *sunnah*. His famous *Four Basic Qur'ānic Terms* expresses his political ideology. Maulānā Maudūdī argues that the meaning of the original four Qur'ānic terms, *ilāh* (God), *rabb* (lord), *ibādat* (worship) and *dīn* (religion) were lost as the centuries passed.[77] This implied that a correct understanding of these terms was not possible without contextualising them against the backdrop of an Islamic order. Maulānā Nadwī contends that Maulānā Maudūdī propagated new religious ideas, in fact a new approach to religious theology.

> The way in which he (Maulānā Maudūdī) interpreted and explained the terms and the emphasis he laid on them being the core and focal points of the real spirit, led to a new type of exegesis of the Qur'ān, which had a political colouring and revolved around "Kingdom of God" and "Sovereignty of God" and the purpose of the revelation of the Qur'ān and Islamic teachings was reduced to the establishment of the "Kingdom of God."[78]

In Maulānā Maudūdī's formulation the four terms also meant obeying the ultimate political authority. For example, he equates rituals like prayer (*salāh*) to military training and considered them tools to achieve the goal of an Islamic state. Likewise Maulānā Maudūdī interpreted *dīn* (religion)

---

76. For a detailed history on the JI see Nasr, Seyyed Vali Reza Nasr, *The Vanguard of the Islamic Revolution: The Jamā'at-i-Islami of Pakistan*, Berkeley: University of California Press, 1994, 3-46.

77. Maudūdī, *Four Basic Qur'ānic Terms*, 5-6.

78. Nadwī, *Appreciation and Interpretation . . .*, 21-22.

politically, in fact the word *dīn* approximately has the same meaning as the word "state" has in the contemporary age.[79] Interestingly Maulānā Maudūdī's theorisations echo the spirit of modern politics in terms of his understanding of Islam as a movement and Muslims as a party.[80] For Maulānā Maudūdī, Islam and his conception of the Islamic state are synonymous. Thus *dīn* is inseparable from Ḥākimiyyah as both these concepts promote the Islamic way of life in its totality. Maulānā Maudūdī says:

> Acknowledging that someone is your ruler to whom you submit means that you have accepted His *dīn*. He now becomes your sovereign and you become his subjects. . . . *Dīn*, therefore, actually means the same thing as state and government; *shari'ah* is the law of that state and government; and *'ibādah* (worship) amounts to following and complying with that law.[81]

The above statement is too idealistic and negates the levels of spirituality that dominate *dīn* as conceived by the *shari'ah*. The implications of such a position are serious for it reduces liturgical rituals (*'ibādah*) as a means to an end. It indirectly challenges the efficacy of *'ibādah* as a Divinely sanctioned relationship between Allah and his servants. Maulānā Nadwī shares a similar view, in refutation of Maulānā Maudūdī's Ḥākimiyyah that an exclusive focus on politics makes Islam formalistic, arid, worldly, narrow and devoid of inner sensibilities.[82]

ḤĀKIMIYYAH: QUṬB'S VIEWS

A detailed study of *Milestones* reveals Quṭb's analysis of

79. Maudūdī, *Four Basic Qur'ānic Terms*, 6-8.
80. For a critical assessment on the JI's failure to mobilise its success on both political and ideological fronts, see Nasr, *The Vanguard of Islamic Revolution*, 219-21.
81. Cited in Nasr, *Maudūdī and the Making of Islamic Revival*, 82.
82. Cited in Zaman, *The 'Ulamā in Contemporary Islam*, 231 fn.

Jāhiliyyah in its varied forms. Our focus is on Quṭb's view of Ḥākimiyyah and its relation to Jāhiliyyah. Quṭb observes:

> If we look at the sources and foundations of modern ways of living, it becomes clear the whole world is steeped in Jāhiliyyah and all the marvellous material comforts and high-level inventions do not diminish this ignorance. This Jāhiliyyah is based on rebellion (*ṭāghut*) against God's sovereignty (Ḥākimiyyah) on this earth. It transfers to man one of the greatest attributes of God, sovereignty and makes some men lords over others. . . .[83]
>
> We are also surrounded by Jāhiliyyah today which is of the same nature as it is during the first period of Islam, perhaps a little deeper. Our whole environment, people's beliefs and ideas, habits and art, rules and law is Jāhiliyyah, even to the extent that what we consider to be Islamic culture, Islamic sources, Islamic philosophy and Islamic thought, are also constructs of Jāhiliyyah.[84]

The above passages reflect the trend and tenor of Quṭb's formulation of Ḥākimiyyah. A summative assessment reveals Quṭb's projection of this concept to societies that do not acknowledge the sovereignty of God. The dualism of theory and practice of the "Islamic ideal and the un-Islamic state of the world"[85] is emphasised in *Milestones.*

Quṭb's problem is the contradiction between divine sovereignty (Ḥākimiyyah) and humanity's transgression (*ṭāghut*). The binary opposites are not restrictive as they also apply to Muslim societies who do not acknowledge the universal system (*shumuliyyat*) of Islam. This demarcation has serious implications for a Muslim society: there can be no social circumstances or situation which is largely Islam or

83. Quṭb, *Milestones,* 15.

84. Ibid., 32.

85. Binder, *Islamic Liberalism,* 180.

partly *jāhili*.[86] According to Quṭb, whatever is not Islam is Jāhiliyyah. Quṭb's assessment of Jāhiliyyah and Ḥākimiyyah does not tolerate political alternatives in Muslim societies which embrace trends of Western democracy that have also influenced the process of Islamic resurgence.

The complementarity of views between Quṭb and Maulānā Maudūdī on Ḥākimiyyah restricts Islam as a *dīn*. In other words if anyone acknowledges the greatness of other than God and in any matter of life obeys him, he is neither a Muslim nor has he anything to do with Islam. But one who believes in Ḥākimiyyah and is not subservient to man is a Muslim and in the fold of Islam.[87] This approach according to Maulānā Nadwī is problematic for two reasons: firstly, it rejects the idea that God should permit to devise for themselves administrative arrangements or laws that may regulate any sphere of their lives. Secondly, Ḥākimiyyah has created exaggerated and perverse notions among several Islamic organisations that tend to pursue a hostile approach to Muslim societies that do not reflect Quṭb's ideal of *dīn*.

THE ESTABLISHMENT OF DĪN

As discussed in the previous sections Maulānā Nadwī presents his understanding of *dīn* which is in marked contrast to both Maulānā Maudūdī's and Quṭb's presentation of Ḥākimiyyah. Another important scholar Maulānā Wahiduddin Khan's views are also examined to show how the concept of *dīn* is linked with the Islamic order.

MAULĀNĀ NADWĪ'S VIEW ON DĪN

For Maulānā Nadwī, the tradition of the revivalists (*mujaddids*) shows clearly that the duty of establishing religion (*iqāmat-i-*

86. Binder, *Islamic Liberalism*, 181.

87. Cited in Nadwī, *Appreciation and Interpretation of Religion*, 60-61.

dīn) consists of a sustained effort to "please Allah" and "to follow the Prophet." The pillars of faith were observed in its original spirit and so was the duty of "promoting good and forbidding evil." The Caliphate and Muslim political powers were established to serve all these purposes.[88]

Maulānā Nadwī argues that Maulānā Maudūdī's one-sided reductionist stress on a theocratic state is too narrow and pessimistic. The continuity of *iṣlāḥi* and *tajdīd* has been uninterrupted throughout the course of Islamic history[89] and that "every link of this golden chain is linked with another and no link is missing."[90]

There have been in all ages true renovators of Islam who have made remarkable efforts towards establishing *dīn-i-Islam*[91] in its totality, always employing practical wisdom (*hikmat-i-amali*)[92] in ever-changing circumstances. Maulānā Nadwī insisted that "wisdom" demanded that strategies for attaining the goal be worked out in response to the existing social conditions. In Maulānā Nadwī's estimation it was necessary to "prepare people's minds" for an Islamic government through a "silent revolution." The pragmatic approach, he

---

88. Nadwī, *Appreciation and Interpretation of Religion*, 78-81.

89. The multi-volume *Saviours of Islamic Spirit* elaborates on this aspect which Nadwī considers, important to appreciating the role of the reformers.

90. Nadwī, *Appreciation and Interpretation of Religion*, 52.

91. The emphasis on *dīn* in its comprehensiveness differs fundamentally with Maulānā Maudūdī's theorisation of *dīn* as a political entity. Cf. Nadwī, *Islamic Concept of Prophethood*, Lucknow: Academy of Islamic Research and Publications, 1976, 56-57.

92. Nadwī is largely inspired by the Indian reformer Mujaddid Alf-i-Thāni (d. 1624) who in his interaction with notables and royalty used practical wisdom (*hikmat-i-amali*). See Nadwī, *Saviours of Islamic Spirit*, vol. 4.

maintains, could also be employed by Islamists advocating an Islamic government in Muslim majority countries.

The pragmatic approach is also reflected in Maulānā Nadwī's formulation of an Islamic order which is examined in Chapter 5. Maulānā Maudūdī, as Nasr observed, has been portrayed by the JI as a charismatic leader and *mujaddid*. Beyond the Jamā'at, Maulānā Maudūdī's authority has become the basis for the systematic articulation of an all-encompassing reinterpretation of Islam that forms the foundation for a novel religious and intellectual orientation in Muslim life and thought.[93] The point of disagreement on the Islamic order between Maulānā Nadwī and Maulānā Maudūdī reinforces their respective approaches to an Islamic order.

DĪN: MAULĀNĀ WAHIDUDDIN KHAN'S CRITIQUE

Maulānā Wahiduddin Khan (b. 1925),[94] a contemporary of Maulānā Nadwī, is a leading scholar of Islamic thought among Muslims today. What sets Khan apart from contemporary scholars is his interpretation of *dīn*. He sees Islam as a "personal struggle for faith in God and sincere reaching out to God in pursuit of a life of piety."[95] He is unequivocally opposed to any political understanding of Islam. In his view politics is a matter of choice whereas Islam is not. In this context Khan criticises the trend in much of contemporary Islam to give primary importance to the establishment of an Islamic political system:

---

93. Nasr, *Maudūdī and the Making of Islamic Revivalism*, 140.

94. For a brief account on Wahiduddin Khan's life and thought see Irfan Omar, "Islamic Thought in Contemporary India: The Impact of Maulānā Wahiduddin Khan's Al-Risala Movement" in Ibrahim Abu-Rabi' (ed.), *The Blackwell Companion to Contemporary Islamic Thought*, 75-87.

95. Ibid., 77.

He notes:

> These people, because of their mental attitude, have come to view *dīn* in the form of a political order. For them *dīn* has to do with things of the government and not with personal reform. They conceive it as their religious responsibility to establish and to implement *dīn* as a political order on this earth.[96]

The quietist personal affirmation of Islam as a faith is self-evident in the above passage. Khan offers an alternative view that emphasises the separation between politics (read *Islamic state*) and Islam. The discourse is expressed in a somewhat different form by the Tabligh Jamā'at which has developed its *dīn-duniyā* (other-worldly/worldly) discourse[97] in their reformist activities. (This aspect is examined in Chapter 3.) Likewise, Maulānā Nadwī differed with Quṭb and Maulānā Maudūdī in their presentation of an Islamic state which is focused largely on Jāhiliyyah and Ḥākimiyyah. Instead he envisaged an Islamic order which was applicable for his formulation of an Islamic order and had a direct bearing on Indian Muslims who constituted a minority in a largely Hindu-dominated majority. The implications of an alternative political system is examined in the next section.

Islamic Order: Historical Developments in the Indian Subcontinent

Any attempts to understand Maulānā Nadwī's interpretation of an Islamic order must be contextualised in a historical setting. As much as Maulānā Nadwī avoided politics his active

96. Wahiduddin Khan, *Dīn Kya Hai,* New Delhi: Risala Books, 1982, 22.

97. Yoginder Sikand remarks: "[in] a striking parallel with the Protestant revolution, the TJ might actually be seen as helping to promote a more *personalised* (emphasis added) form of Islam divorced from concern with control of state structures, with its clear division, in practice if not in theory, between the *dīn* and *duniyā*." *The Origins and Development of the Tablighi-Jama'at,* 262.

involvement in the *millat*'s (Indian Muslim community) affairs invariably drew him to the political processes of the day.[98] Two historical developments influenced his vision of an Islamic order: the '*ulamā*'s association with the Indian Congress party and the Partition of India in 1947.

The Jamia'at-ul-'Ulamā Hind (JUH) was established in 1920 with the exclusive purpose of safeguarding the *shar'iah* and providing the Muslim community religious and political guidance according to Islamic principles.[99] JUH advocated the freedom of India which was Muslims' homeland too from British imperialism. The '*ulamā* were in favour of an unconditional co-operation with the Congress as far as freedom was concerned. The spiralling communal riots[100] between Muslims and Hindus largely caused by Hindutva (extremist religious organisations) posed a threat to the co-operation movement between the JUH and the Congress. Against this backdrop was the rival organisation, Muslim League, led by Muhammad Ali Jinnah[101] which advocated a

98. It was a paradox of Nadwī's persona that although he was a reluctant politician, he could not remain politically indifferent. "In the formation of the Muslim Mashwarat (Council)," Nadwī remarks, "began a new epoch of my life, which brought me out of my corner of a recluse into the field of service to the *millat* and the *ummah* and which brought me very close to the problems faced by the Muslims." Cited in Alavi, Shariq *The Fragrance of East*, Lucknow, 2000, 123.

99. Zia-al-Hasan Faruqi, *The Deoband School and the Demand for Pakistan*, Lahore: Progressive Books, n.d., 67-69.

100. The communal riots during pre- and post-Pakistan have been a subject of extensive research. The sectarian bias in presenting the causes of such conflicts is reflected in the writings of nationalists who castigate Muslims for maintaining their corporate Islamic identity.

101. For Jinnah's contribution to the Pakistan movement, see Stanley Wolpert, *Jinnah of Pakistan*, New York: Oxford University Press, 1984; Ayesha Jalal, *The Sole Spokesman: Jinnah, the Muslim League and the Demand for Pakistan*, Cambridge: Cambridge University Press, 1985.

separate homeland for Muslims. The *'ulamā* were not prepared to follow the Western-oriented Muslim intelligentsia whom they suspected to be the representatives of a different culture.[102] The conflict highlighted the divergent perspectives to the vision of an Islamic order.

TWO-NATION THEORY OR COMPOSITE NATIONALISM

The influence of nationalism in Muslim countries has been critically examined by Maulānā Nadwī elsewhere in the chapter. Paradoxically, it was the JUH which aligned itself with the Congress that advocated composite nationalism. Religious scholars and Muslim activists intensely debated the issue whether Indian Muslims in spite of their heterogeneous cultural and linguistic character constituted a separate nation. This discourse was significant as it showed a marked departure from their condemnation of nationalism in the West.[103] Even Maulānā Maudūdī who initially opposed the creation of Pakistan later reconciled himself to the "territorial concept for an Islamic society."[104]

It would be worthwhile to examine the concept of nationalism and the divergent opinions associated with it. The JUH and Maulānā Ḥusayn Aḥmad Madani in particular defended composite nationalism.[105] It was however Iqbal, the

---

102. The conflictual relationship between the Deobandi *'ulamā* and the intelligentsia is examined in several writings. Two works may be mentioned in this regard: Qureshi, *Ulema in Politics*, 240-74; Zaman, *The 'Ulamā in Contemporary Islam*, 68-74.

103. For an incisive analysis of this ambivalence towards the West, see Robinson, *Islam and Muslim History in South Asia*, New Delhi: Oxford University Press, 2001, 156-219.

104. Reetz, *Islam in the Public Sphere*, 234.

105. The theory of composite nationalism has been much debated among scholars in South Asia. For an objective assessment of this theory, see Reetz, *Islam in the Public Sphere*, 233-6; Zaman, *The 'Ulamā in Contemporary Islam*, 32-38; Metcalf, *Islamic Contestations*, 184-87.

poet-philosopher, who argued that religion was the sole basis of nationhood. "According to the Qur'ān it is the religion of Islam alone which sustains a nation in its true cultural or political sense. It is for this reason the Qur'ān openly declares that any system other than that of Islam must be deprecated or rejected.[106] In a similar vein, Maulānā Maudūdī ridiculed Maulānā Madani for his obsession to bring about the end of British colonial rule while ignoring the dangers a Hindu-dominated India would pose to the religion and culture of the Muslim community.[107] The discourse of the significant "other" reinforced his idealised conception of an Islamic state, Pakistan, in defining and shaping a nascent Muslim community.

Maulānā Madani, in reply to these scathing criticisms, argued that composite nationalism was distinct from a *millat* (Muslim community): the latter he identified as community based on shared textual tradition, while the former on "shared residence."[108] There was no correlation between these two concepts. Thus both Muslims and Hindus could constitute a nation without Muslims losing their religious autonomy. Maulānā Nadwī's assessment of Maulānā Madani's commitment to the "composite nationalism" is expressed in the following words.

> Maulānā Madani strove to the best of his ability to make the Muslims realise the folly of the Pakistan demand. . . . It is tragically true that the high hopes he had entertained from freedom remained largely unfulfilled . . . but during the struggle he remained firm like a rock, and even after the Independence had been won there appeared no change in his political views and convictions.[109]

106. Cited in Zaman, *The 'Ulamā in Contemporary Islam*, 34.

107. Ibid., 35.

108. Metcalf, *Islamic Contestations*, 186.

109. Nadwī, *Muslims in India*, 121-22.

Maulānā Nadwī too emphasised the loyalty and devotion of Indian Muslims to the nation-state despite his critique of Arab nationalism and his discomfort with Muslim communalism,[110] both of which led to the establishment of Pakistan. Like Maulānā Madani he insisted on the need for communal harmony between Muslims and Hindus[111] which is a salient feature of his interpretation of an Islamic order. The shared similarities between Maulānā Nadwī and nationalist *'ulamā* on communal harmony in a secular nation-state do not suggest the former's total agreement on this idea. Rather Maulānā Nadwī believed that for Muslims "the sources of this identity lie not in the historical experience of Islam in India but in being part of the greater Muslim world and an awareness of being such.[112] The Islamic authenticity which Maulānā Nadwī envisioned for the Indian Muslims permits the *millat* to exercise its "religious autonomy" within a broader Islamic framework.

On the subject of Hindu-Muslim unity, Abul Kalam Āzād, a nationalist *'ālim* has expressed his views poignantly in his famous speech:

> I am a Muslim and profoundly conscious of the fact that I have inherited Islam's glorious traditions of the last thirteen hundred years. I am not prepared to lose even a small part of that legacy. . . . As a Muslim, I have a special identity within the field of religion and culture and I cannot tolerate any undue interference with it. But with these feelings, I have another deep realisation, born out of my life's experience, which is strengthened, not hindered by the spirit of Islam. I am equally proud of the fact

110. On Nadwī's assessment of communalism see *Kārwān-i-Ẓindagī*, vol. I, 496-503; *Kārwān*, vol. 5, 112-15.

111. The *iṣlāḥī* series and monographs focus on communal harmony and the restoration of ethical values. On this theme, see Nadwī, *Reconstruction of Society: What Muslims Can Do?*, Lucknow: Academy of Islamic Research and Publications, n.d.

112. Zaman, *The 'Ulamā in Contemporary Islam*, 167.

> that I am an Indian, an essential part of that indivisible unity of Indian nationhood, a vital factor in its total make-up without which this noble edifice will remain incomplete. I can never give up this sincere claim.[113]

This assumption of separate identities as the building blocks of Indian society is also evident in the following passage:

> It was India's historic destiny that many human faces and cultures and religions should flow to her, finding a home in her hospitable soil. . . . One of the last of these caravans . . . was that of the followers of Islam. . . . This led to a meeting of the culture-currents of two different races. . . . We brought our treasures with us, and India too was full of the riches of her own precious heritage . . . we gave her what she needed most, the most precious of gifts from Islam's treasury, the message of democracy and human equality.[114]

The rhetoric of composite nationalism couched in Islam's rich contributions to democracy and human equality is a narrative line of Āzād. The universal individualism enshrined in the Indian constitution, according to Āzād is also based on Islam's message of equality and democracy.

In his creed of harmony between their two complementary identities, Āzād saw no reason why Muslims should have any apprehension about their role in this emerging nation-state. The echoes of a distinct Muslim identity[115] rooted in an Indian soil are concerns raised by Maulānā Nadwī in a post-Partition context.

MUSLIMS IN POST-1947 INDIA

With the Partition of India in 1947 Indian Muslim leaders

113. Hameed, Syeda Saiyidain, *Islamic Seal on India's Independence*, op. cit., 190.
114. Mushirul Hasan, *India's Partition: Process, Strategy and Mobilization*, New Delhi: Oxford University Press, 67.
115. Nadwī, *Muslims in India*, 67-76.

were forced to come to terms with the grave threats[116] which the community was faced with. Even Maulānā Maudūdī's evocative call for "the rule of God" (*hukumat-e-ilāhiyah*) was abandoned by the Jamā'at-i-Islami in India in favour of secularism and democracy,[117] twin concepts that were once considered evil of Western political thought by Islamists. Secularism in particular was advocated as an alternative to the growing Hindu fascism (Hindutva).[118] It (secularism) was initially not embraced by the Muslim community as it was perceived to be an irreligious movement (*lā-madhabiyat*).[119] The concept was built in the Muslim psyche that it negated core values of religion and promoted an atheistic worldview. This apprehension has been analysed by Muslim scholars in India. Asghar Ali Engineer, a Muslim activist, believes that Islam is not incompatible to secularism if it does not mean the rejection of faith. He argues that throughout the world there is an increasing emphasis on harmonious co-existence of different religions and Islam. Engineer rejects the notion that Islam and politics cannot be separated. His line of argument in support of secularism is stated in the following words:

While the state should not interfere in religious autonomy,

116. These grave threats have been analysed by Nadwī, *Muslims in India*, 125-40.

117. For a critique on secularism and religion, see Talal Asad, *Formation of the Secular: Christianity, Islam and Modernity*, Stanford: Stanford University Press, 2003, 180-201. The writer criticises the flawed thinking of secularists' opposition to religious intrusion into private life and the public sphere.

118. The rise of a religious consciousness and the Hinduisation of Hindu life in the public sphere has been critically examined.in Robinson's *Islam and Muslim History in South Asia*, 156-76.

119. It was natural for Indian Muslims to react apprehensively to this unfamiliar concept of secularism as their religious traditions were autonomous and as such resisted assimilation from their Hindu-majority co-religionists.

> religious authorities should not poke their noses into the affairs of the state. The Indian *'ulamā* had accepted this position with a good conscience throughout the freedom struggle and it was on this basis that they became allies of the Indian National Congress.[120]

The rhetoric of secularism is self-evident in Engineer's understanding of Islam's role in a multi-religious Indian state. An alternative view is presented by the noted scholar, Syed Shahabuddin in his article, "Secularism and Democracy in Contemporary India: An Islamic Perspective." He laments the fact that Muslims as minority group have faced discrimination in a secular and democratic India. This problem he attributes to the religious majority who act as state functionaries. Their antipathy towards the Muslims and disregard for their democratic rights send mixed signals to the Muslims as a minority group. Firstly, the state is in complicity with the Hindu majority against Islam and secondly, the state's secular character is a mere tokenism.[121] Shahabuddin reassures the Muslims that the Muslim minority has to "evolve a mindset which does not see secularism as anti-religion or anti-Islam.

> [It should not see] the secular order as a mask for anti-Islamic repression, but as a humane system which may at times fail to deliver and yet is the only viable course for the peaceful co-existence of many religions within a nation-state and in the world.[122]

Maulānā Nadwī too exhorted Muslims to adopt a pragmatic strategy that would enable them, on the one hand, to reconcile

---

120. Asghar Ali Engineer, "Islam and Secularism" in Abu Rabi', *Blackwell Companion to Contemporary Islamic Thought,* 344.

121. Syed Shahabuddin, "Secularism and Democracy in Contemporary India" in Abu Rabi', *Blackwell Companion to Contemporary Islamic Thought,* 366-69.

122. Ibid., 370-71.

their commitment to Islam, and on the other, carry out their responsibilities towards their country.[123] This approach was in response to the anti-Muslim violence and the spiralling aggression towards Muslims which was bent on a "cultural genocide"[124] and aimed at turning India into "another Spain." Likewise, the noted anthropologist, Akbar Ahmed has remarked in his book *Discovering Islam: Making Sense of Muslim History and Society*, that the *Andalus Syndrome*[125] a metaphor for Muslim decline had left a permanent scar on India and was regularly challenged by Hindutva.[126] The metaphor was also an allusion to medieval Muslim rule in India idealised by Maulānā Nadwī.

Maulānā Nadwī was pragmatic to realise that efforts to build an Islamic society was imperative without which no Islamic state could be established. In this regard he appealed to the Muslims to focus their energies on strengthening their commitment to Islam and be actively involved in *da'wah* among other important responsibilities. Interestingly, Maulānā Maudūdī shared a similar sentiment in his later years that the reconstruction of the Muslim society in Pakistan[127] was a prerequisite for a viable Islamic state.

Conclusion

Writing after the Partition of 1947, the noted Islamic scholar Wilfred Cartwell Smith remarked that there was a pressing

123. Nadwī, *Kārwān-i-Ẓindagī*, vol. 3, 82-83.

124. Ibid.

125. The Andalus Syndrome refers to Christian reconquest of Spain in 1492. For details see Philip Hitti, *History of the Arabs*, London: Macmillan, 1986, 537-56. Iqbal has immortalised the grandeur of Cordova in his poetry. See Nadwī, *Glory of Iqbal*, 137-48.

126. Akbar Ahmed, *Discovering Islam: Making Sense of Muslim History and Society*, London: Routledge, 1988.

127. Nadwī, *Kārwān-i-Ẓindagī*, vol. 2, 269.

need for Indian Muslims as a minority community to develop new interpretations of the faith (Islam). He argued that Indian Muslims required a realistic appreciation of the context in which they were placed and "inspiring them to come to creative grips with the problems and opportunities they were confronted with."[128] Some Muslim scholars notably among whom is Maulānā Nadwī have been engaged in articulating an "understanding of faith" and addressing themselves to issues of contemporary concern.

The diversity of ways of interpreting Islam does indicate the manner in which individuals and organisations examined in the chapter relate to the Indian polity. The advocacy of an ideal society rather than ideal polity reflects their respective responses to changing political situations. Maulānā Nadwī, for example, envisaged an Islamic order operating in a secular, democratic state. He invoked the institution of the Indian Constitution which provides safeguards for religious minorities like Muslims to maintain their corporate Islamic identity. The affirmation of democracy by Maulānā Nadwī in promoting an Islamic order in a religiously plural society is in line with the core values of *Payām-i-Insāniyat*. Islamic faith and practice, according to Maulānā Nadwī, is not exclusionary in an Indian context; rather it can contribute positively in building the moral fibre of a community. Dialogue as an instrument of *da'wah* can promote goodwill and peace between people of different faiths and more particularly the significant other, the Hindu majority.

The contesting discourse of an Islamic order must be examined against the emergent Hindu ideology, Hindutva. Maulānā Nadwī's support for composite nationalism endorsed by nationalist *'ulamā* like Maulānā Madani and Āzād did not materialise. Rather the Partition had serious implications for

128. Cited in Sikand, *Muslims in India Since 1947*, 7.

an Islamic order. Pakistan, established in the name of Islam, was envisaged as an ideal Islamic state governed by Ḥākimiyyah. Maulānā Maudūdī believed a theocratic state that would mirror the ideal past of the Prophet model. The last 50 years since Partition has seen a nation grappling with the challenges of implementing the *shari'ah*. The Jamā'at-i-Islami, Maulānā Maudūdī's ideological movement, has not achieved any real success in promoting an Islamic state. On the contrary its members have either contested in elections as a political party or aligned themselves with the ruling party for a partial implementation of the *shari'ah*. Not surprisingly, the Jamā'at members have employed democratic tools in their attempts to define their understanding of an Islamic state. This position does not depart from Maulānā Maudūdī's own perceptions of Ḥākimiyyah which incorporated features of Western democracy. The ambiguities and contradictions of such an approach challenges the notion of Ḥākimiyyah as an Islamic ideal.

On the other side of the spectrum is the Jamā'at-i-Islami Hind (India) which was founded by Maulānā Maudūdī in 1941. Recognising the impossibility of establishing an Islamic state in India in the foreseeable future, the Jamā'at argued that the secular democratic state is the best option for a Muslim minority in the country. These contesting discourses reveal the complexities of establishing a uniform Islamic order. Furthermore they illustrate the need for pragmatism in reworking an Islamic order in specific socio-political circumstances.

Perceptions of an Islamic order as the study suggests vary in the different Islamic discourses represented by both Islamists and *'ulamā*. Both Quṭb and Maulānā Maudūdī's Jāhiliyyah and Ḥākimiyyah doctrines continue to dominate movements sharing similar ideological orientations. Their impact in presenting Islam as a *dīn*, comprehensive in content and scope, has not gone unchallenged in the last decades. Not surprisingly, the tools of the Western political system are employed to remodel their interpretation of an Islamic order. Islamists have to contend with the forces of secularism, democracy and globalisation in re-defining their perceptions of an Islamic state/order.[129] As Robinson has rightly observed, it is the political economies of societies and geo-politics of environment that will determine the interaction between Islamist groups and the West at present and in the future.[130]

Likewise, the Islamic order that Maulānā Nadwī envisioned for Indian Muslims is not a parallel model bearing on the Islamist understanding of the Islamic state. Rather it is rooted in a historical process embodying democratic structures and the impact of globalisation. As we observed in Chapter 1 the critique on secularism implied Islam's rejection of this concept. However, the ambivalence towards accommodating secularism by *'ulamā* in particular as Zaman noted showed the multiple discourses that have existed side by side in the world of the *'ulamā*. As interpreters of the *shari'ah* they have done so by "drawing on the earlier juristic tradition and by striving to adapt themselves to the changes around them."[131] Maulānā Nadwī is no exception to this phenomenon. The new challenges and opportunities for Indian Muslims in such an Islamic order are issues that are investigated in the next chapter.

---

129. The Islamist response to democracy and secularism has been analysed in recent works. Rachid Ghannoucchi, an Islamist Activist of Tunisia represents a new generation of Islamists attempting to reconcile democracy with Islam. See Azzam Tamimi, *Rachid Ghannouchi: A Democrat within Islamism*, London: Oxford University Press, 2001.

130. Robinson, *Islam, South Asia and the West*, 204.

131. Zaman, *The 'Ulamā in Contemporary Islam*, 187.

5

Islamic Order in an Indian Society

As the study suggests, Islamic resurgence in relation to the Islamic order offers several interpretations. Conceptual differences of an Islamic order by Maulānā Nadwī and his contemporaries examined in the previous chapter have assumed a somewhat ideological character. This chapter however attempts to investigate Maulānā Nadwī's conceptual framework in a specific setting with Indian contemporaries whose contributions on the Islamic order either express a divergence of opinion or complementarity of views shared by Maulānā Nadwī. More importantly, the Islamic order is defined in terms of tools of Western democracy, a clear departure from Ḥākimiyyah which is analysed in Chapter 4. The primary focus is on Maulānā Nadwī's interpretation based largely on his views on Islamic authenticity and *tajdīd* which are salient features of our study on Islamic resurgence.

The Ḥākimiyyah theories presented by Maulānā Maudūdī and Quṭb and their respective responses to democracy have clear implications for an Islamic order. Maulānā Maudūdī's Ḥākimiyyah bẹtrays traces of democracy that is Western in origin. While not advocating a theocratic state, Maulānā Maudūdī sought to locate democratic practice in an Islamic framework by suggesting that it is a viable option to promote the custodial role of man as envisaged by the Qur'ān. Less unequivocal was Maulānā Maudūdī in acknowledging the widespread presence of democracy (in whatever form) in Muslim countries. In a sense the implementation of Ḥākimiyyah was untenable as it had to contend with the incursion of Western models of democracy even in Pakistan which was created in the name of Islam.

On the other hand, Quṭb was opposed to any reconciliation with democracy. He reaffirmed the belief that Western democracy was incompatible with Islamic values and a product of man-made systems. Quṭb's worldview of Islam reflected an extremist position and insulated against socio-political realities. Set against this background, it was predictable that the Quṭbian ideology would create competing discourses of Islamic resurgence with specific reference to an Islamic order. A central theme to the Islamic order is the representation of a corporate Muslim identity (*tashakhkhuṣ*) which depending on its socio-political setting may have important implications for Islamic resurgence. The following section is based on Maulānā Nadwī's understanding of *tashakhkhuṣ* and its relevance to the Muslims in India.

Corporate Muslim Identity (Tashakhkhuṣ)

Maulānā Nadwī's intellectual and political career offers useful insights into efforts to preserve a corporate Muslim identity in the framework of a secular nation-state as well as into the conflicting bases of the *'ulamā* leadership and Islamist influence in the Indian Muslim community.

The motivation for Maulānā Nadwī's active involvement in Indian politics since the 1960s is suggested in the following passage:

> [This is] an age when the sphere of governmental operations is no longer confined to collecting taxes, administering the state, and defending the nation. [The government] can interfere in all spheres of life and can make new laws to regulate all its aspects; it can create a uniform civil code for the entire country; it can

> create a new curriculum for the intellectual and moral formation of the youth and thereby influence even their accepted religious beliefs and sever their link with their past, their culture and their civilisation; it can change the language, or alter the script in which the language is written. . . . In a country where there is no other means for protecting oneself against danger than through the right to express one's opinion [in the general elections], and through political influence and practical wisdom, it is inconceivable for the [Muslim] community to abstain from democratically exerting its influence on national politics. [To so abstain would be especially inconceivable] given that this community's concept and sphere of religion encompasses the entirety of life. . . . [Those who believe that Muslims should stay away from politics, or that they ought to concentrate] merely on establishing welfare and charitable institutions or only on strengthening their economic position or the standards of their education, are, in fact, recommending a path of collective suicide. For [in abstaining from politics] Muslims would not be able to defend their collective identity, nor their rituals and family law; they would not be able to preserve their doctrinal or cultural integrity; and quite apart from leading others and proselytising to them — which is the proper role of this community — they would not even be able to live a free and respectable life.[1]

This lengthy extract reveals Maulānā Nadwī's view of contemporary India as government-regulated. He also weighs divergent strategies and decides that Muslim involvement in mainstream political activities is linked to their corporate identity. It would be worthwhile to consider the implications such involvement entail for Indian Muslims with a minority status. In this respect Maulānā Nadwī's message is clear to the Muslim community: abstinence from politics would jeopardise the collective identity of Muslims in respect of their

1. Nadwī, *Kārwān*, vol. 2, 85-105.

distinctive characteristics that set them apart from their Hindu co-religionists. Maulānā Nadwī's political philosophy has clear underpinnings of a religious autonomy that co-exists with democratic institutions.

RELIGIOUS AUTONOMY

Maulānā Nadwī's reference to a religious autonomy has political connotations. This term suggests that Indian Muslims have maintained an unbroken link with Islamic faith and culture. However, there are no extraneous political influences that are likely to shape Indian Muslims' understanding of a religious autonomy. Put simply, Maulānā Nadwī rejects the view that political institutions in the Arab world which have misrepresented Islamic authenticity are readily acceptable to Indian Muslims. Rather Maulānā Nadwī reminds the Arab world to acknowledge Indian Muslims' contributions to the development of Islamic civilisation.[2] In his view, Arabs need to re-claim their role as the first torchbearers of Islam and also forerunners of Islamic culture and civilisation. According to Maulānā Nadwī, Indian Muslims in their own chequered history did not lag behind in making significant Islamic contributions. The statement seeks to show the importance of Indian Muslims' contributions in shaping the cause of Islamic authenticity. One such example were the medieval Muslim rulers whose exemplary conduct[3] maintained the spirit of Islamic authenticity in Muslim India dominated by a strong Hindu presence. Like the Arab rulers they too "professed the same ideology" and assimilated the same ideals of Islam to be important contributors of this great civilisation.

In addressing the Arabs against the nationalistic trends in the Arab world in the 1950s and in drawing attention to

2. Nadwī, *Islam and the World*, 87.
3. Nadwī, *Islam and Civilisation*, Lucknow: Academy of Islamic Research and Publications, 1986.

the challenges faced by Muslims in a secular, Hindu-dominated India, Maulānā Nadwī draws an important distinction. Even if the Arabs succumbed to the Jāhiliyyah of nationalism, Indian Muslims would continue with their commitment to Islam.

> If the entire world were to abandon Islam, our determination would not be weakened. Even if the Turks return to their "Turani" nationhood and to the customs, beliefs and glories of their first Jāhiliyyah . . . and the people of Arabia — may God not will this — to their Jāhiliyyah and their heroes: [let it be known that] we have not bound our future to any community or nation. We have pledged to God that we will persevere in His religion. And God has vouched for the permanence of His religion and for the continued existence of a group in the community that will hold on to it.[4]

The rhetoric of religious autonomy exercised by Indian Muslims, according to Maulānā Nadwī, is linked to an Islamic authenticity rather than an unconditional acceptance of the Arab understanding of this concept. The criterion, Maulānā Nadwī contends, is based on the foundational sources of Islam which have been validated over the centuries and consolidated an Islamic *turāth* (culture and civilisation). In his inaugural address at the eighty-fifth anniversary of the inception of Nadwah, Maulānā Nadwī stated:

> By the Grace of God, the Muslims of India are to a large extent autonomous as regards Islam. They draw guidance from the sources of Islam — the Qur'ān and the *sunnah* and from the lives of Islam's earliest representatives. . . . Their faith and their lives are tied to the radiance of Islam, not the ephemeral glimmerings of Muslim nations or Islamic states.[5]

4. Nadwī, *Kārwān*, vol. 2, 171-95.

5. Nadwī, Muhammad, *Ru ād-i-Chaman*, 117. This sentiment is expressed in several of Nadwī's writings.

"Indian Muslims, by God's Grace, are self-sufficient in matters →

The religious autonomy is not meant to deny Indian Muslims as being a segment of the global *ummah* or impervious to developments across the Muslim world. Rather Maulānā Nadwī highlights this aspect to demonstrate Indian Muslims' commitment only to ideologically committed Arabs. Maulānā Nadwī maintains that Indian Muslims will draw their inspiration from Arabs who are attached to Islam.

The Islamic authenticity advocated by Maulānā Nadwī does not deny the outside influences or local traditions that tend to give meaning and direction even to a reformist Islam.

ISLAMIC CULTURE WITHIN INDIA

The cultural structure of Muslims everywhere is determined by two major factors. Firstly Islamic belief and way of life; and secondly the indigenous civilisation and local customs which are bound to make their presence as a result of the intermingling with the indigenous population. The Indian Muslims are not exempt from the general principle. According to Maulānā Nadwī "their culture, which has taken centuries to evolve itself, is a combination of both Islamic and Indian influences. This twofold aspect has, on the one hand, endowed it with a beauty and richness which is characteristically its own, and on the other, it holds forth the assurance that this culture will operate here not like an alien or a traveller but as a natural permanent citizen who has built his home in the light of his peculiar needs and circumstances. . . ."[6]

Maulānā Nadwī's evaluation of Indo-Islamic culture must

→ of Islam. They derive their [understanding] from the primary sources — Qur'ān and *sunnah* — and the lives and sacrifices of the earliest precursors. They have tied their faith and life to the radiance of Islam's sun."

Nadwī, *Millat-i-Islam Tārikhi Kardār,* Lucknow: Shu'bah Da'wat wa Irshād, 2004, 20.

6. Nadwī, *Muslims in India*, 67-68.

be seen in a broader context of his Islamic resurgence paradigm. The confluence of cultures according to Maulānā Nadwī does not diminish the pioneering role Islam has played as a transmitter of universal values of Divine unity, equality and brotherhood to a society steeped in a hierarchical caste system. The impact of Islamic civilisation in shaping attitudes of the people and their cultural advancement during the heyday of its glory is elaborated by Maulānā Nadwī in *Islam and the World.* Maulānā Nadwī says:

> The rejuvenating currents of Islam ran through the world, infusing men everywhere with a new life and unparalleled enthusiasm for progress. . . . Even nations that did not come directly under the influence of Islam, profoundly, though unconsciously, benefited by the freshness and vitality of the new creative impulses released by its impact on larger parts of the world. Numerous aspects of their thought and culture bear evidence to the magic touch of Islam.[7]

In a similar vein, Maulānā Nadwī admits that identification of influences of Islam on different cultures is an extremely difficult task as people themselves cannot indicate whether "they are extrinsic or intrinsic, borrowed from Islam or evolved by them internally." The impact of Islam on different cultures and its pioneering role in shaping positive values is a central theme in Maulānā Nadwī's works dealing with Islam and civilisation.

Likewise the synthesis of Muslim culture[8] as opposed to syncretism or eclecticism, Maulānā Nadwī argues, does not

7. Nadwī, *Muslims in India,* 10-12.

8. The noted anthropologist, Akbar Ahmed has analysed the concept of culture and change to show that diversity in culture in South Asia, with its rich and colourful tapestry is as varied in its lifestyles as it is in the range of its philosophical ideal. On this incisive discussion, see Akbar Ahmed, *Postmodernism and Islam,* London: Routledge, 1992, 1-51.

betray the influences of the Ibrāhimī civilisation. In *Islam and Civilisation*[9] Maulānā Nadwī delineates the essential features of Islamic culture which as a network crisscrosses Muslim societies across the world. Maulānā Nadwī observes:

> Islamic cultural unity depends, by and large, on the *shari'ah* and the moral norms prescribed by it, though the standards may vary in proportion to their compliance with the teachings of Islam. These apparent variations are inevitable, too, owing to the inherent variety in Muslim nations, countries, times and their political and social organisations, but each of these would be found to carry a distinctive stamp of Islam. The common features tracing their origins to Islam in all the Muslim societies can be seen in their unshaken faith in the Oneness of God, a sense of human dignity and equality, modesty and courtesy. . . . The religious and cultural unity of Muslim societies becomes even more distinct in religious observances and festivals. . . .[10]

This ideal vision is in consonance with Maulānā Nadwī's notion of Islamic authenticity which defines the tenor of Islamic resurgence.

Yet when it comes to describing Indian influences on Islamic culture and thought, Maulānā Nadwī makes an honest assessment.[11] "Indian Muslims have adopted numerous rites and customs of the soil that are not found among Muslims elsewhere." These practices include rites of marriage, social hierarchies and public festivals all of which

---

9. Nadwī, *Islam and Civilisation*, Lucknow: Academy of Islamic Research & Publications, 1986. Nadwī's dedication of this work to the Centre of Islamic Studies, University of Oxford (United Kingdom) assumes greater importance in his efforts to bridge the Islam – West divide. On a similar theme, see Nadwī, *Islam and the West*, 1993.

10. Ibid., 83-84.

11. Nadwī, *The Musalman: Social Life, Beliefs and Customs of the Indian Muslims*, 25.

are borrowed from Hinduism.[12] This approach is in line with his *Payām-i-Insāniyat* which is discussed elsewhere in the chapter. Despite the critique of Indian Muslims' cultural practices, Maulānā Nadwī insists on a need for communal harmony between Muslims and Hindus. Maulānā Nadwī is candid when he says that the ethical values and standards have "suffered a distinct transfiguration in India"[13] which is unavoidable: "When two civilisations meet, the transmission of cultural effects and impulses between them is a two-way process. Human existence is based essentially on the noble principle of give-and-take. In it lies its strength and glory."[14]

The "distinct transfiguration" to which Maulānā Nadwī refers is reflected in the Barelwi sect which advocated "a custom-laden style of Sūfīsm, closely tied to the *pīrs* (saints) of the medieval tombs."[15] They opposed the Deoband and Nadwah *'ulamā* on their reformist programme which criticised shrine-based Islam and cultural accretions borrowed from Hinduism. Maulānā Nadwī's appreciative annotation on an influential work, *Taqwiyat-ul-Imān*[16] by Shah Ismā'il Shahid (1831)[17] is illustrative of the reformist trends among the Nadwah and Deobandi *'ulamā*. This polemical tract, labelled by the Barelwis as a Wahhābi/*salafi* inspired ideology set the

12. Nadwī, *Muslims in India*, 74-76.

13. Ibid., 76.

14. Ibid.

15. Metcalf, *Islamic Revival in British India*, 267.

16. Muhammad Ismā'il Shahīd, *Taqwiyat-al-Imān*, Lucknow: Al-Maktaba Maulānā Nadwīyyah, 1991.

17. For a brief biography on Shah Ismā'il Shahīd, see Mohiuddin Ahmad, *Saiyid Ahmad Shahid*, Lucknow: Academy of Islamic Research and Publications, 1975, 196-387; Nadwī, *Saviours of Islamic Spirit*, vol. 4, 269-72. Shāh Isma'il Shahid is considered to be the ideologue of Sayyid Ahmad Shahid's (Nadwī illustrious ancestors who are mentioned in Chapter 3) *jihād* movement.

tone for doctrinal dissensions[18] over the next century in the Indian subcontinent.

A somewhat different approach from Maulānā Nadwī's approach to Indo-Muslim culture is Wahiduddin Khan's multi-culture model. Tracing the history of conflict between Muslims and Hindus, Khan puts the blame squarely on the Partition of India in 1947. For a multi-culture to succeed, Khan insists that Muslims after acknowledging their minority status must accept their role of "no-problem" community.[19] This will also mean Muslims co-operating with the Hindu majority to ensure stability and harmony in the country. Khan concludes: "Peaceful co-existence is the only viable state for their [Muslim] community in this day and age but it will become a reality only when they make peace and not communal prestige their supreme goal."[20] Maulānā Nadwī also insists that cultural and religious homogeneity are not in accordance with the principles of nature and history. According to Khan "culture follows its own logic of evolution" and any attempts to eliminate its differences will only magnify the problems between different religious communities.[21] Therefore peaceful toleration and co-existence are the only solutions. Khan's analysis of Indo-Muslim culture have interesting connotations for Indian Muslims. Muslims' penchant with their past is counter-productive to the present realities they face. Instead Muslims should have a participative role in mainstream Indian life in order to retain their corporate religious identity.

---

18. A critical assessment on the polemics between the Barelwis and the reformist *'ulamā* appears in Habib-ul Haq Nadvi, *Islamic Resurgent Movements in the Indo-Pak Subcontinent*, 221-43.

19. Wahiduddin Khan, *Indian Muslims: The Need for a Positive Outlook*, New Delhi: Al-Risala Books, 1997, 1-50.

20. Ibid., 154.

21. Wahiduddin Khan, *Aman-e-'Alam*, New Delhi: Goodword Books, 2005, 95-97.

The views presented by Maulānā Nadwī and Khan reinforce the challenges Indian Muslims have to face to retain their corporate Islamic identity while acknowledging the presence of a dominant Hindu culture. These approaches offer pragmatic solutions to the challenges faced by Indian Muslims and in a specific sense discourage them from remaining insular to the realities of mainstream Indian life.

Reconstruction of Muslim Society

Maulānā Nadwī's theorisation of an Islamic society is drawn largely from two ideals: the Prophetic model and medieval Muslim India. In his discussion on the role of the prophets, Maulānā Nadwī asserts that they did not summon their respective communities to accept only a creed and a law. "Rather they (prophets) also laid the foundation of a new way of life on which a society was built.[22] Thus the Ibrahimi [Abrahamic-Muhammadan] culture[23] perpetuated the basis of an Islamic society whose influence is still felt across the Muslim world." Likewise the medieval societies of Muslim India, in Maulānā Nadwī's view, mirrored in many ways an ideal Islamic society.[24] The Muslim rulers of India "diffused the most valuable treasure they had with them — the wealth of faith in One God and prophethood. [They] dispersed their conviction in virtues of human dignity and equality, their administrative skill and practical genius and their refined taste of arts and culture among the people of their adopted land.[25]

22. Nadwī, *Islamic Concept of Prophethood,* 90.

23. Ibid., 91-98 for Nadwī's discussion on the characteristics of Ibrahimi culture.

24. A useful study on medieval societies in Muslim India is Waheed-uz Zaman, *Islam in South Asia,* Islamabad: NIHCR, 1993.

25. Abdul Hai, *India During Muslim Rule,* Lucknow: Academy of Islamic Research and Publications, 1977, 3. The introduction to this book is written by Nadwī.

In fact two volumes of his *Saviours of Islamic Spirit*[26] are devoted to the achievements of Muslim intellectuals in the sub-continent who endeavoured to establish an ideal Islamic society. Maulānā Nadwī's aim was to show the unbroken link between Muslim India and the rest of the Muslim world. It also articulated the Islamic authenticity embedded in Maulānā Nadwī's own worldview and reinforced his claims that Muslim India played a pivotal role in developing models of Islamic society[27] rather than operating in a vacuous state.

The following sections highlight Maulānā Nadwī's view of an Islamic society which attempts to integrate its broader Islamic principles in a specific socio-political setting.

Maulānā Nadwī's idealised vision of an Islamic past in India has important implications for his presentation of his Islamic order. Firstly, Islam has had a major influence on Indian civilisation and any attempt to ignore it would be "a sad reflection on the innate human richness of our land."[28] For Indians in general Muslim reformers and their singular contributions to Indian culture represent "models of conduct,"[29] a strong reminder of Indian Muslim commitment to ideals that are embedded in the Indian Constitution. Secondly Maulānā Nadwī's Islamic order takes into account the inseparable destinies that link Indian Muslims and the significant "other." In other words, the Islamic order that Maulānā Nadwī envisages does not function independently

26. *Saviours of Islamic Spirit,* vols. 3 & 4 deal with contributions of Shaykh Ahmad Sirhindi and Shah Wali-allah respectively. Nadwī discusses the social milieu and the reformers' impact on their respective societies in the subcontinent.

27. The noted historian, Khaliq Ahmad Nizami (d. 1997) has written prolifically on Muslim India during the medieval period. See Khaliq Ahmad Nizami, *On Islamic History and Culture,* vols. 1 and 2, Delhi: Idarah-i-Adabiyat-i-Delli, 1995.

28. Nadwī, *Muslims in India,* 3.

29. Ibid.

of the currents of political developments in the country but is influenced in some ways to give it a local character. Maulānā Nadwī says:

> Unity, trust and harmony among the diverse elements that go to make the Indian people, which are a prerequisite of national integration and progress, cannot be produced till we remain unaware of each other's spiritual and emotional make-up, history and social background and the possibilities we hold for the future.[30]

ISLAMIC SOCIETY WITHIN AN INDIAN CONTEXT: DEFINITION AND SIGNIFICANCE

Maulānā Nadwī outlines the salient features of a society that are based on Islamic values and ethical standards:

> History bears an irrefutable evidence to the fact that the society at any given time is much more important than languages and literatures, cultural patterns and folklores of any country. The existence of a vigorous society having a flicker of life in its veins, endowed with a conscience that discriminates between virtue and wickedness and taking offence of all cruel acts is a great blessing from God.[31]

A basic postulate of an Islamic society in Maulānā Nadwī's view is the establishment of justice and morality. Justice, according to Maulānā Nadwī, has been promoted by Prophet Muhammad (SAW) in its perfect form. His Companions (*ṣahābah*) exemplified this value in their exemplary conduct. An unbroken link was maintained to sustain this core value in an Islamic society. Maulānā Nadwī eulogises an Islamic society where justice reigns. Therefore his reference to "models of excellence" means invariably the *ṣalf-al-ṣāliḥ* and to an Indian audience the early Muslim society in India. The unbroken link with the past sets a precedence for a

30. Nadwī, *Muslims in India,* 2.

31. Nadwī, *Reconstruction of Indian Society: What Muslims can do,* 4-5.

reformulation of an Islamic order in changed situations. Maulānā Nadwī sees a "corporate effort" as an effective instrument for reformatory (*iṣlāḥi*) changes and maintaining patterns of upright behaviour through which justice and morality can prevail. The paradigm of *iṣlāḥ* and *tajdīd* defines the scope of Maulānā Nadwī's presentation of an Islamic order although there is no evidence to suggest that there is a radical departure from the conventional understanding of what constitutes an Islamic society. On the contrary Maulānā Nadwī adopts a pragmatic approach to advance his views on this concept.[32]

Here again it must be noted that the Islamic society he refers to is rooted in an Indian soil. The broad framework suggested by Maulānā Nadwī incorporates elements of a civil society which promotes democratic values and provides checks and balances against excesses by political powers of self-centred individuals. Maulānā Nadwī envisages an Islamic society that is not insular;[33] it embraces a worldview that is also compatible to the temperament of its Hindu counterparts.

Maulānā Nadwī juxtaposes Islamic teachings with universal values for his conceptual framework of an Islamic order. The religious boundaries that are rigidly upheld by *salafi*s for example in their formulation of an Islamic order are blurred in Maulānā Nadwī's attempt to contextualise the universal values brought by Islam:

> Islamic civilisation is a realistic and living issue which relates not only to the prophethood of Muhammad (SAW) and the

32. For a discussion on the contribution of the *sahābah* and the early Muslim society to the promotion of justice and morality, see Nadwī, *Islam and the World*, 49-90.

33. This standpoint is in keeping with Nadwī's belief that co-existence and harmonious relationship between Muslims and Hindus are a prerequisite to a stable Indian society. Ibid., 21-22.

> teachings of Islam, but also to the reality of life itself, the present and future of mankind, the historic role played by Muslims in the development of culture and building up a flourishing civilisation.[34]

The focus on Islamic civilisation is directly linked to the pivotal role it has played in influencing other faiths on monotheism and human dignity. These values are given a salience in Maulānā Nadwī's Islamic order. Thus justice and morality are universal values linked to the Muslim past which can have a positive influence on the Indian society at large.

FEATURES OF AN ISLAMIC SOCIETY

Let us examine some of the features that Maulānā Nadwī has for an Islamic order in India:

These features are relevant in our study for two purposes: Firstly, Maulānā Nadwī asserts that Islamic civilisation through its redeeming values of *tawḥīd* and equality has maintained a corporate Islamic identity in India. Secondly, the features mentioned hereunder have equal relevance for the Hindu compatriots in carving out a future for all Indians which are free from the hierarchical caste system. Moreover, these features have a resonance in the contributions made by *mujaddid*s drawn from the Indian subcontinent by Maulānā Nadwī in his *Saviours of Islamic Spirit*. The universal influence of Islam can also impact positively on the Indian society in general. This approach conforms to Maulānā Nadwī's interpretation of *da'wah* which is elaborated elsewhere in the chapter. In contrast to Maulānā Nadwī's Islamic society formulation is Quṭb's view of society which is rigidly Islamic and therefore precludes communities of other faiths. Likewise Maulānā Maudūdī's "holy community" has an explicit agenda: an Islamic society upholding utopian ideals.

34. Nadwī, *Islam and Civilisation*, 3.

WORTH OF HUMANITY

Maulānā Nadwī states that Islam restored the dignity of man by declaring that he is the most respectable and prized being in the universe and nothing has a greater claim to honour and protection than him.[35] The unity of mankind is integral to an Islamic society that seeks to promote peace and harmony among all its citizens regardless of their religious affiliation. It has repeatedly emphasised the fact that the Creator of human beings is one, and so is their progenitor, and hence the entire humankind belongs to one family, has one father and one Lord.[36] Maulānā Nadwī makes an impassioned appeal to the Muslim community in India to "spread the gospel of human dignity and strengthen the hands of all well-wishers of this land by acting on the precepts of the Qur'ān and teachings of the holy Prophet (SAW).[37] Two points merit our attention. Firstly, Maulānā Nadwī makes the above statement against the backdrop of communal violence that had beset the country. The litany of indiscriminate killings in the name of religion was spawned after the Partition in 1947 and continues to dominate Indian religious and political life. Maulānā Nadwī remarked that in the aftermath of the Partition communal harmony and peace became fragile with a corresponding wave of religious intolerance.[38] Secondly, there is a reminder for the Muslims to promote human

35. Nadwī, *Islam and Civilisation*, 29.

36. This statement is emphatically stated in the Qur'ān. See Qur'ān 4:1.

37. Nadwī, *Reconstruction of Indian Society*, 20. Cf. Nadwī, *Basis of a New Social Order*, 7-8.

38. Nadwī, *Muslims in India*, 120. Nadwī lamented the lack of foresight of Hindu leaders who did not forcefully address the concerns of Muslims who now held a minority status. Communalist tendencies, according to Nadwī, could have been checked if they did not alienate the sympathies of Muslim leaders who were in the vanguard of the nationalist movement, the Congress.

dignity[39] regardless of religious distinctions and not to fall prey to religious intolerance. The above sentiment is echoed in his inaugural address at the University of Kashmir in 1981:

> The art of leading a good, useful and dignified life consists basically of God-fearingness, humanitarianism, self-restraint and willingness to subordinate one's own advantage to the common good. Unselfish in the welfare of others, respect for mankind, the urge to protect the life, property and honour of fellow men . . . the courage to speak the truth at all times . . . these are the essential conditions of a good and noble life, and the fundamental requirements of a healthy society, and a strong and honourable nation.[40]

Human dignity is equated with the Prophetic mission of restoring the position of man as the custodian of Allah's sovereignty on this earth. The Prophetic model, explains Maulānā Nadwī, is imbued with the spirit of equality and brotherhood of man and has the potential to weld mankind into one family.[41] The ethical implications of human dignity extend to both Muslims and Hindus. Maulānā Nadwī reaffirms the view that Muslim corporate identity is the harbinger of the spirit of equality and brotherhood which must be vigorously promoted by Indian Muslims.

CULTURAL AND LINGUISTIC TOLERANCE

The evolution of Islamic civilisation in India was not immune from the cultural influence of Hinduism. Cultural and linguistic chauvinism, deeply entrenched in the Hindu psyche had also made its mark on the Muslim behaviour as a result of social interaction between them over the centuries.

---

39. Nadwī, *Kārwān*, 121-22.

40. Nadwī, *The Place of Knowledge and Responsibilities of Those Who Acquire It*, Lucknow: Academy of Islamic Research and Publications, n.d., 17.

41. Nadwī, *Islam and the World*, 63.

On a positive note, Maulānā Nadwī believes Indian Muslims can overcome these shortcomings and promote human equality[42] as an alternative to the caste system embedded in Hindu life and thought. This implies an acceptance of cultural and linguistic differences. Maulānā Nadwī states:

> The variations on languages and mode of living have helped man to evolve new patterns of culture and enrich and beautify his life; and indeed as the Qur'ān reminds us, these are all Divine blessings conferred on man by the grace of the Lord.
>
> And of His Signs is the creation of the heavens and the earth, and the differences of your languages and colours. Lo! Herein indeed are portents for men of knowledge.[43]

Maulānā Nadwī's assessment of cultural and linguistic tolerance has far-reaching implications for Muslims in South Asia. For Indian Muslims, this approach not only promotes the Prophetic dictum of human dignity but it also strikes at the root of Jāhiliyyah. Maulānā Nadwī refers to the period of the *ṣalf-al-ṣāliḥ* where merit supplanted racial and cultural affiliation.[44] Any deviation from this path resurrected the *jāhilī* past of chauvinism in its various forms. The prophetic model combined with Islamic authenticity are criteria for Maulānā Nadwī's concept of an Islamic order. In contrast, Maulānā Nadwī is critical of Muslim societies in Pakistan and Bangladesh which have not removed the shackles of cultural and linguistic chauvinism[45] from their lives. Maulānā Nadwī

42. Nadwī, *Reconstruction of Indian Society*, 25-26.

43. Surah 33:20.

44. Nadwī describes the *sahābah* as "new men" who were elevated by the Prophet to be the standard bearers of learning and culture in the world. See Nadwī, *Islam and the World*, 71-74.

45. The *Tuḥfah* (Gift) series written by Nadwī on Pakistan and Bangladesh highlights the issues on culture and language. See Chapter 2 for more details.

is critical of these Muslim countries which were separated after the civil war in 1971. The cause is attributed to linguistic and cultural prejudice. "The idol of language prevailed upon the faith in the unity of God (*tawḥīd*) and brotherhood of man. National and racial zealotry smashed the brotherhood of Islam and Jāhiliyyah overcame the unifying bonds of the Islamic faith."[46] The image of Jāhiliyyah permeating Muslim countries, Pakistan and Bangladesh which have a shared history with Indian Muslims, is employed by Maulānā Nadwī to emphasise the salutary effects of cultural and linguistic tolerance. A solution proferred by Maulānā Nadwī is the all-encompassing value of love:

> The quality of love permeating through the human heart is a very precious gift of God. When something stirs it, it assumes a strange power. It rises above the considerations of religion, community, nation and motherland. It then only sees another man's heart and feels its suffering and is drawn to it by nature as is pulled an iron chip towards a magnet.[47]

Maulānā Nadwī draws his understanding on the dynamics of a stable society from the prophetic model. The prophet served as an exemplum and his life mirrors the possibilities of co-existence and communal harmony. To this end, Maulānā Nadwī's writings bearing the titles *Iṣlāhiyāt*[48] (Reforms) and *Khuṭbāt*[49] (Public Lectures) are aimed at providing guidelines for a healthy and stable Muslim society. He also critiques the Muslim society for their shortcomings and prejudices. However, these writings maintain an

46. Nadwī, *Calamity of Linguistic and Cultural Chauvinism*, 5.
47. Nadwī, *Islam: An Introduction*, Lucknow: Academy of Islamic Research & Publications, 1998, 152.
48. Nadwī, *Iṣlāhiyāt*, Karachi: Majlis Nashriyat-i-Islam, 1987.
49. Nadwī, *Khuṭbāt-i-Mufakkir-i-Islam*, vols. 1-4, Lucknow: Dār-al-Qalam, 2000.

optimistic tone and do not reflect a polemical approach. The Islamic appeal of love for mankind which transcends racial and religious barriers are a viable alternative to the entrenched Hindu caste system that denies individuals of their rights to equality and freedom.

RECONSTRUCTION OF MUSLIM SOCIETY

Maulānā Nadwī argues that a reconstruction of Muslim society must take into account the social norms derived from Islamic teachings. A progressive Islamic society maintains a healthy balance in matters that define its corporate identity. In this respect Maulānā Nadwī cautions Muslims against imitating social customs of Hindus that are antithetical to Islam's uncompromising view on correct beliefs (*'aqīdah*).

Similarly, Maulānā Nadwī believes that the economic disparities among Muslims must be bridged through sustainable economic development programmes. Again Maulānā Nadwī refers to the exemplary lives of the early generations of Muslims who alleviated the economic plight of impoverished Muslims to remind Indian Muslims of their commitment to the ideals of the *ṣalf-al-ṣāliḥ*.

Maulānā Nadwī extends the scope of social norms to theological issues which impinge on the very fabric of Islam in its pristine form. Muslims' penchant for legal minutiae has embroiled them in hair-splitting theological issues which have undermined their distinctive corporate identity. Maulānā Nadwī lamented the unity of the *ummah* was compromised resulting in splinter theological groups advancing their respective sectarian cause. Muslims, Maulānā Nadwī argued, should focus their energies on the reconstruction of their society which in turn can exercise a positive influence on the nation.[50]

---

50. Harun Rashid Siddiqui, "Unity of Muslim Ummah" in *Tameer-i-Hayat: Special Issue*, 2000, 91-96.

CONCLUSION

The building of bridges between Muslims and Hindus by Maulānā Nadwī to remove distrust and animosity[51] was the key issue faced by him. He envisaged a movement to crystallise his thoughts which would bring peace to the Indian nation. The *Payām-i-Insāniyat* was established for this purpose which mirrored the need for interreligious dialogue. The "Indian influences" on Muslims are by and large acknowledged by Maulānā Nadwī for the sake of a putative Hindu audience. This acknowledgement does serve "to sharpen the sense of an immutable Islamic essence"[52] which Muslims have preserved and sustained over the centuries in the Indian soil as pure and distinct from outside (Indian) influences.

At the same time, Maulānā Nadwī emphasises the loyalty and patriotism of Muslims to India in order to defuse the effects of Muslim communalism that led to the creation of Pakistan. He insists on the need for communal harmony between Muslims and Hindus. It is in the context of a secular nation-state that Maulānā Nadwī states that the distinct identity of the Muslim *ummah* can co-exist with a dominant religious group without any form of assimilation.

Interreligious Dialogue

According to Nadwī, the potential growth of *da'wah* could not be realised through *tablighī* activities alone. Pragmatism dictated an interactive approach to the prevailing realities — the presence of a dominant Hindu majority in India. The theme of religious dialogue and communal harmony

---

51. Nadwī advocated self-restraint and taking recourse to the judiciary on communal matters. He cautioned for calm in Hindu-Muslim conflict and sought ways to defuse the tension between them. See *Kārwān,* vol. 4, 147-51.

52. Zaman, *The 'Ulamā in Contemporary Islam,* 166.

characterised his *da'wah* writings after 1950, a clear indication of Maulānā Nadwī's formulation of interfaith relations. In the wake of communal conflicts of which Muslims were largely the victims, interreligious dialogue assumed a particular urgency for Maulānā Nadwī. His involvement with the Tabligh Jamā'at in the early 1950s also raised the need to reach out to the wider society.

The changing landscape in India had brought about a new set of social conditions which had a direct impact on Muslims. In this regard Maulānā Nadwī commented:

> If you make Muslims one hundred per cent mindful of their optional prayers (*tahajjud guzār*) making them all very pious, but leave them cut off from the wider environment, ignorant of where the country is heading and of how hatred is being stirred up in the country against them, then, leave alone the optional prayers, it will soon become impossible for Muslims to say even their five daily prayers. If you make Muslims strangers in their own land, blind them to social realities and cause them to remain indifferent to the radical changes taking place in the country and the new laws that are being imposed and the new ideas that are ruling people's hearts and minds, then let alone, [acquiring] leadership [of the country] it will become difficult for Muslims to even ensure their own existence.[53]

The concern for Indian Muslims to be active citizens meant that their Islamic identity could be protected. This approach, Maulānā Nadwī noted, was the only safeguard for Muslims.

Accordingly, Maulānā Nadwī initiated efforts at religious dialogue between Muslims and Hindus. He established close ties with the Bangalore-based *Dalit Voice* through which he advocated an alliance between the marginalised communities which included Dalits, Backward classes, Sikhs, Christians

53. Muhammad Nafis Hasan, *Merī Tamām Sarguẓasht: Sayyid Abul Hasan 'Ali Nadwī*, Delhi, 2000, 35.

and Muslims against the oppressive policies of the "upper caste" Hindus.[54] Similarly Maulānā Nadwī was instrumental in setting up a fortnightly *Nation and the World*, a name tactfully chosen to show that Muslims also were part of the Indian nation. The primary focus of the journal as its editor Sayyid Hamid writes was to promote "balance and goodwill"[55] among people of different communities.

The motivation for interreligious dialogue as Maulānā Nadwī envisaged was to establish joint efforts for building a more harmonious and just society. This interaction in the past saw the emergence of numerous Hindu reformers who influenced by Islam advocated the unity of God and the oneness of mankind.[56] The emergence of Sikhism in the sixteenth century as a religious movement is illustrative of Islam's influence on Hindu faith and culture. The role of the Sūfīs in spreading the message of Islam combined with their proverbial religious tolerance gave birth to such religious movements with distinct syncretic orientations. This was a result of the interaction of Islam with social, cultural and intellectual processes native to India.[57] In other words, Islam benefited from the cultural heritage of India which defined its peculiar character and distinct corporate identity (*tashakhkhuṣ*).

While not advocating a form of interfaith dialogue which would suggest that Muslims compromise on their faith,

---

54. Nadwī showed much interest and support for the *Dalits*, a marginalised community that has suffered discrimination over the centuries at the hands of the "upper caste" Hindus. For details, see *Kārwān*, vol. 1, 156-63. Cf. Barbara Metcalf, *A Concise History of Modern India*, Cambridge: Cambridge University Press, 2006.

55. Sayyid Hamid, "Mawlana Ali Miyan" in *Rabita*, Delhi, 2000, 49-50.

56. Nadwī, *Muslims in India*, 75-76.

57. Ibid., 76.

Maulānā Nadwī presented an alternative: *waḥdat-i-akhlāq* (unity of morality). For Maulānā Nadwī, this was a "dialogue of life" appealing to people of different faiths to work towards a common purpose. The twofold strategies could easily be achieved through this forum:

- to douse the flames of hatred and animosity, and
- to teach Muslims that they could live in a religiously plural society that "their beliefs could be free from the stain of communal prejudices and conflict."[58]

Maulānā Nadwī urged the Indian Muslims that they could "live in a religiously plural society in such a way that their beliefs could remain free from the stain of communal prejudices and conflict."[59] This was only possible if Indian Muslims could live together with others in harmony by respecting each other's religious beliefs.

In retrospect, Maulānā Nadwī acted as a "facilitator" in the interreligious dialogue and boosted the confidence of the Muslim community to express their support for such an initiative.

PAYĀM-I-INSĀNIYAT (MESSAGE OF MANKIND): AN OVERVIEW

The origins of *Payām-i-Insāniyat* (hereafter *Payām*) go back in the early 1950s when in the wake of communal riots Maulānā Nadwī began addressing joint Hindu-Muslim public rallies calling for communal peace and harmony.

The 1950s period was a turning point in Maulānā Nadwī's chequered career. His return from Egypt had broadened the maturity of his outlook[60] as a result of his close association

58. Sayyid Hamid, *Mawlana Ali Miyan*, 50-51.
59. Cited in Sikand, *Muslims in India Since 1947*, 44.
60. Nadwī refers to his stay as a productive period in his intellectual career. See *Kārwān*, vol. 1, 363-94.

with the Ikhwān movement and its influential members. The *Payām* was established also in the wake of attacks on Muslims by the chauvinist Hindu groups steeped in the Hindutva ideology.[61] Maulānā Nadwī, through the forum of the *Payām* movement advocated better relations between Muslims and members of other faiths. The inspiration, according to Maulānā Nadwī, was the Qur'ānic dictum exhorting Muslims to "enjoin what is good and forbid what is evil."[62] The Qur'ānic message served as an impetus for the Muslim community to join hands with members of other faiths in the country. Maulānā Nadwī began addressing joint Hindu-Muslim public rallies calling for communal harmony and peace. It was in 1974 when the *Payām* was formally launched. Central to his vision was the protection of state from baneful influences which undermined the religious character of the Indian nation.[63] Although Maulānā Nadwī engaged the *Payām* as a popular movement it achieved limited success. This was partly due to the movement not having any registered office or members and the fact it revolved around the charismatic personality of Maulānā Nadwī. Despite these limitations, the *Payām* later gave birth to pro-active organisations like the Forum for Communal Understanding and Synthesis (FOCUS)[64] which attracted a considerable number of both Hindu and Muslim intellectuals.

The activities of the *Payām* were twofold: the communities in India could progress only in a climate of peace, free from

---

61. The rise of communalists and communal violence is critically examined in Reetz, *Islam in the Public Sphere,* 218-28.

62. Nadwī invoked the Qur'anic dictum to reassure wary *'ulamā* and other concerned groups that the Islamic character of *Payām-i-Insāniyat* was not compromised.

63. Nadwī, *Reconstruction of the Indian Society,* Cf. Nadwī, *Kārwān,* vol. 2, 118, 33-35.

64. Hasan, *Meri Tamam Sarguzasht,* 132-33.

inter-communal violence.[65] Bringing Muslims and others to work together, Maulānā Nadwī believed, would provide a means for the Muslims to carry out their responsibilities of *tablīgh* (missionary work). The paradigm shift from Maulānā Nadwī's association with the TJ to his broad-based articulation of *tablīgh* became more visible. The TJ activities were restricted to Muslims and advocated an idealised Islamic society. As opposed to this, Maulānā Nadwī's *Payām* adopted a pragmatic approach in dealing with issues affecting Muslims in a multi-religious and plural society. In a public gathering at Moradabad in 1978, Maulānā Nadwī declared that "the prophets always strove to make sure that the beads of humanity always remained strung in one necklace."[66] Maulānā Nadwī's reference to the Prophet reinforced his belief that the core message of the *Payām* was embedded in the prophetic ideals.

Between 1974 and 1980 Maulānā Nadwī addressed large Hindu-Muslim public rallies to remind the audience that Islam as a religion of peace (*aman*) and security (*salāmat*) fostered in its true followers love and not hatred for humanity.[67] Implicit in his discussion was the need for Muslims to exhibit love for their land (*hubb-al-watan*). Simply put, patriotism and *da'wah* were integral to the Muslim community's survival in the country. Maulānā Nadwī, however, argued that religious freedom was essential in a plural society in which secularism (the state's neutrality towards all religions) and democracy could chalk out the nation's future.[68] Ironically, the *Payām* could not stem the tide

65. Nadwī, *Kārwān*, vol. 2, 119-23.

66. Hasan, *Merī Tamām Sarguẕasht*, 123.

67. The terms *aman* and *salamati* are used as a *leitmotif* in Nadwī's nation-building vision. See Nadwī, *Tameer-i-Insāniyat*, Karachi: Majlis Nashriyat-i-Islam, n.d., 136-59.

68. Cited in *The Fragrance of the East*, 85-91, Nadwī, *Kārwān*, vol. 6, 143-44.

of communal violence which erupted sporadically.[69] Hence the challenges for Maulānā Nadwī and his *Payām* became more intense with an aggressive Hindutva looming larger on the Indian horizon. Likewise, Maulānā Nadwī was not spared by his critics, particularly the *salafis*,[70] who ridiculed his efforts for communal harmony through such forums as the *Payām*.

The *Payām* movement was largely a symbolic expression for Indian Muslims to consolidate their presence and make meaningful contributions in the larger interest of India as a nation. It must be noted that the *Payām* was not the only forum through which the message of communal harmony could be spread. Efforts to either complement or provide alternatives to the *Payām* by Maulānā Nadwī's contemporaries are provided hereunder.

MAULĀNĀ WAHIDUDDIN KHAN'S MODEL OF INTERFAITH DIALOGUE

Maulānā Wahiduddin Khan believes that Muslims must engage with others with the intention of *tablīgh* because of the present realities of Indian policy. It will be prudent for Muslims to "develop inter-cultural, interreligious, and inter-ethnic relations in order to co-operate on issues such as providing greater access to education and inculcating moral values."[71] Likewise his effort to engage with the "other" is radically different from other scholars. Khan invokes an Islam that stands for peace and does not "otherwise"[72] seek to alienate the Hindus. In this regard he has made great inroads

69. For an incisive analysis of the communal violence, see *Milli Gazette*, Delhi, 2007. January-December issues. Cf. Nadwī, *Kārwān*, vol. 5, 112-15.

70. 'Abdullāh 'Abbās Nadwī, *Mīr-i-Kārwān*, 423-24.

71. Cited in Abu-Rabi' *The Blackwell Companion to Contemporary Islamic Thought*, 80.

72. For a critical assessment on the "other", see Khan, *Indian Muslims*, 95-108.

in establishing conversations between Hindus and Muslims to cover a range of issues. This direct talk approach, Khan insists, is more productive in resolving conflicts than relying on help from the government to seek redress. Unlike Khan who insists present realities in India should redress past injustices committed by both Muslims and non-Muslims, Maulānā Nadwī says Muslims' contributions in the past must be acknowledged to promote better relations between Muslims and non-Muslims in secular India. Maulānā Nadwī's view is to reinforce Islam's impact on Indo-Islamic culture. Another point Maulānā Nadwī advances is that Muslims in the past have been integral to the building of a stable Indian society.

The Islamic state in India, Khan argues, is implausible for various reasons. Even if an Islamic state can be established, the manifestation of the Islamic laws cannot be agreed upon largely because of sectarian differences.[73] Therefore Khan reminds Muslims as minorities they must engage with other religious communities "in contributing to the demands of their specific socio-cultural ethos."[74] Like Maulānā Nadwī, Khan says that Muslims must accept multiple ethical models drawn from the Indian experience in relation to worldly matters. He is optimistic that the secular system safeguards the religious and cultural principles of Muslims as minorities.

Genuine dialogue for Khan does not mean the removal of all differences between the different religions. On this issue he is in agreement with Maulānā Nadwī that the *waḥdat-al-adyān* (unity of faiths) or a new syncretic

73. Khan refers to the intra-sectarian disagreements that have hampered any form of consensus. Despite this criticism, the Fiqh Academy (India) has made considerable progress in redefining the role of *shar'iah* in the Indian Muslim community.

74. Cited in Abu-Rabi', *Blackwell Companion to Contemporary Islamic Thought,* 81.

religion[75] is unacceptable. The Qur'ān, writes Khan, clearly accommodates religious pluralism which is opposed to "religious unity" in the following verse: "You have your religion and I have mine." Therefore it is the principle of tolerance that should guide genuine dialogue between Muslims and other religions.

Unlike the Islamists, Khan argues, "the secular state allows Muslims to govern their personal lives according to the *shari'ah*. In all other matters, he insists, Muslims must follow the secular laws which safeguard the constitutional rights for its citizens including Muslims in consonance with Islam."[76] Two points emerge from Khan's understanding of Islamic state. Firstly, the Islamists pursue a political ideology which inflames hostility towards non-Muslims. As opposed to the Islamist viewpoint, the dichotomy between state and religion in India ensures the security of the Muslim community's religious and cultural practices.

It must be noted that Khan's approach thus differs significantly from the Jamā'at-i-Islami of which he was a former member. His resignation was based on ideological differences with Maulānā Maudūdī[77] which is evident in his presentation of interfaith dialogue.

INTERFAITH DIALOGUE: AN ISLAMIST APPROACH: THE JAMĀ'AT-I-ISLAMI OF INDIA

Given the Jamā'at-i-Islami Hind's (hereafter JIH)

75. Muslim India had witnessed the emergence of a syncretic religion. *Din-i-ilahi* by the Mogul Emperor Akbar, which was regarded as the "greatest tumult of the tenth century Islamic calendar". See, Nadwī, *Saviours of Islamic Spirit*, vol. 3, 45-102; Cf. Khaliq Ahmad Nizami, *Akbar and Religion*, Delhi: Idarah-i-Adabiyat-i-Delli, 1989.

76. Cited in Sikand, *Muslims in India Since 1947*, 55.

77. Wahiduddin Khan, *Ta'bir ki Ghalati*, New Delhi: Maktaba al-Risala, 1987.

understanding of Islam as the only completely true religion as a means of salvation the question of Muslims as a minority relating to people of other faiths is crucial. The JIH like several other Islamic organisations have begun to strike a "balance between what might seem conflictual demands as members of the worldwide Muslim *ummah* and as citizens . . . in a secular, non-confessional democratic state."[78]

The JIH has adopted a pragmatic approach to this conflictual relationship. It has called for a critical re-examination of the contemporary condition to seek from the Qur'ān and *sunnah* how they should relate to other people of different faiths. Like the *Payām* movement, it has contextualised its *tablīgh* activities to transform society and "usher in a new social order based on Islamic values."[79]

In a spirit of communal harmony the JIH has called on Muslims to join hands with other religious communities to promote moral regeneration and undertake social service activities.[80] These include sustained efforts to oppose discrimination based on the caste system which militates against the Islamic concept of human dignity. Similarly the JIH has called Muslims to review their understanding of their relations with the other communities, which they term a self-reflection exercise. This approach, the JIH claims, is a means of promoting inter-communal harmony and presenting a vision that Islam is for all mankind.[81] The *da'wah* thrust by the JIH is self-evident. Defending the JIH from the charge of being "communal"[82] its ideologue, Maulānā Abu Lais Nadwī, insists

78. Sikand, *Muslims in India Since Partition*, 80.

79. Ibid., 82.

80. Jamā'at-i-Islam Hind: *Policy and Programme, April 1999-2003*, 7-8.

81. Abu Lais Nadwī, *Mulk-o-Millat ka Masā'il Aur unka Hal*, Delhi: Markazi Maktaba-i-Islami, 21-23.

82. This term is generally understood in India to mean hatred and hostility to people of other faiths.

that the JIH's concern for the protection of property, culture and language of Muslims is not a violation of the Indian Constitution. The convergence of views by Maulānā Nadwī and JIH reflects the realities confronted by Muslim scholars and organisations in promoting the best interest of the Muslim community. The JIH's perception of issues affecting the Muslims have a direct bearing on the Islamic order that Maulānā Nadwī envisaged. Although the JIH is opposed to democracy it opposes its founder's (Maulānā Maudūdī) theory of Ḥākimiyyah (sovereignty) and adopts a pragmatic approach to the issue. It maintains that under the present circumstances democracy is the best form of politics and a defence against Hindu fascism.[83] Similarly it echoes the views of Maulānā Nadwī that Indian Muslims have a dual responsibility as Muslims and as Indian citizens which demands them to take an active interest in the affairs of the country.[84]

In retrospect, for the JIH dialogue and *da'wah* are complementary concepts. Maulānā Nadwī too promoted these concepts from his own perspective bearing in mind his multi-faceted career. These conceptual frameworks of an Islamic order by Maulānā Nadwī, Khan and JIH respectively represent efforts to implement an Islamic order in changed political circumstances.

STRATEGIES FOR THE IMPLEMENTATION OF THE ISLAMIC ORDER IN AN INDIAN CONTEXT

The *shari'ah* as an all-embracing system had guided the Muslims in the subcontinent for almost a millennium.[85] It was implemented by *qāḍis* (judges) and the *farmāns* (ordinances)

83. Nadwī, *Mulk-o-Millat . . .* , 9-12.

84. *Policy and Programme,* 6-7; Cf. Nadwī, *Mulk-o-Millat,* 12-13.

85. For details on the *shari'ah* in South Asia, see Habibul Haq Nadvi, *Islamic Legal Philosophy and the Qur'ānic Origins of Islamic Law,* Durban: Academia, 1989, 358-61. Cf. Abdur Rahman Doi, *Shari'ah: The Islamic Law,* London: Ta Ha Publishers, 1984.

of the Sultans. British rule had diluted the corporate presence of the *shari'ah* into Muslim Personal Law[86] which was both restrictive in its content and scope. The Partition of India in 1947 brought in its wake fresh challenges for the Muslim community in the understanding of the *shari'ah* which would govern their lives and a secular system that promoted a uniform civil code. The inherent contradiction between the *shari'ah* and uniform civil code did not suggest a blatant conflict of religious interests; rather it pointed to the urgency of establishing an organisation that represented the collective will of Muslims who wished to be governed by the *shari'ah*. Maulānā Nadwī's leading role in promoting the *shari'ah* as an alternative to the uniform civil code reinforced his vision of a corporate Muslim identity by invoking the constitutional safeguards which every Indian citizen was expected to enjoy. The challenges to the *shari'ah* were made by the governance arbitrary decisions which infringed on the Muslim corporate identity. These aspects are examined in the next sections.

MUSLIM PERSONAL LAW BOARD

The Muslim Personal Law Board (hereafter MPLB)[87] was established in 1973. The objective was to safeguard Muslim Personal law and train *qāḍis* (judges) to oversee the *shari'ah* courts in different parts of the country. The MPLB under Maulānā Nadwī who was elected as its President in 1983 was to play a major role in Muslim politics in the coming years. The Board's resistance to any government initiatives towards the creation of a uniform civil code for all Indian citizens was tested in the Shah Bano case of 1985. The Supreme Court gave its judgement in favour of Shah Bano who filed for continuing financial support from her husband after the end

86. Habibul Haq Nadvi, *Islamic Legal Philosophy and the Qur'ānic Origins of Islamic Law*, Durban: Academia, 1989, 360-61.

87. Quraishi, Abdur Rahim, *Muslim Personal Law Tahrik: Mawlana 'Ali Miyān ke Daura-i-Ṣadārat Mein*, in *Rabita*, Delhi, 2000, 112.

of her "waiting period" (*'iddat*) following her divorce. The husband had argued the *shari'ah* did not stipulate any maintenance beyond the *'iddat* period. The Supreme Court upheld its verdict quoting arbitrarily from the Qur'ān and *sunnah*.[88] This interpretation, Maulānā Nadwī stated, infringed on the constitutional rights of Muslims to conduct their personal law along clear mandates of the *shari'ah*. Maulānā Nadwī together with *'ulamā* of almost all sectarian persuasion galvanised large segments of the Muslim population into action to protest against the verdict. The Congress-led government of Rajiv Gandhi met with Maulānā Nadwī and other members of the MPLB.[89] In 1986 the Muslim Women Bill[90] (Protection of Rights on Divorce) was passed and dealt a major blow to prospects of a uniform civil code.

The Shah Bano case was seen as threatening Muslim identity in a country where they (Muslims) were a beleagured minority. The course of events in this case strengthened the role of *'ulamā* as legitimate authoritative representatives of the Muslim community which the government readily acknowledged. Maulānā Nadwī's influential position in the Muslim world and his assertion that Indian Muslims were a

88. The deliberate distortion and interpretation of Qur'anic verses by the judges in the Supreme Court was the prelude to the Uniform Civil Code which Muslims in India were expected to adopt. The consequences of such a move were clear — a dissolution of Muslim Personal Law, loss of Muslim corporate identity and assimilation into Hindutva ideology. Nadwī, *Kārwān*, vol. 3, 116-17.

89. On the maintenance (*nafaqah*) debate, see ibid., 116. The memorandum passed by the MLPB to the Prime Minister documented in SAH Rizvi, *A Supreme Court and the Muslim Personal Law*, Delhi: Markaz-i-Maktab Islami, 1985, See the correspondence and meeting between Nadwī and Prime Minister, Rajiv Gandhi, in *Kārwān*, vol. 3, 131-40.

90. Nadwī, *Kārwān*, vol. 3, 139-48.

religious autonomy[91] contributed significantly to the success of the Shah Bano case.

Maulānā Nadwī's stature as an authoritative voice of the Muslim community was tested again in the Babri mosque destruction in 1992.[92] Hindu zealots destroyed the mosque in Ayodhyā which they alleged had been built on the ruins of a temple dedicated to the god-king Rāma. The "aggressive revivalism"[93] as Maulānā Nadwī called it, unleashed a wave of attacks against Muslims. In the climate of communal tension, Maulānā Nadwī counselled restraint and dialogue and met with several Hindu leaders "to evolve a mutually acceptable solution."[94] Maulānā Nadwī called for a reconstruction of the mosque on the original site and a ban on all organisations preaching communal violence. Especially Maulānā Nadwī was unsparing in his condemnation of Muslims in Pakistan and Bangladesh who attacked Hindu temples citing their retributive action as a negation of the Islamic teachings.[95]

---

91. For a discussion on the aspects, see Zaman, *'ulamā in Contemporary Islam*, 169-70. Zaman states: The perception of Nadwī's stature in the Muslim world strengthened . . . [which] signified greater [Islamic] authenticity, a superior and more authoritative claim to respect the interests of the community and those of the faith.

92. The Babri mosque dispute deepened the crisis of confidence between Muslims and Hindus. The extremist elements resisted a negotiated settlement which Nadwī and other influential religious leaders put forward. See *Kārwān*, vol. 4, 98-111. Jan-Peter Hartung in his article, "The Land, the Mosque, the Temple: 145 Years of Dispute Over Ayodhya" [Erfurt, 2003], has traced the conflict of the Babri mosque dispute and the rippling effects it had in the Muslim world after its destruction. Nadwī and leading Muslim personalities played a pivotal role in "globalising" the Babri mosque dispute. Ibid., 20-25.

93. Ibid., 73.

94. Sikand, *Muslims in India Since 1947,* 41.

95. Hasan, *Merī tamām Sarguzasht*, 156-58.

The Babri mosque dispute brought to the surface two conflicting positions. Firstly, the collective will of the Muslim community to maintain its corporate identity (*tashakhkhuṣ*) was strengthened. Secondly, the rise of Hindu nationalism (Hindutva)[96] posed a serious threat to prospects of communal harmony in the country. Against all odds, Maulānā Nadwī urged Muslims to refrain from agitational politics and instead strive for peaceful co-existence with people of other faiths and work towards social justice. These prescriptions Maulānā Nadwī advocated would serve as counterweight against Hindu-oriented India.

Likewise Khan's response to the Babri mosque dispute is based on a three-point formula. Firstly Muslims should receive assurance that after the Babri mosque dispute, no other mosque's right of continued existence will be challenged. Secondly, Muslims should maintain a strict silence on the Babri mosque issue. This means that the Muslims should leave it to the conscience of the nation about the destruction of the mosque. Lastly, the government should provide constitutional safeguards that places of worship will be respected. Khan's "personalised" Islam and quiet diplomacy did not get much support from the Muslim community. Instead he has been accused of being an "Indian agent"[97] because of his conciliatory and self-critical tone.

The peceptions of Maulānā Nadwī and Khan on the Babri dispute represent a spectrum of views and opinions shared by Muslim scholars of varied backgrounds. Likewise, Muslims

---

96. The movement consolidated its position under the BJP government. Hindutva too is synonymous with nationalism and it denounces the policy of appeasement towards Muslims and Christians. See Zafarul-Islam Khan, "Hindu Fundamentalism in Contemporary India" in Abu-Rabiʿ (ed.), *The Blackwell Companion to Contemporary Islamic Thought*, 509-26.

97. Cited in *The Blackwell Companion . . .*, 76.

responded vociferously when the state apparatus interfered in educational issues that had a direct bearing on their religious identity. Maulānā Nadwī's influential role points out to the strategies for implementing an Islamic order which possess variables of his Islamic resurgence paradigm.

EDUCATIONAL SYSTEM: MUSLIM RESPONSE

The Indian Constitution in its efforts to promote communal harmony envisioned secularism as a benchmark for promoting neutrality to its largely diverse population. The educational system which was expected to reflect this secular orientation did not meet up to the marginalised Muslim expectation. The curriculum was designed to articulate a Hindu-ideology ethos. Therefore it was no surprise that the rabid rise of aggressive Hindu revivalism spared no efforts to give the curriculum a communal character.[98] Maulānā Nadwī argued:

> [the] basic reader incorporated material that was inundated with Hindu mythology and polytheistic (*shirk*-laden) stories. . . . This [step] if it gained momentum would negatively impact on the faith, practice and pristine *tawḥid* of the corporate Islamic identity (*millat-i-Ibrāhim/ummati* — Muhammad) of the new Muslim generation. The ignorance and unfamiliarity of their own Islamic faith would make them vulnerable to the polytheistic and syncretic practices of Hinduism.[99]

The climate of uncertainty in schools provoked a definite response from concerned Muslim individuals to redress this imbalance. The proliferation of *makātib* (primary muslim schools) which incorporated secular subjects to impart

---

98. On the problems of discrimination faced by Indian Muslims, see Barbara Metcalf, "Madrasas in Secular India", in Hefner (ed.), *Schooling Islam*, 87-106.

99. Nadwī, *Kārwān*, vol. 1, 460 (adapted).

elementary Islamic education was an alternative to the state's prescription of a syllabus that undermined the belief system of Muslims. This scenario assumed alarming proportions in Uttar Pradesh (north India) and as a corollary the thrust of educational reforms took place in this state. The element of Islamic authenticity was central to Maulānā Nadwī's formulation of an educational policy that would remain unaffected by the pervasive influence of the Hindutva ideology.

DĪNI TĀ'LIMI COUNCIL (RELIGIOUS EDUCATION COUNCIL)

To meet the challenges of this new threat the Dīni Tā'limi Council was established in 1959. Influential members like Qāzi Muhammad 'Adil Abbāsi,[100] a visionary of this movement, Maulānā Manzur Nu'māni and Maulānā Nadwī who was elected President steered the destinies of the Council. It was an institution which exposed and refuted the harmful impact of the wrong policies of the state.

Maulānā Nadwī served as president of the Dīni Tā'limi Council for 40 years until his death in 1999. The *Musalsal Takbir,* a collection of presidential addresses by Maulānā Nadwī, is a pioneering work which embodied the progress of the Council over a period of 50 years. The following extract by Maulānā Nadwī succinctly captures the spirit of the Dīni Tā'limi Council:

> . . . We are completely successful in our endeavours. The non-religious form of the educational system which is encouraged [by the state] will not overshadow the need to impart to our children *dīnī* (religious) education and moral training. The existence of the Muslim community is anchored on sound, established beliefs (*'aqidah*).[101]

---

100. For 'Abbāsi's contributions, see Masud-ul-Hasan 'Uthmāni, *Musalsal Takbīr*, Lucknow: Dīni Tā'limi Council, 2002, 17-54.

101. Nadwī, *Kārwān*, vol. 1, 434.

Correct Islamic beliefs, Maulānā Nadwī insisted, was integral to a stable Islamic society. This resolute standpoint was challenged by Hindu nationalists working in complicity with state apparatus. In 1998 the government issued directives for the compulsory singing of the national anthem, *Vande Mātaram* at all educational institutions.[102] Reaction from the Muslim community was predictable: a strong opposition to its introduction.[103] Maulānā Nadwī categorically rejected the mandatory singing of *Vande Mātaram* for Muslims as it "militated against *tawḥid* (Unity of God) and was a breach of the spirit of secularism enshrined in the Constitution." The bold declaration by Maulānā Nadwī forced the prime minister and the home minister to revoke the directive.[104] This decision by the state was also prompted by the wave of protests across the country by Muslims. Maulānā Nadwī's bargaining power with state structures and his established position as a leader in the Muslim community is evident in the *Vande Mātaram* controversy.

Conclusion

The variations of an Islamic order in India by Maulānā Nadwī and his contemporaries have important implications in a contemporary context. The ideal Islamic order that emerged in the early period of the *ṣalf-al-ṣāliḥ* underwent significant mutations over the centuries in response to changing socio-political situations. Maulānā Nadwī's pragmatism in acknowledging these changes allowed him to work on an alternative model to Maulānā Maudūdī's and Quṭb's conceptions of an Islamic order. The *iṣlāḥi-tajdīdī* elements are conspicuous in his Islamic order and his promotion of Islamic authenticity is set against the backdrop of democracy. This

102. Nadwī, *Kārwān*, vol. 7, 204-8.

103. Ibid., vol. 7, 204. Cf. Iqbal Zaheer, *Abul Hasan Ali Nadwī*, 85.

104. Nadwī, *Kārwān*, vol. 7, 207-8.

contradiction between Islamic resurgence and Western-oriented model is reconciled by Maulānā Nadwī to illustrate a useful point: Islamic order can function in diverse situations without compromising on the broad framework of Islamic resurgence. The views presented by Khan and JIH are examples of how an Islamic order can be flexible and adaptable in specific settings.

Maulānā Nadwī's ability to use institutional tools like the *Payām-i-Insāniyat* in augmenting the sphere of *da'wah* is significant. The interfaith dialogue is not confined in India but resonates in Western countries where Muslims constitute a minority. The following extracts echo his vision of the *Payām-i-Insāniyat* for Muslims residing in the United Kingdom.

> You must earn your place in this country. You should leave an imprint on the host community of your usefulness. You must demonstrate your existence here is beneficial. You must impart to them the lessons of humanity. You should demonstrate how noble and principled you are, and that there cannot be found more upright humans elsewhere besides you. You need to establish your worth for this country.
>
> However if you remain preoccupied with just working and partying, and in personal prayers, indifferent to what is happening in the country, insulated within Muslims, apathetic to what is happening outside, which direction the country is taking, you will not be able to save yourselves if problems emerge.[105]

Muslim participation in political issues in countries where they constitute a minority is a focus of Maulana Nadwī's appeal. His vision offers a parallel understanding of Muslims reorganising their lives to preserve a corporate Islamic identity taking into account the political realities they have to face.

---

105. *Al-Ahsan Magazine*, 2001, vol. 3, 25-26 (Al-Ahsan Foundation).

Conclusion

THE concept of *iṣlāḥ* and *tajdīd* in the study in Islamic thought has had a chequered history. From its very inception, the period of the *ṣalf-al-ṣāliḥ* (early representatives of Islam) to the present times, these concepts have become adaptable and flexible that are consistent with the dynamics of change. Ibn Taymiyyah as the ideologue of the tradition had invoked the Qur'ān and *sunnah* to confront the challenges of his times. His exercise of *ijtihād* unshackled the intellectual sterility that characterised the existing Islamic society. The *tajdīdī* tradition highlighted both the process of decay and regeneration, the binary opposites, that manifested themselves in various forms in Islamic history. In a particular sense *tajdīd* did not present a coherent system that could be rigidly applied to all reformist movements. Instead, the study showed how reformist thought was responsive to change and evolved with distinct characteristics in different Muslim societies. The founder of the Wahhābi movement, for example, claimed legitimacy for a *salafi* interpretation of Islam while Afghānī and 'Abduh of Egypt reinterpreted Islamic thought against the backdrop of colonialism. Similarly Maulānā Maudūdī and Quṭb re-defined *tajdīd* in the light of the Western civilisation and its pervasive influence in the Muslim world. Likewise Maulānā Nadwī contextualised this concept to the changing scenarios in the Arab world and the Indian subcontinent.

The Islamist and *salafi* profiles are no different in their interpretation of *tajdīd*. These movements sought to shape an Islamic order which though rooted in the *ṣalf-al-ṣāliḥ* tradition employed models of Western experience. Two other movements though set apart from other *tajdīdī* trends imbibed *islāh* in an exclusive sense to promote their respective Islamic vision. The *'ulamā* in the context of the Indian subcontinent and the Tabligh Jamā'at which were largely offshoots of the Shāh Wali-allah tradition strove for the reconstruction of the Muslim society. The Tabligh Jamā'at made major strides as a transnational movement; however it represented a pietistic Islam tied to the Deoband scripturalist formulation of *tajdīd*.

The study on the *mujaddid* raises an important question: is there a clear-cut definition for this phenomenon in Islamic history? The salient features of a *mujaddid* as described in the *hadīth* literature have been examined in Chapter 1. A detailed study of *tajdīd* reveals conflicting perspectives of which Maulānā Maudūdī and Maulānā Nadwī are representatives of this trend. Maulānā Maudūdī's politicised understanding of the role of the *mujaddid*s differs widely from Maulānā Nadwī's appreciation of their unbroken contribution to *iṣlāḥ* and *tajdīd*. This divergence is shown in their respective approaches to an Islamic order. In a similar vein, the *'ulamā* are pitted against Islamists who reject *taqlīd* in their reformulation of contemporary reformist thought. Thus the conflicting viewpoints point paradoxically to the dynamic nature of *tajdīd*. It has no immutable principles, is not time-bound and offers scope for re-interpretation.

In the study, primary sources largely related to autobiographical and biographical works were examined. The focus was on reformist thought in the writings of important scholars, *'ulamā* and intellectuals who have articulated their vision of *iṣlāḥ* and *tajdīd*. As Maulānā Nadwī is the primary focus of our study in relation to his contemporaries, some interesting points emerge. There are definite strands of reformist thought from different intellectual backgrounds defined by several milieus that had influenced Maulānā

Nadwī's formulation of *tajdīd* (Chapter 2). His *Kārwān-i-Ẓindagī* offers interesting insights to his admiration of these reformers. It is evident that his evaluation reflect his independence of thought. Maulānā Nadwī's frame of reference is the *ṣalf-al-ṣāliḥ* through whose lenses he develops his own *tajdīdī* model. Again the dynamics of change are discernible both in his interaction and assessment of contemporary reformers. In this regard one may compare and contrast the influence of Muḥammad Asad on Maulānā Nadwī's writings. Asad's *The Road to Mecca*, an autobiographical account and his *Islam at the Crossroads* — a critique of Western civilisation — are acknowledged by Maulānā Nadwī as important sources in his own critique of the West. It may be noted that Asad's formative intellectual career was in the Indian subcontinent and his contributions had influenced a number of reformers and intellectuals in this region.

As the title of the study suggests, Maulānā Nadwī's contemporaries are drawn from Egypt and the Indian subcontinent. It is quite evident that their respective ideological orientations have had a significant influence in Maulānā Nadwī's theorisation. The *turāth* paradigm that Maulānā Nadwī advocates revolves around reformist personalities who represent an unbroken link to *iṣlāḥ* and *tajdīd* traditions. A comparative study of Maulānā Maudūdī and Quṭb's contributions to Islamic resurgence reinforces our views that Maulānā Nadwī's choice of reformers is linked to the *ṣalf-al-ṣāliḥ* lineage. Even so both Quṭb and Maulānā Maudūdī had discernible influence on Maulānā Nadwī's *tajdīdī* presentation. An interesting observation emerges from such interaction: the contrasting discourse of reformist thought is evident between Maulānā Nadwī and his contemporaries. Chapter 4 reinforces this viewpoint in respect of the Jāhiliyyah and Ḥākimiyyah theories formulated by Quṭb and Maulānā Maudūdī.

Transnational networks closely associated with a scholarly tradition defined Maulānā Nadwī's intellectual career. His rapport with the Ikhwān movement with its *iṣlāhi* orientations permitted him to develop his presentation of Islamic thought. Likewise translocal scholarship helped link Maulānā Nadwī to the Arab world where contesting forces of secularism and Arab nationalism posed a threat to Islam. These networks, heralded, albeit in a limited way, the era of globalisation, a phenomenon that had a direct impact on the world of Islam. Islamic discourse is not immune from this global impact which offers possibilities of dialogue between Islam and the West on common issues that affect mankind.

Islamic history during the nineteenth and twentieth centuries gave rise to several Islamic movements presenting alternative models of an Islamic state at variance with established practices embodied by the Caliphate rule. The twentieth century also saw the emergence of Islamic movements calling for Ḥākimiyyah (sovereignty) in the wake of Western incursion. The system presented by Quṭb and Maulānā Maudūdī was rooted in a political milieu and pointed out to an incongruity: an Islamist formulation of an Islamic order employing Western tools for a Muslim constituency. The multiple identities of Islamic political expression assume greater importance in Maulānā Nadwī's interpretation of an Islamic order (Chapter 4).

Two possible reasons may explain this contradiction. Firstly, the products of modern and partly Westernised education themselves with non-traditional Islamic learning, the leaders of the Islamic movements borrowed modern methods of mobilisation, organisation, and mass activism. In their expressed goals of an Islamic order, they embraced modernity without having an operative programme to shape modernity itself. Their activism was not as a result of an outflow of Islamic response to modernity. Rather it accentuated an ambivalence that shaped their Islamic discourse *vis-à-vis* the West. Secondly, in the public sphere the role of the *'ulamā* also underwent a transformation. As custodians of Islamic tradition they too could not remain immune from the dynamics of change largely introduced by Western culture. The reformist discourse formed the basis of the re-interpretation of Islamic categories to accommodate changes in politics and society. However, the radical re-interpretation of the Islamic sources was not possible because of the stronghold of *taqlid* in their Islamic discourse. Maulānā Nadwī as a traditional *'ālim* added new dimensions to the reformist discourse. His articulation of an Islamic authenticity and his own international stature were motivating factors of an Islamic order. Even in his critique of Arab nationalism he saw no contradiction in accepting this concept in a secular state, India. Islamic order, as Maulānā Nadwī saw it, did not reflect a duality of worldviews; rather it created the possibility of Muslims as a minority co-existing with the significant "other." Maulānā Wahiduddin Khan and Jamā'at-i-Islami Hind echoed similar sentiments on this crucial issue. The success of Maulānā Nadwī's initiative was inextricably linked with the Muslim community's pragmatic approach to the realities they were confronted with. Maulānā Nadwī highlighted the challenges and opportunities that his Islamic order offered.

Maulānā Nadwī's guidelines for communal harmony are clearly spelt out in Chapter 5. Peace would remain elusive if one community sought to impose its belief and culture on the other. In a climate of political volatility, religious freedom in a plural society could only be achieved, Maulānā Nadwī argued, through secularism and democracy. The recent unfolding of events — the wave of communal violence incited by Hindutva against the Muslim community — is truly prophetic of Maulānā Nadwī's concerns on ideological extremism.

In retrospect, Maulānā Nadwī's Islamic order illustrates the possibilities of Muslims re-modelling their lives even in different political settings. Peace, security and social justice are the salient features of Maulānā Nadwī's ideal society. Keeping in mind the unpredictable geo-politics and increasing presence of militant Islamic groups, Maulānā Nadwī's realism and pragmatism reflected in his *Payām-i-Insāniyat* may be a starting point for a reassessment of the challenges confronting the Muslim world.

Bibliography

Ansari, Muḥammad Abdul Haq, *Sufism and Shari'ah: A Study of Shaykh Ahmad Sirhindi's Effort to Reform Islam*, Leicester: The Islamic Foundation, 1986.

Abu-Rabi', Ibrahim, *Contemporary Arab Thought: Studies in Post-1967 Arab Intellectual History*, London: Pluto Press, 2004.

———, *Islam and the Search for a Social Order in Modern Egypt: An Intellectual Biography of Shaykh Abd-al Halim Mahmud*, PhD thesis, Temple University, 1987.

———, *Intellectual Origins of Islamic Resurgence in the Modern Arab World*, New York: SUNY Press, 1996.

———, (ed.), *The Blackwell Companion to Contemporary Islamic Thought*, London: Blackwell, 2006.

Abul-Fadl, Mona, *Where East Meets West*, Herdon: IIIT, 1992.

Abu Zahra, Muḥammad, *The Four Imams: Their Lives, Works and the Schools of Thought*, London: Dar-al-Taqwa, 2001.

Aḥmad, Aziz, *Islamic Modernism in India and Pakistan, 1857–1964*, London: Oxford University Press, 1967.

Aḥmad, Israr, *Tahrik Jamā'at-i-Islami: Ek Tahqiqi Mutāla*, Lahore: Markazi Maktaba Tanzim-i-Islami, 1983.

Aḥmad, Khurshid (ed.), *Islamic Perspectives in honour of Sayyid Abul A'la Maulānā Maudūdī*, Leicester: The Islamic Foundation, 1979.

Ahmed, Akbar, *Discovering Islam: Making Sense of Muslim History and Society*, London: Routledge, 1988.

———, *Postmodernism and Islam*, London: Routledge, 1992.

Akhtar, Hakim Muḥammad, *Maulānā Maudūdī, Akābir-i-ummat ki nazar me*, Lahore: Maktaba-al-Qāsim, n.d.

Alam, Muḥammad Manzoor, *100 Great Muslim Leaders of the 20th Century*, New Delhi: Institute of Objective Studies, 2005.

Al-Bannā, Ḥasan, *Mudhakarāt al-da'wah wa'l dā'iyah*, Beirut, 1970.

Ali, Yusuf, *The Holy Qur'ān: English Translation of the Meanings and Commentary*, Medina, 1990.

Allen, Roger, *The Arabic Novel: A Historical and Critical Introduction*, Syracuse: New York Press, 1982.

Al-Matroudi, Abdul Hakim, *The Hanbali School of Law and Ibn Taymiyyah*, Oxon: Routledge, 2005.

Andrabi, Abroo, *Muḥammad Asad: His Contribution to Islamic Learning*, New Delhi: Goodword Books, 2007.

Asad, Muḥammad, *The Road to Mecca*, London: Max Reinhardt, 1954.

———, *Islam at the Crossroads*, Lahore: Ashraf Publications, 1969.

Asad, Talat, *Formation of the Secular: Christianity, Islam and Modernity*, Stanford: Stanford University Press, 2003.

———, *The Idea of an Anthropology of Islam*, Washington: Centre for Contemporary Arabic Studies, 1986.

Assmann, J., *Das Kulturelle Gedächtnis: Schrift Erinnerung und Politsche Identität in fròhen Hochkulturen*, Munich: Verslag CH Beck, 1992.

Āzād, Abul Kalam, *Tadhkirah*, New Delhi: Sahitya Academy, 1985.

Baalbaki, Rohi, *Al-Mawrid: A Modern Arabic-English Dictionary*, Beirut, 2004.

Barakat, Muḥammad Tawfiq, *Sayyid Quṭb*, Beirut: Dār-al-Da'wah, n.d.

Binder, Leonard, *Islamic Liberalism: A Critique of Development Ideologies*, Chicago: The University of Chicago Press, 1988.

Brass, Elizabeth, *Autobiographical Acts*, Baltimore: John Hopkins University Press, 1976.

Brown, Daniel, *Rethinking Tradition in Modern Islamic Thought*, Cambridge: Cambridge University Press, 2006.

Carre, Olivier, *Mysticism and Politics: A Critical Reading of Fī-Zilāl-al-Qur'ān* by Sayyid Quṭb, 1906-66, Leiden: Brill, 2000.

Choughley, A.K., *Da'wah, Peace and Dialogue in the Writings of Sayyid Abul Hasan 'Ali Nadwī, 1913-99*, M.A. Thesis, University of Johannesburg, 2004.

Chughtai, Ikram, *Muḥammad Asad, Europe's Gift to Islam*, Lahore: The Truth Society, 2006.

Doi, Abd al-Rahman, *Shaikh Uthmān Don Fodio: The Grand Mujahid and Mujaddid of Africa*, Pretoria: Al-Madinah Publishers, 1998.

Douglas, Ian Henderson, *Abul Kalam Azad: An Intellectual and Religious Biography*, Delhi: Oxford University Press, 1993.

Elbaz, Robert, *The Changing Value of the Self: A Critical Study of the Autobiographical Discourses*, London: CroomHelm Ltd., 1998.

Esposito, John (ed.), *The Oxford Encyclopedia of the Modern Islamic World*, Oxford: Oxford University Press, 1995.

———, *Makers of Contemporary Islam*, Oxford: Oxford University Press, 2001.

Farah, Caesar, *'Abdul Hamid 11 and the Muslim World*, Istanbul, ISAR, 2008.

Faruqi, Ziya-al-Hasan, *The Deoband School and the Demand for Pakistan*, Lahore, n.d.

Gerard, Genette, *Figures III*, Paris: Edutions du Sevil, 1972.

Ghazali, Muḥammad, *The Socio-Political Thought of Shah Wali Allah*, Islamabad: Islamic Research Institute, 2001.

Ghazi, Mahmood Aḥmad, *Islamic Renaissance in South Asia 1707-1867*, Islamabad: Islamic Research Institute, 2007.

Ghorab, Aḥmad, *Subverting Islam: The Role of Orientalist Centres*, Kuala Lumpur: The Open Press, 1995.

Goyal, D.R., *Maulana Husain Ahmad Madani: A Biographical Study*, Kolkata: Anamika Publishers, 2004.

Hai, Abdul, *India during Muslim Rule*, Lucknow: Academy of Islamic Research, 1977.

Hajjan, Shaikh Muhammad, *Maulana Ubaid Allah Sindhi: A Revolutionary Scholar*, Islamabad: NICHR, 1986.

Hameed, Saiyida Saiydian, *Islamic Seal on India's Independence: Abul Kalam Azad: A Fresh Look*, Karachi: Oxford University Press, 1998.

Hartung, Jan-Peter, *'Ulamā of Contemporary South Asia: Globalising the Local by Localising the Global*, Berlin, n.d.

Hasan, Masudul, *Sayyid Abul A'la Maudūdī and His Thought*, vols. 1 and 2, Lahore: Islamic Publications Pvt. Ltd., 1984.

Hasan, Muḥammad Nafis, *Merī Tamām Sarguẓasht: Maulānā Sayyid Abul Hasan 'Ali Nadwī*, Delhi, 2000.

Haykel, Bernard, *Revival and Reform in Islam: The Legacy of Muḥammad Al-Shawkāni*, Cambridge: Cambridge University Press, 2003.

Hitti, Philip, *History of the Arabs*, London: Mcmillan, 1986.

Husain, Mohammad Anwer, *The Prisoners of Malta*, New Delhi: Manak Publishers, 2005.

Hourani, Albert, *Arabic Thought in the Liberal Age 1798-1939*, Oxford: Oxford University Press, 1983.

Hussaini, I.M., *The Muslim Brethren: The Greatest Modern Islamic Movement*, Beirut: Khayat College Book Cooperative, 1956.

Hodgson, Marshall G.S., *Venture of Islam, Conscience and History in a World Civilisation*, Chicago, 1974.

Iyer, Subromani, *The Role of Mawlana Abul Kalam in Indian Politics*, Hyderabad: Oriental Research Institute Publications, n.d.

Izutsu, Toshihiko, *God and Man in the Qur'ān: Semantics of the Qur'ānic Weltanschauung*, Kuala Lumpur: Islamic Book Trust, 2002.

Iqbal, Muḥammad, *The Achievement of Love: The Spiritual Dimension of Islam*, Vermont: Amana Books, 1987.

Jalal, Ayesha, *The Sole Spokesman: Jinnah, the Muslim League and the Demand for Pakistan*, Cambridge: Cambridge University Press, 1985.

Jameelah, Maryam, *Western Civilisation Condemned by Itself*, Lahore: Yusuf Khan, 1970.

———, *Islam and Modernism*, Lahore: Yusuf Khan, 1975.

———, *Who is Maudoodi*, Lahore: Yusuf Khan, n.d.

Jeppie, Shamil, *Language, Identity, Modernity*, Pretoria: HSRC, 2007.

Kamal, Mohammad, *Heterodoxy in Islam: A Philosophical Study*, Karachi: Royal Book Company, 1993.

Khalid, Adeeb, *The Politics of Muslim Cultural Reform: Jadidism in Central Asia*, Berkely: University of California Press, 1999.

Khan, Shams Tabrez, *Tarikh Nadwat-ul-'Ulamā*, Lucknow: Daftar Nizāmat Nadwat-al-'ulamā, 1984.

Khan Wahiduddin, *Islam and Peace*, New Delhi: Maktaba-al-Risala, 1999.

———, *Ta'bir ki Ghalati*, New Delhi: Maktaba al-Risala, 1987.

———, *Tablīgh Movement*, New Delhi: The Islamic Centre, 1986.

———, *Dīn Kya Hai*, New Delhi: Risala Books, 1982.

———, *Indian Muslims: The Need for Positive Outlook*, New Delhi: Al-Risala Books, 1997.

———, *Aman-e-'Alām*, New Delhi: Goodword Books, 2005.

Khatab, Sayed, *The Political Thought of Sayid Quṭb: The Theory of Jāhiliyyah*, London: Routledge, 2006.

———, *The Power of Sovereignty: The Political Philosophy of Sayyid Quṭb*, Abingdon: Routledge, 2006.

Lewis, Bernard, *Islam and the West*, New York: Oxford University Press, 1993.

Makdisi, George, *The Rise of Colleges: Institutions of Learning in Islam and the West*, Edinburgh: Edinburgh University Press, 1981.

Makris, G.P., *Islam in the Middle East: A Living Tradition*, Malden: Blackwell Publishing, 2007.

Malti-Douglas, Fedwa, *Autobiography and Blindness: Al-Ayyam of Taha Husayn*, Princeton: Princeton University Press, 1988.

Maudūdī, Abul A'lā, *A Short History of the Revivalist Movements in Islam*, Lahore: Islamic Publications Ltd., 1972.

———, *Khilāfat wa Malukiyyat*, Lahore: Islamic Publications, 1966.

———, *Wathā'aq-i-Maulānā Maudūdī*, Lahore, 1986.

———, *The Sick Nations of the Modern Age*, Lahore: Islamic Publications Ltd., 1966.

———, *The Islamic Movement: Dynamics of Value, Power and Change*, Leicester: The Islamic Foundation, 1984.

———, *Four Basic Qur'ānic Terms*, Delhi, 1980.

———, *Towards Understanding the Qur'ān*, vol. 1-7, Leicester: The Islamic Foundation, 1988.

———, *Towards Understanding Islam*, Kuwait: IIFSO, n.d.

Masud, Khalid (ed.), *Travellers in Faith: Studies of the Tablīghi Jamā'at as an International Islamic Movement for Faith Revival*, Leiden: Brill, 2000.

Metcalf, Barbara Daly, *Islamic Revival in British India: Deoband 1860-1900*, Karachi: Royal Book Company, 1989.

———, *Islamic Contestations, Essays of Muslims in India*, New Delhi: Oxford University Press, 2004.

Moosa, Ebrahim, *Ghazāli and the Poetics of Imagination*, Chapel Hill: University of North Carolina Press, 2005.

Murad, Mehr Afroz, *Intellectual Modernism of Shibli Nu'mani*, Lahore: Institute of Islamic Culture, 1976.

Mousalli, Aḥmad, *Moderation and Radical Islamic Fundamentalism*, Gainesville: University Press of Florida, 1999.

Musallam, A.A., *The Formative Stages of Sayid Quṭb's Intellectual Career and His Emergence as an Islamic Da'iyan, 1906-52*, Phd. Thesis, University of Michigan, 1983.

Nadvi, Syed Habibul-Haq, *Islamic Resurgent Movements in the Indo-Pak Subcontinent*, Durban: Academia, 1987.

———, *The Dynamics of Islam*, Durban: Academia, 1987.

———, *Islamic Fundamentalism: A Theology of Liberation and Renaissance*, Durban: Academia, 1987.

———, *Islamic Legal Philosophy and the Qur'ānic Origins of Islamic Law*, Durban: Academia, 1989.

Nadwī, 'Abdullah 'Abbās, *Mīr-i-Kārwān*, Karachi: Majlis-i-'Ilmī, 1999.

Nadwī, Abu Lais, *Mulk-o-Millat ka Masā'il Aur unka Hal*, Delhi: Markazi Maktaba-i-Islami, n.d.

Nadwī, Muḥammad Na'im Siddiqui, *'Allāmah Sayyid Sulāyman Nadwī, Shakhsiyat wa Adab-i-Khidmat*, Lucknow: Maktaba Firdaus, 1985.

Nadwī, Muhsin 'Uthmān, *Mutāla wa Tasnifāt Sayyid Abul Hasan 'Ali Nadwī*, Delhi: Arshad Publications, 2002.

Nadwī, Sayyid Abul Hasan 'Ali, *Islam and the World*, Lucknow: Academy of Islamic Research and Publications.

———, *Western Civilisation, Islam and Muslims*, Lucknow: Academy of Islamic Research and Publications, 1974.

———, *Kārwān-i-Ẓindagī*, vols. 1-7, Lucknow: Majlis Nashriyāt-i-Islam, 1985.

———, *Saviours of Islamic Spirit*, vols. 1-4, Lucknow: Academy of Islamic Research and Publications, 1993.

———, *Al-Islam wa-al-Mustashriqun*, Lucknow: Nadwat-ul-'ulamā, 1983.

———, *The Life and Mission of Moulana Mohammad Ilyas*, Lucknow: Academy of Islamic Research and Publications, 1979.

———, *The Life of Caliph Ali*, Lucknow: Academy of Islamic Research and Publications, 1991.

———, *Appreciation and Interpretation of Religion in the Modern Age*, Lucknow: Academy of Islamic Research and Publications, 1982.

———, *Muslims in India*, Lucknow: Academy of Islamic Research and Publications, 1976.

———, *Purān-i-Chirāgh*, vols. 1-3, Karachi: Majlis Nashriyāt-i-Islam, 1994.

———, *Tadhkirah Maulānā Fazlur Rahmān Ganj-Murādabādi*, Karachi: Majlis Nashriyāt-i-Islam, 1985.

———, *Qadianism, A Critical Study*, Lucknow: Academy of Islamic Research and Publications, 1974.

———, *Hadhrat Shaykh-ul-ḥadīth Maulānā Muḥammad Shaykh Zakariyyah,* Karachi: Majlis Nashriyat-i-Islam, 1982.

———, *Calamity of Cultural and Linguistic Chauvinism,* Lucknow: Academy of Islamic Research and Publications, 1972.

———, *Reconstruction of Islamic Society: What Muslims Can Do?,* Lucknow: Academy of Islamic Research and Publications, n.d.

———, *Tuḥfah-i-Pakistan,* Karachi: Majlis Nashriyāt-i-Islam, 1984.

———, *Tuḥfah-i-Insāniyat,* Lucknow: Majlis Tahqiqāt wa Nashriyāt-i-Islam, 1992.

———, *Da'wat-i-Fikr,* Lucknow: Majlis al 'Ilmi, 1999.

———, *Mukhtārāt min al-adab al-'Arabi,* Beirut Dār-al-Fikr, 1965.

———, *Sīrat-i-Sayyid Ahmad Shahīd,* vols. 1-2, Karachi: Majlis Nashriyāt-i-Islam, 1987.

———, *A Misunderstood Reformer,* Lucknow: Academy of Islamic Research and Publications, 1974.

———, *Rabbāniyyah la Rahbāniyyahi,* Lucknow: Al-Majma'ul-Islami-al-'Ilmi, 1979.

———, *Aḍwā,* Lucknow: Majlis Tahqiqāt wa Nashriyāt-i-Islam, n.d.

———, *Meri 'Ilmi aur mutāl'āti Ẓindagī,* Rae Bareli: Sayyid Aḥmad Shahīd Academy, n.d.

———, *The Place of Knowledge and Responsibilities of Those Who Acquire It,* Lucknow: Academy of Islamic Research and Publications, n.d.

———, *Islam and Knowledge,* Oxford: OCIS, 1988.

———, *Sawānih Hadhrat Maulānā 'Abdul Qādir Raipuri,* Lahore: Maktaba Rashidiya, 1977.

———, *Muslims in the West: The Message and Mission,* Leicester: The Islamic Foundation, 1983.

———, *Islam and the West,* Lucknow: Academy of Islamic Research and Publications, 1983.

———, *Islámic Concept of Prophethood,* Lucknow: Academy of Islamic Research and Publications, 1976.

———, *Islam and Civilisation,* Lucknow: Academy of Islamic Research and Publications, n.d.

———, *Millāt-i-Islam ka Tārikhi Kardār,* Lucknow: Shu'bah Da'wat wa Irshād, 2004.

———, *The Musalman: Social Life, Beliefs and Customs of the Indian Muslims*, Lucknow: Academy of Islamic Research and Publications, 1972.

———, *Islam: An Introduction*, Lucknow: Academy of Islamic Research Foundation, 1998.

———, *Iṣlāhiyāt*, Karachi: Mājlis Nashriyāt-i-Islam, 1987.

———, *Khuṭbāt-i-Mufakkir-i-Islam*, Lucknow: Dar-al-Qalam, 2000.

———, *Ta'meer-i-Insāniyat*, Karachi: Majlis Nashriyāt-i-Islam, n.d.

Nasr, Seyyed Hossein, *Islamic Spirituality Foundation*, New York: The Crossroad Publishing Company, 1985.

Nasr, Seyyed Vali Reza, *The Vanguard of the Islamic Revolution*, Berkeley: University of California Press, 1994.

———, *Maudūdī and the Making of Islamic Revivalism*, Oxford: Oxford University Press, 1996.

Nicholson, R.A., *A Literary History of the Arabs*, Delhi: Adam Publications, 1996.

Nizami, Khaliq Aḥmad, *On Islamic History and Culture*, Delhi: Idarah-i-Adabiyat-i-Delli, 1995.

Qureshi, Ishtiaq Hussain, *Ulema in Politics*, Karachi: Ma'arif Press, 1972.

Quṭb, Sayyid, *Milestones*, IIFSO, 1977.

———, *Social Justice in Islam*, New York: Islamic Publications International, 2000.

———, *Fī-Zilāl al-Qur'ān*, vols. 1-6, Cairo: Dār-ul-Shuruq, 1992.

Reynolds, Dwight, *Interpreting the Self: Autobiography in the Literary Arab Tradition*, Berkeley: University of California Press, 2001.

Rahman, Fazlur, *Islam and Modernity: Transformation of an Intellectual Tradition*, Berkeley: University of California Press, 2001.

———, *Revival and Reform in Islam*, Oxford: Oneworld, 2000.

Rahnema, Ali, *Pioneers of Islamic Revival*, London: Zed Books Ltd., 1994.

Reetz, Dietrich, *Islam in the Public Sphere*, New Delhi: Oxford University Press, 2006.

Rippin, Andrew, *Approaches to the History of the Interpretation of the Qur'ān*, Oxford: Clarendon Press, 1988.

Rizvi, SAH, *A Supreme Court and the Muslim Personal Law*, Delhi: Markaz Maktab-i-Islami, 1985.

Robinson, Chase, *Islamic Historiography*, Cambridge: Cambridge University Press, 2003.

Robinson, Francis, *Islam and Muslim History in South Asia*, New Delhi: OUP, 2001.

———, *Islam, South Asia and the West*, New Delhi: Oxford University Press, 2007.

———, *The 'Ulamā of Farang-i-Mahal*, Delhi: Permanent Black, 2001.

Roy, Olivier, *Globalised Islam: The Search for a New Ummah*, London: C. Hurst & Co., 2002.

Sambhali, Atiqur-Rahmān, *Hadhrat Maulānā Muḥammad Manzur Nu'māni*, Lucknow, 1997.

Sanyal, Usha, *Devotional Islam and Politics in British India: Ahmad Riza Khan Barelwi and His Movement*, 1870-1920, New Delhi: Oxford University Press, 1996.

Sawlat, Sarwar, *Maudūdī*, Karachi: International Islamic Publications, 1984.

Schulze, Reinhard, *A Modern History of the Islamic World*, London: I.B. Tauris Publishers, 2000.

Shahīd, Muḥammad Ismā'il, *Taqwiyat-ul-Imān*, Lucknow: Al-Maktaba al Nadwāyyah, 1991.

Siddiqui, Mazheruddin, *Modern Reformist Thought in the Muslim World*, Islamabad: Islamic Research Institute, 1982.

Sikand, Yoginder, *Muslims in India Since 1947: Islamic Perspectives on Interfaith Relations*, London: Routledge, 2004.

———, *The Origins and Development of the Tablīghi Jama'at*, 1920-2000, New Delhi: Orient Longman, 2002.

Tayob, Abdul Kader, *Islamic Resurgence in South Africa*, Cape Town: UCT Press, 1995.

Tamimi, Azzam, *Rachid Ghannouchi: A Democratic within Islam*, London: Oxford University Press, 2001.

'Uthmāni, Mas'ud-ul-Ḥasan, *Musalsal Takbīr*, Lucknow: Dīnī Ta'līmī Council, 2002.

Wolpert, Stanley, *Jinnah of Pakistan*, New York: Oxford University Press, 1984.

Zaman, Muḥammad Qasim, *The 'Ulamā in Contemporary Islam: Custodians of Change*, Princeton: Princeton University Press, 2002.

———, *Schooling Islam*, Princeton: Princeton University Press, 2007.

Zaman, Waheed-uz, *Islam in South Asia*, Islamabad: NICHR, 1993.

Journals

Al-Ahsan Magazine, 2003:3.

Hamdard Islamicus, vol. xxx, no. 4.

International Journal of Middle Eastern Studies, 2005:37; 2003:35.

Islamic Studies: 31:4; 44:4; 42:2.

Meria Journal, vol. 5, no. 94.

Middle East Affairs, 1993, 1:3.

Milli Gazette, January-December 2007.

Muslim Education Quarterly, vol. 44:4.

Ta'meer-i-Hayāt, July-August 2000.

The Fragrance of the East, 2004.

The Muslim World, vol. 81, July-October 1991; vol. 63:96.

Websites

http://www.oxfordIslamicstudies.com/articles Accessed on 24/04/09

http://www/algonetse/pmanzoor Accessed on 27/07/08

Index